# Lecture Notes of the Institute for Computer Sciences, Social Informatics and Telecommunications Engineering 269

More information about this series at http://www.springer.com/series/8197

João L. Afonso · Vítor Monteiro
José Gabriel Pinto (Eds.)

# Green Energy and Networking

5th EAI International Conference, GreeNets 2018
Guimarães, Portugal, November 21–23, 2018
Proceedings

 Springer

*Editors*
João L. Afonso ⓘ
University of Minho
Guimaraes, Portugal

José Gabriel Pinto ⓘ
University of Minho
Guimaraes, Portugal

Vítor Monteiro ⓘ
University of Minho
Guimaraes, Portugal

ISSN 1867-8211          ISSN 1867-822X   (electronic)
Lecture Notes of the Institute for Computer Sciences, Social Informatics
and Telecommunications Engineering
ISBN 978-3-030-12949-1          ISBN 978-3-030-12950-7   (eBook)
https://doi.org/10.1007/978-3-030-12950-7

Library of Congress Control Number: 2019931003

This Springer imprint is published by the registered company Springer Nature Switzerland AG
The registered company address is: Gewerbestrasse 11, 6330 Cham, Switzerland

# Preface

We are pleased to present the proceedings of the fifth edition of the International Conference on Green Energy and Networking (GreeNets), promoted by the European Alliance for Innovation (EAI) in collaboration with the University of Minho, Portugal. The GreeNets 2018 conference was part of the fourth annual Smart City 360° Summit Event, realized in Guimarães, Portugal, and promoted a multidisciplinary scientific meeting to solve complex societal, technological, and economic problems of emerging Smart Cities. As a contribution to reduce the impact of climate change, while maintaining social prosperity as a priority, the broad themes of green energy and networking are vital for ensuring a balance between economic growth and environmental sustainability. In this context, the growing global concern has led to the adoption of new technological paradigms, especially for the operation of future Smart Cities. All of the topics related to these subjects were addressed during the GreeNets 2018 conference.

The technical program of GreeNets 2018 consisted of 15 full papers in oral presentation sessions in the main conference tracks. All of the accepted papers were subjected to a peer-review blinded process with a minimum of four reviews per paper. It was a great pleasure to work with the excellent organizing team of the EAI, which was absolutely essential for the success of the GreeNets 2018 conference. In particular, we would like to express our gratitude to Kristina Lappyova and Marek Kaleta for all the support they provided throughout. We would also like to express our gratitude to all the members of the Technical Program Committee, who helped in the peer-review process of the technical papers and allowed us to have a high-quality technical program. We would like to thank the external reviewers from several areas of expertise and from numerous countries around the world.

The GreeNets 2018 conference provided a good scientific meeting for all researchers, developers, and practitioners to discuss all science and technology aspects that are relevant to a Smart City perspective. With the success of the GreeNets 2018 conference, as demonstrated by the contributions presented in this volume, we expect a successful and stimulating future series of this conference.

January 2019

João L. Afonso
Vítor Monteiro
J. G. Pinto

# Conference Organization

## Steering Committee

Imrich Chlamtac      Bruno Kessler Professor, University of Trento, Italy

## Organizing Committee

### General Chair

João L. Afonso      University of Minho, Portugal

### General Co-chairs

Vítor Monteiro      University of Minho, Portugal
J. G. Pinto      University of Minho, Portugal

### TPC Chair and Co-chair

Carlos Couto      University of Minho, Portugal

### Technical Program Committee Co-chairs

| | |
|---|---|
| Jesus Doval-Gandoy | University of Vigo, Spain |
| João A. Peças Lopes | University of Porto, Portugal |
| Rune Hylsberg Jacobsen | Aarhus University, Denmark |
| Carlos Hengeler Antunes | University of Coimbra, Portugal |
| Marcelo Cabral Cavalcanti | Federal University of Pernambuco, Brazil |
| João P. S. Catalão | University of Porto, Portugal |
| Jose A. Afonso | University of Minho, Portugal |
| António Pina Martins | University of Porto, Portugal |
| Hfaiedh Mechergui | University of Tunis, Tunisia |
| Luis Origa | São Paulo State University, Brazil |
| Chunhua Liu | City University of Hong Kong, SAR China |
| Luis Monteiro | Rio de Janeiro State University, Brazil |
| Marcin Jarnut | University of Zielona Gora, Poland |
| João P. P. Carmo | University of São Paulo, Brazil |
| Luis A. S. B. Martins | University of Minho, Portugal |

### Sponsorship and Exhibit Chair

Joao Aparicio Fernandes      University of Minho, Portugal

### Local Chairs

Madalena Araujo      University of Minho, Portugal
Julio S. Martins      University of Minho, Portugal

## Workshops Chairs

Marcello Mezaroba             UDESC – Santa Catarina State University, Brazil
M. J. Sepulveda               University of Minho, Portugal

## Publicity and Social Media Chair

Paula Ferreira                University of Minho, Portugal

## Publications Chair

Joao C. Ferreira              ISCTE – University Institute of Lisbon, Portugal

## Web Chair

Andres A. Nogueiras           University of Vigo, Spain
  Melendez

# Contents

# Improved Voltage Control of the Electric Vehicle Operating as UPS in Smart Homes

Vítor Monteiro[1]([✉]), Joao P. S. Catalão[2], Tiago J. C. Sousa[1],
J. G. Pinto[1], Marcello Mezaroba[3], and João L. Afonso[1]

[1] ALGORITMI Research Centre, University of Minho, Guimarães, Portugal
vmonteiro@dei.uminho.pt
[2] INESC TEC and Faculty of Engineering of the University of Porto,
Porto, Portugal
[3] Santa Catarina State University, Joinville, Brazil

**Abstract.** As a contribution for sustainability, electric vehicles (EVs) are seen as one of the most effective influences in the transport sector. As complement to the challenges that entails the EVs integration into the grid considering the bidirectional operation (grid-to-vehicle and vehicle-to-grid), there are new concepts associated with the EV operation integrating various benefits for smart homes. In this sense, this paper proposes an improved voltage control of the EV operating as uninterruptible power supply (UPS) in smart homes. With the EV plugged-in into the smart home, it can act as an off-line UPS protecting the electrical appliances from power grid outages. Throughout the paper, the foremost advantages of the proposed voltage control strategy are comprehensively emphasized, establishing a comparison with the classical approach. Aiming to offer a sinusoidal voltage for linear and nonlinear electrical appliances, a pulse-width modulation with a multi-loop control scheme is used. A Kalman filter is used for decreasing significantly the time of detecting power outages and, consequently, the transition for the UPS mode. The experimental validation was executed with a bidirectional charger containing a double stage power conversion (an ac-dc interfacing the grid-side and a dc-dc interfacing the batteries-side) and a digital stage. The computer simulations and the acquired experimental results validate the proposed strategy in different conditions of operation.

**Keywords:** Electric vehicle · Bidirectional converter · Uninterruptible power supply · Kalman filter · Smart home

## 1 Introduction

The intensification use of electric vehicles (EVs) leads to new challenges for the grid controlling with respect to the energy needed for the batteries charging (grid-to-vehicle, G2V mode), particularly when assuming a substantial amount of VEs plugged-in [1–3]. As example, a strategy to minimize the peak load caused by a fleets of EVs is presented in [4], the contribution of EVs for demand response in distributed power grid is proposed in [5], an analysis of the EVs integration through different dynamics in the power grid is presented in [6], and a review of the impact caused by EVs on distribution power grid is presented in [7]. In response to the G2V and V2G tasks that the

J. L. Afonso et al. (Eds.): GreeNets 2018, LNICST 269, pp. 1–12, 2019.
https://doi.org/10.1007/978-3-030-12950-7_1

EVs incorporation entails, and with the creation of the communication network connecting all the players, there are new opportunities in terms of distributed storage to help to stabilize the power grid operation [8]. Some of these opportunities are related with distributed energy resources (DER) in microgrids: the collective process of EVs and solar PV panels for the energy generation portfolio is analyzed in [9], a DER with EVs controlled by a collaborative broker is presented in [3], an EV charging on an office building with DER is presented in [10], a smart distribution grid with EVs is experimentally analyzed in [11], and optimized energy management of EVs in microgrids is presented in [12]. In these circumstances are expected EVs prepared to accomplish a bidirectional operation, i.e., consuming or delivering energy from or to the grid (vehicle-to-grid, V2G mode) [13, 14]. Besides the bidirectional operation, new concepts for the EV functioning in smart grids and smart homes are emerging [15, 16], highlighting assistances for improving power quality [17, 18].

In addition to the G2V and V2G modes, the spread of the EVs will also consent the emergence of new concepts for the EV utilization framed with new technologies for smart homes. One of these new concepts is the possibility of the EV operation as an uninterruptible power supply (UPS). This option is only accessible when the EV is plugged-in at the smart home. Since in this operation mode the EV is used to provide additional functionalities for the smart home, it is identified as vehicle-to-home (V2H). This operation mode consists in use the energy stored in the EV batteries to supply the electrical appliances during power outages, which is different of the scheduling management between EVs and electrical appliances [19, 20]. The V2H operation mode was initially proposed for isolated locations, where there is no connection to the grid, however, without the UPS functionality [21]. Commercially, this concept was initially introduced by Nissan under the name "LEAF-to-Home", however, it requires a "EV Power Station", letting the V2H approach only where it is installed, but it does not allow the operation as a UPS in case of power outages. The possibility of the V2H mode as UPS was introduced in [22], however, without a satisfactory experimental validation in terms of synthetized voltage in the UPS mode. The main contributions of this paper are: Improved voltage control of the EV operating as UPS in smart homes; Faster transient from the G2V to the V2H mode; Experimental validation of the EV charger prototype operating with the proposed voltage control.

The paper is organized as follows. After the contextualization, Sect. 2 presents the EV integration, Sect. 3 introduces a description of the EV charger, Sect. 4 presents the multi-loop voltage control for the V2H mode, Sect. 5 presents the most relevant experimental results, and, finally, Sect. 6 presents the main conclusion.

## 2   EV Integration into Smart Homes

In a smart home perspective, the operation of some of the electrical appliances are on/off controlled according to the energy management and the user comforts and conveniences. These electrical appliances require two fundamental things for a properly operation: power and an internal communication. Since the EV is plugged-in at the smart home, in case of power outages, it can provide uninterrupted power for the electrical appliances according to the battery state-of-charge (cf. Sect. 1). However, in order to prevent a fully battery discharging, some of electrical appliances can be turned-off at the same time of the power outage occurrence (e.g., heating systems or secondary lights), but others not (e.g., internal communication system, main lights, or the alarm system). The criteria to select the electrical appliances supplied by the V2H mode as UPS is established by the smart home energy management. The introduction of the EV charger into a smart home during the operation in G2V mode (charging the batteries) and in V2H mode (as an off line UPS to supply the smart home electrical appliances) is presented in Fig. 1.

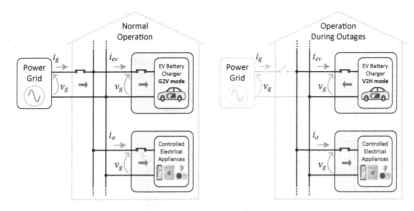

**Fig. 1.** Introduction of the EV charger into a smart home during: (a) Operation in G2V mode (charging the batteries); (b) Operation in V2H mode (as an off-line UPS to supply the smart home electrical appliances).

## 3    EV Battery Charger Description

In a smart home perspective arises the occasion to integrate a bidirectional EV charger with new functionalities, representing a pertinent influence for the home energy management. Therefore, the presented EV charger also allows the V2H mode as an off-line UPS. In the scope of this paper, the developed EV charger comprises two power converters linked by a dc-link. One of the converters interfaces the grid-side and the other interfaces the batteries-side. For the converter that interfaces the power grid a fully-controlled active full-bridge rectifier is used to make the current consumption sinusoidal with unitary power factor (in G2V and V2G modes) [23–26]. During the V2H mode as an UPS, the ac-dc converter operates as a voltage source controlled to synthesizing a voltage signal with the amplitude and frequency needed to supply the electrical appliances connected in the smart home. The converter that interfaces the batteries (dc-dc), during the G2V mode, acts as a buck converter, controlling the periods of the battery charging. During the V2G mode, it acts as a boost converter, discharging the batteries. During the V2H mode as an UPS, the dc-dc converter is responsible for regulating the voltage of the dc-link for the correct operation of the ac-dc converter.

The introduction of the EV charger into a smart home is presented in Fig. 2, showing the internal arrangement of the EV charger, where LC low-pass filters are used at the grid-side and at the batteries-side to filter the high frequencies produced by the converters. In the grid-side, targeting to smooth the gain response of the LC filter at the cut-off frequency, a damping resistor is used in series with the capacitor. In the battery-side, a capacitor with low equivalent series resistor is used, targeting to attain a low current ripple in the batteries. All of the semiconductors (IGBTs) are switched at 20 kHz and the components were selected establishing a conciliation among the filter performance and size.

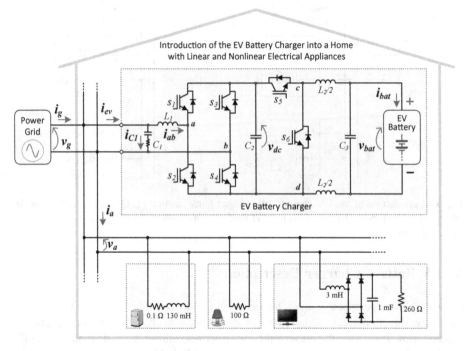

**Fig. 2.** Introduction of the EV charger into a smart home and its internal arrangement in terms of power electronics converters.

## 4   Multi-loop Voltage Control

A meticulous explanation of the proposed multi-loop voltage control applied to the V2H mode as UPS is introduced in this section, which is based on a predictive control strategy deducted from the circuit topology shown in Fig. 2. The multi-loop voltage control has as main purpose the EV charging control for producing an ac-side voltage with the nominal rms and frequency values of the grid voltage, i.e., the nominal values before the outage. Since the proposed algorithm does not require any gain in its modulation, it is only dependent of the converter parameters, represents a pertinent benefit due to the unpredictability operation of the linear or nonlinear electrical appliances connected into the home. By applying the first Kirchhoff law, the relation among the grid-side current ($i_{ev}$), the current in the passive filter C1 ($i_{C1}$), and the current of the converter ($i_{ab}$), can be expressed by:

$$i_{ev} = i_{C1} + i_{ab}. \tag{1}$$

On the other hand, in order to obtain the relation among the voltage produced by the converter (denoted by $v_{ab}$ in Fig. 2), the voltage in the passive filter L1 ($v_{L1}$), and the voltage applied to the electrical appliances is used the second Kirchhoff law, as expressed by:

$$v_{ab} = -v_{L1} + v_g. \tag{2}$$

Since the voltage across the inductor $L_1$ is expressed by:

$$v_{L1} = L_1 \frac{di_{ab}}{dt}, \tag{3}$$

substituting the Eq. (3) in the Eq. (1) is attained the subsequent relation:

$$v_{ab} = -L_1 \frac{di_{ab}}{dt} + v_g. \tag{4}$$

Knowing that the current $i_{ab}$ is provided by the Eq. (1), and existing the possibility to determine the current in the capacitor $C_1$ using the equation (it was considered that the damping resistor is negligible):

$$i_{C1} = C_1 \frac{dv_g}{dt}, \tag{5}$$

the final equation is obtained from:

$$v_{ab} = -L_1 \frac{d}{dt} \left( i_{ev} - C_1 \frac{dv_{C1}}{dt} \right) + v_g. \tag{6}$$

Reorganizing the terms of Eq. (6), and considering the grid side voltage ($v_g$) equal to the voltage variation at the capacitor $C_1$, is obtained the equation:

$$v_{ab} = L_1 C_1 \frac{d^2 v_g}{dt^2} - L_1 \frac{di_{ev}}{dt} + v_g. \tag{7}$$

The derivatives can be estimated by linear variations without leading noteworthy error due to the high sampling frequency. Therefore, the Eq. (7) is simplified for:

$$v_{ab} = \frac{L_1 C_1}{T_a^2} \left( v_g^*[k] - 2v_g[k] + v_g[k-1] \right) -$$
$$+ \frac{L_1}{T_a} \left( i_{ev}[k] - i_{ev}[k-1] \right) + v_g[k]. \tag{8}$$

## 5   Experimental Results

In this section, the experimental results of the tests that were carried out with the EV charger are presented. These results were attained for validating the proposed multi-loop voltage control presented in Sect. 4, mainly, under the V2H mode as UPS. Figure 3 shows the laboratory workbench where all the experimental tests were carried out. It should be noted that all the experimental results were obtained using the Yokogawa DL708E oscilloscope.

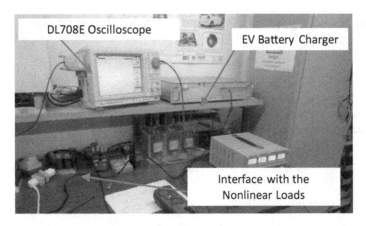

**Fig. 3.** Laboratory workbench used for the experimental tests.

With the purpose to control the EV charger according to the objectives outlined, it is indispensable to implement a synchronization algorithm with the fundamental component of the grid voltage. Thereby, a phase locked-loop (PLL) was used to attain such synchronization. In Fig. 4(a), it can be observed the synchronism of the PLL signal ($v_{PLL}$) with the grid voltage during 50 ms. It should be noted that this result was attained in steady state, i.e., after the PLL is completely synchronized with the voltage. A detail of both signals is presented in Fig. 4(b).

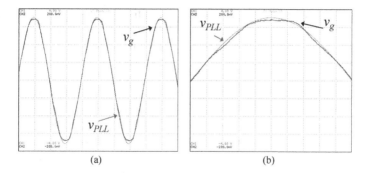

**Fig. 4.** Experimental results: (a) Synchronism of the PLL signal ($v_{PLL}$) with the power grid voltage ($v_g$); (b) Detail of both signals.

As mentioned in Sect. 2, the current control strategy for the ac-dc converter of the EV charger needs a sinusoidal reference, which is compared with the measured grid-side current for obtaining the PWM signals of the IGBTs. As validate through the result shown in Fig. 5(a), the grid-side current is sinusoidal with the same phase of the voltage, demonstrating the excellent operation of the current control loop. In order to charge the EV batteries, a constant reference of current was selected. As can be validated through the Fig. 5(b), in steady, the charging current state is constant, validating the current control and the operation of the dc-dc converter. However, as can be seen in figure, the reference of current value does not immediately take the maximum value, i.e., the value is gradually increased until reaching the desired value. This plan is used in order to prevent oscillations of the dc-link voltage, which was perfectly achieved, as demonstrated in this figure.

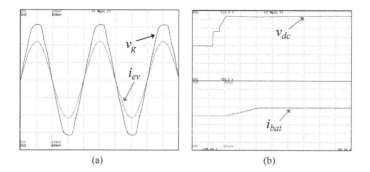

**Fig. 5.** Experimental results: (a) Power grid voltage ($v_g$) and EV current ($i_{ev}$) in G2V mode; (b) EV battery current ($i_{bat}$) and dc-link voltage ($v_{dc}$) in the G2V mode.

During the tests carried out with the EV charger operating in the V2H mode, a comparison was established in terms of the calculation of the rms voltage using a traditional method and a method based on the Kalman filter. The main purpose of this comparison was to verify if the calculation based on the Kalman filter is faster than the traditional approach. A set of computer simulations were obtained for different amplitudes of outages and considering its occurrence in different angles of the voltage, showing that the Kalman filter offers better results for all the operating scenarios. However, since this study is out of the scope of this paper, they were omitted. Therefore, an experimental validation was carried out using a Kalman filter. As can be validated through the Fig. 6, the power outage was detected by the control system about in 0.4 ms after the outage, time in which the EV charger starts its operation as energy source, i.e., the required time for the operation as UPS.

In order to confirm the EV charger operation and to evaluate the performance of the multi-loop voltage control in V2H mode as UPS considering a real scenario, linear and nonlinear electrical appliances were used in the experimental validation. The tests began with a representative linear electrical appliance of heating systems (in the laboratory, a resistor of 26 Ω was selected for such purpose). In Fig. 7(a) can be observe the voltage synthesized by the EV charger and applied to the linear electrical appliance, as well as the consumed current. In this first test the voltage synthesized by the EV charger is totally sinusoidal, does not present any distortion as intended, thus being validated the multi-loop voltage control applied to the ac-dc converter. After the initial test performed with a linear electrical appliance, experimental tests were carried out with nonlinear electrical appliances to evaluate the proposed multi-loop voltage control. In Fig. 7(b) it is possible to observe the results of this experimental test, where a resistive load with a value of 26 Ω and a diode rectifier with a capacitive output filter with a capacitance value of 470 μF are coupled to the EV charger during the operation as UPS. As shown in the result obtained in Fig. 7(b), due to the proposed multi-loop voltage applied to the ac-dc converter, it was possible to synthesize a sinusoidal voltage with reduced harmonic distortion.

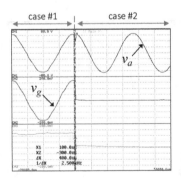

**Fig. 6.** Experimental result showing the detection of a power outage and the beginning of the V2H mode as UPS.

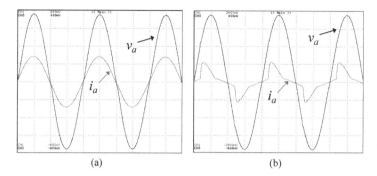

**Fig. 7.** Experimental results of the produced voltage ($v_a$) and consumed current ($i_a$) during the V2H mode as UPS considering: (a) linear electrical appliances; (b) nonlinear electrical appliances.

During the tests performed on the EV charger operating as an UPS, the dc-link voltage and the current in the EV batteries were also analyzed in order to see if the dc-link voltage control is operating correctly. The result of this experimental test can be seen in Fig. 8. Initially, the dc-link regulation is achieved through the EV charger operating as G2V. When the dc-link voltage is at its reference value a power outage occurs and, subsequently, the charging is interrupted, the EV charger is unplugged from the grid and initiates the operation in V2H mode as UPS. As shown in Fig. 8(a), during the transition from the G2V mode to the V2H mode as UPS, a voltage sag in the dc-link occurs, which is readily recovered by the control algorithm inherent to the dc-dc converter, keeping the dc-link voltage at a steady state voltage close to the defined reference. It should be noted that the voltage sag on the dc-link can be minimized, however, the discharging current of the batteries at that time would have a high current peak. Taking into account this factor, a cost-benefit ratio was chosen, opting to reduce the peak current of the batteries and increase the voltage sag of the dc-link during the transition from operating modes. In Fig. 8(a) it is also possible to verify the discharging current with a constant stage during the operation in the V2H mode as UPS. It should be noted that throughout the V2H mode, and for all the electrical appliances, the result of the dc-link voltage and of the EV battery current is comparable, changing only the discharge value of the batteries. In addition to the above-mentioned results, a shift from the V2H to the G2V mode was attained. As shown in Fig. 8(b), a transition is obtained without the existence of any type of transient, either in the current or in the voltage. This is because the transition does not happen instantly after the power grid is reestablished, but rather after the signal resulting from the PLL is fully synchronized with the grid voltage and the control system waits a period of 5 s in order to verify that there were no other power grid outages.

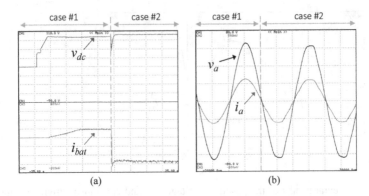

(a)                                          (b)

**Fig. 8.** Experimental results: (a) EV battery current ($i_{bat}$) and dc-link voltage ($v_{dc}$) in the G2V mode during the transition of the G2V mode to the V2H mode as UPS; (b) Voltage ($v_a$) and current ($i_a$) in the electrical appliances during the transition from the V2H mode to the normal mode.

# 6   Conclusions

An improved voltage control for the electric vehicle (EV) operation in vehicle-to-home (V2H) mode as an off-line uninterruptible power supply (UPS) is proposed in the context of smart homes. The V2H mode as UPS represents a complement to the challenges that entails the EVs integration into the grid, representing a pertinent benefit for smart homes, since the EV can be used for protecting the electrical appliances from grid outages. The voltage control is based on a predictive control strategy, deducted from the circuit topology of the EV charger. Its main purpose consists in establish an ac-side voltage with the nominal rms and frequency values of the grid voltage. An EV battery charger based on a double stage power conversion was developed for the experimental validation, showing the correct action in the V2H mode as UPS, mainly characterized by a fast transition from the normal mode to the UPS mode and by a sinusoidal voltage even with nonlinear loads.

**Acknowledgment.** This work has been supported by COMPETE: POCI-01-0145-FEDER-007043 and FCT – Fundação para a Ciência e Tecnologia within the Project Scope: UID/CEC/00319/2013. This work is financed by the ERDF – European Regional Development Fund through the Operational Programme for Competitiveness and Internationalisation – COMPETE 2020 Programme, and by National Funds through the Portuguese funding agency, FCT – Fundação para a Ciência e a Tecnologia, within project SAICTPAC/0004/2015 – POCI – 01-0145–FEDER–016434. This work is part of the FCT project 0302836 NORTE-01-0145-FEDER-030283.

# References

1. Monteiro, V., Ferreira, J.C., Meléndez, A.A.N., Afonso, J.L.: Electric vehicles on-board battery charger for the future smart grids. In: Camarinha-Matos, L.M., Tomic, S., Graça, P. (eds.) DoCEIS 2013. IAICT, vol. 394, pp. 351–358. Springer, Heidelberg (2013). https://doi.org/10.1007/978-3-642-37291-9_38

2. Monteiro, V., Gonçalves, H., Afonso, J.L.: Impact of electric vehicles on power quality in a smart grid context. In: IEEE EPQU International Conference on Electrical Power Quality and Utilisation, pp. 1–6, October 2011

3. Ferreira, J.C., da Silva, A.R., Monteiro, V., Afonso, J.L.: Collaborative broker for distributed energy resources. In: Madureira, A., Reis, C., Marques, V. (eds.) Computational Intelligence and Decision Making. ISCA, vol. 61, pp. 365–376. Springer, Dordrecht (2013). https://doi.org/10.1007/978-94-007-4722-7_34

4. Nguyen, V.L., Tran-Quoc, T., Bacha, S., Nguyen, B.: Charging strategies to minimize the peak load for an electric vehicle fleet. In: IECON 2014 - 40th Annual Conference of the IEEE Industrial Electronics Society, pp. 3522–3528. IEEE, October 2014

5. Wang, Y., Sheikh, O., Hu, B., Chu, C.-C., Gadh, R.: Integration of V2H/V2G hybrid system for demand response in distribution network. In: 2014 IEEE International Conference on Smart Grid Communications (SmartGridComm), pp. 812–817. IEEE, November 2014

6. Lopes, J.A.P., Soares, F.J., Almeida, P.M.R.: Integration of electric vehicles in the electric power system. Proc. IEEE 99(1), 168–183 (2011)

7. Green, R.C., Wang, L., Alam, M.: The impact of plug-in hybrid electric vehicles on distribution networks: a review and outlook. In: IEEE PES General Meeting, vol. 15, no. 1, pp. 1–8. IEEE, July 2010

8. Zhao, J.H., Wen, F., Dong, Z.Y., Xue, Y., Wong, K.P.: Optimal dispatch of electric vehicles and wind power using enhanced particle swarm optimization. IEEE Trans. Ind. Inform. 8(4), 889–899 (2012)

9. Vithayasrichareon, P., Mills, G., MacGill, I.F.: Impact of electric vehicles and solar PV on future generation portfolio investment. IEEE Trans. Sustain. Energy 6(3), 899–908 (2015)

10. Van Roy, J., Leemput, N., Geth, F., Büscher, J., Salenbien, R., Driesen, J.: Electric vehicle charging in an office building microgrid with distributed energy resources. IEEE Trans. Sustain. Energy 5(4), 1389–1396 (2014)

11. Gouveia, C., et al.: Experimental validation of smart distribution grids: development of a microgrid and electric mobility laboratory. Elsevier Electr. Power Energy Syst. 78, 765–775 (2016)

12. Zhang, M., Chen, J.: The energy management and optimized operation of electric vehicles based on microgrid. IEEE Trans. Power Deliv. 29(3), 1427–1435 (2014)

13. Jin, C., Tang, J., Ghosh, P.: Optimizing electric vehicle charging: a customer's perspective. IEEE Trans. Veh. Technol. 62(7), 2919–2927 (2013)

14. Kisacikoglu, M.C., Ozpineci, B., Tolbert, L.M.: EV/PHEV bidirectional charger assessment for V2G reactive power operation. IEEE Trans. Power Electron. 28(12), 5717–5727 (2013)

15. Galus, M.D., Vayá, M.G., Krause, T., Andersson, G.: The role of electric vehicles in smart grids. Interdiscip. Rev.: Energy Environ. 2, 384–400 (2013)

16. Gungor, V.C., et al.: Smart grid and smart homes - key players and pilot projects. IEEE Ind. Electron. Mag. 6, 18–34 (2012)

17. Monteiro, V., Pinto, J.G., Afonso, J.L.: Operation modes for the electric vehicle in smart grids and smart homes: present and proposed modes. IEEE Trans. Veh. Technol. 65(3), 1007–1020 (2016)

18. Boynuegri, A.R., Uzunoglu, M., Erdinc, O., Gokalp, E.: A new perspective in grid connection of electric vehicles: different operating modes for elimination of energy quality problems. Elsevier Appl. Energy **132**, 435–451 (2014)
19. Tushar, M.H.K., Assi, C., Maier, M., Uddin, M.F.: Smart microgrids: optimal joint scheduling for electric vehicles and home appliances. IEEE Trans. Smart Grid **5**(1), 239–250 (2014)
20. Monteiro, V., Carmo, J.P., Pinto, J.G., Afonso, J.L.: A flexible infrastructure for dynamic power control of electric vehicle battery chargers. IEEE Trans. Veh. Technol. **65**(6), 4535–4547 (2016)
21. Pinto, J.G., et al.: Bidirectional battery charger with grid to vehicle, vehicle to grid and vehicle to home technologies. In: IEEE IECON Industrial Electronics Conference, Vienna Austria, pp. 5934–5939, November 2013
22. Monteiro, V., Exposto, B., Ferreira, J.C., Afonso, J.L.: Improved vehicle-to-home (iV2H) operation mode: experimental analysis of the electric vehicle as off-line UPS. IEEE Trans. Smart Grid **8**(6), 2702–2711 (2017)
23. Monteiro, V., Ferreira, J.C., Meléndez, A.A.N., Afonso, J.L.: Model predictive control applied to an improved five-level bidirectional converter. IEEE Trans. Ind. Electron. **63**(9), 5879–5890 (2016)
24. Monteiro, V., Ferreira, J.C., Meléndez, A.A.N., Couto, C., Afonso, J.L.: Experimental validation of a novel architecture based on a dual-stage converter for off-board fast battery chargers of electric vehicles. IEEE Trans. Veh. Tech. **67**(2), 1000–1011 (2018)
25. Monteiro, V., Meléndez, A.A.N., Couto, C., Afonso, J.L.: Model predictive current control of a proposed single-switch three-level active rectifier applied to EV battery chargers. In: IEEE IECON Industrial Electronics Conference, Florence, Italy, pp. 1365–1370, October 2016
26. Monteiro, V., Ferreira, J.C., Pedrosa, D., Sepúlveda, M.J., Aparício Fernandes, J.C., Afonso, J.L.: Comprehensive analysis and comparison of digital current control techniques for active rectifiers. In: Garrido, P., Soares, F., Moreira, A. (eds.) CONTROLO 2016. LNEE, vol. 402, pp. 655–666. Springer, Cham (2017). https://doi.org/10.1007/978-3-319-43671-5_55

# Energy End-Use Flexibility of the Next Generation of Decision-Makers in a Smart Grid Setting: An Exploratory Study

Inês F. G. Reis[1]([⊠]) , Marta A. R. Lopes[1,2] ,
Paula F. V. Ferreira[3] , Carlos Henggeler Antunes[1,4] ,
and Madalena Araújo[3]

[1] INESC Coimbra - Institute for Systems Engineering and Computers, DEEC,
R. Sílvio Lima, 3030-290 Coimbra, Portugal
inesfreis@deec.uc.pt
[2] Department of Environment - ESAC, Polytechnic Institute of Coimbra,
3045-601 Coimbra, Portugal
[3] ALGORITMI Research Centre, University of Minho, Campus Azurém,
4800-058 Guimarães, Portugal
[4] Department of Electrical and Computer Engineering, University of Coimbra,
Pólo II, R. Sílvio Lima, 3030-290 Coimbra, Portugal

**Abstract.** Demand Response (DR) mechanisms have been developed to reshape consumption patterns in face of price signals, enabling to deal with the increasing penetration of intermittent renewable resources and balance electricity demand and supply. Although DR mechanisms have been in place for some time, it is still unclear to what extent end-users are ready, or willing, to embrace DR programs that can be complex and imply adjustments of daily routines. This work aims to understand how the next generation of Portuguese decision makers, namely young adults in higher education, are prepared to deal with energy decisions in the context of the challenges brought by the smart grids. Results demonstrate that cost savings and the contribution to environmental protection are found to be important motivating factors to enroll into DR programs, which should be further exploited in future actions for the promotion of end-user engagement. Moreover, DR solutions are well-accepted by higher education students, although with limited flexibility levels. In addition, there is room to exploit the willingness to adopt time-differentiated tariffs, yet savings should be clearer and more attractive to end-users. Also, the framing effect should be considered when promoting this type of time-differentiated tariffs.

**Keywords:** Energy decision-makers · Smart grids · End-use flexibility · Smart technologies

## 1 Introduction

The process of decarbonizing the economy will depend, to some extent, on the demand-side flexibility, which may be fostered through the use of time-differentiated tariffs, either with static and dynamic options [1]. In these pricing schemes, end-users

J. L. Afonso et al. (Eds.): GreeNets 2018, LNICST 269, pp. 13–23, 2019.
https://doi.org/10.1007/978-3-030-12950-7_2

are encouraged to adopt more flexible consumption patterns, adjusting their demand profile by reducing or increasing consumption in different time periods, shifting load operation to cheaper time periods or redefining thermostat settings [2, 3]. According to [2] and [4], some factors may influence end-users' enrolment in DR programs, such as: end-user's energy literacy level; the complexity of DR programs and dynamic tariffs; technology costs (when compared to savings and incentives provided); the effort required to search for dynamic pricing information and adjust electrical appliances usage accordingly; risk/loss aversion; and the inertia associated with behavioral change. Moreover, in most European countries, time-differentiated tariffs are not provided to end-users as default, but as an option. Hence, it is relevant to assess end-users' motivations and preferences in what concerns the adoption of those tariffs, enrolment into DR schemes, level of flexibility and adoption of smart technologies, in the context of evolution of electrical networks to smart grids. This work aims to understand how the next generation of Portuguese decision makers, namely young adults in higher education, are prepared to deal with energy decisions in the context of the challenges brought by the smart grids. It presents the combination of two complementary exploratory surveys targeted at Portuguese higher education students exploring their motivations and concerns to be enrolled in DR programs and assessing factors influencing the adoption of time-differentiated tariffs.

## 2 Literature Review

The need to balance energy demand and supply has become more pressing due to the increasing penetration of renewable sources characterized by their intermittent nature. One of the approaches for bridging the demand-supply mismatch in the energy systems is using demand-side management (DSM) techniques to shape demand profiles [5]. DR mechanisms are relevant DSM tools, relying on price signals as the main incentives to change electricity consumption patterns [6]. Some works in the literature exploit end-users' responsiveness to DR programs. For instance, [7] and [8] modeled the influence of pricing in the adjustment of load operation. When comparing these results with a real world experiment conducted by [4], it turns out that simulation results are optimistic and that end-users only accept to change their daily behavior in response to price signals to a certain degree. Usually, end-users are interested in minimizing their energy bills by taking advantage of pricing conditions and transfer home appliance operation to off-peak hours [9]. However, end-users tend to organize their domestic activities based on their preferences; therefore, while some load operations are relatively easy to shift, to interrupt or to re-parameterize, others are more restricted [1]. For instance, a study developed in [10] revealed that residential users in The Netherlands are willing to postpone the start of dishwashers, washing machines, clothes dryers, irons, vacuum cleaners, heating systems and the charging of electric vehicles. Still, lower levels of flexibility were associated with the use of the electric oven. Also, the survey developed in [11] found that Portuguese end-users are more willing to shift the operation of the laundry machine and the dishwasher than of other appliances, identifying electricity savings, not compromising the energy service, and environmental benefits as the main decision factors. In addition, some level of end-users' commitment is required to decode and process complex information on time-differentiated pricing mechanisms. Thus, according to [12] it should be expected that high-literate end-users are more likely to adopt time-differentiated rates since, in principle, people with higher levels of literacy should be more able to understand the advantages of this adoption. In addition, renters generally seek innovative solutions to minimize their costs and therefore are also expected to adopt some type of time-differentiated tariffs. Nevertheless, the literature suggests that end-users show adverse reactions to the adoption of these tariffs due to their complexity. For example, the study in [2] highlights that "*consumers are open to dynamic pricing but prefer simple to complex and highly dynamic programs*". These findings are in accordance with [13], who concluded that end-users are more willing to adopt simpler tariffs, with fixed tariffs being preferred to all others. Although there is a consensus on the preference for simpler tariffs, little is known about how end-users assess time-differentiated tariffs and what is the influence of varying price information presentation on commercial offers [12]. Moreover, no study was found on the preferences of the next generation of energy decision makers.

## 3   Objectives

In this setting, this work aims to understand how end-users perceive the complex energy decision context brought by smart grids, in particular, their preferences and willingness to enroll into DR programs and time-differentiated tariffs to support the design of future energy systems. This work presents the results of two complementary exploratory surveys performed within Portuguese higher education students. Young adults were the target of this work because they will soon be the next generation of energy bill payers and the main energy decision-makers in the context of future smart energy systems. In general, this age group is not in charge of making energy related decisions or paying the energy bill. Young adults are also generally seen as more environmentally and energy aware and driven by personal values, while more cautious about money and time management [14]. This age group is more aware of the advantages and constraints of smart grids, when compared to other segments of the population [10]. Thus, this work aims to contribute to understand how young adults perceive the technological opportunities offered by smart grids and what are their motivations to participate in DR actions and time-differentiated tariffs, which represents a contribution to the existing literature about the topic.

The motivation, context and objectives of this study have been provided in Sects. 1, 2 and 3. Section 4 presents the research methods used and the main results are reported in Sect. 5. Section 6 presents the main conclusions and recommendations for future work.

## 4   Research Methods

Two complementary approaches addressing the general objective of this work were developed using surveys made available through online platforms. The complexity of the topic created important challenges to the design of surveys, as these need to have technical robustness while displaying the ability to be answered by non-experts. The surveys were made available to higher education students enrolled at Portuguese higher education institutions in undergraduate and postgraduate studies. This group was chosen as they are the next energy-related decision makers generation and to ensure higher literacy levels. Different academic backgrounds were included to guarantee diversity. Both approaches addressed the same target audience and the topic assessed, while having their own specificities.

## 4.1  Case Study 1

Case study 1 aims to exploit the motivations and concerns behind the willingness to enroll into DR programs. Table 1 summarizes the dimensions and variables included in the survey.

**Table 1.** Dimensions included in the case study 1 survey

| Dimensions | Variables |
| --- | --- |
| Socio-demographic characterization | Gender, age, on-going level of studies and number of residents at home |
| Level of knowledge and participation in the energy management at home | Monitoring habits on reading the electricity meter, supplier switching rate, knowledge about time-differentiated tariff schemes and ownership of monitoring devices |
| Motivation for participating in DR programs | Main motivations for engaging in DR programs, including potential savings, environmental or other important concerns behind the willingness to enroll into DR programs and on the importance of feedback from peers |
| Flexibility and willingness to change electricity use habits | Willingness to participate in DR programs, delay consumption or change electricity use time, if they could benefit from a reduction on their electricity tariffs |

This survey followed the following steps: first, it was designed and tested by a small group using a face-to-face approach and email; second, it was improved based on the feedback collected; and third, it was implemented through Google Surveys between February and April 2018.

## 4.2  Case Study 2

Case study 2 exploited factors that, to some extent, influence the willingness of end-users to adopt a time-differentiated tariff. The survey included the dimensions and variables presented in Table 2.

**Table 2.** Dimensions included in the case study 2 survey

| Dimensions | Variables |
|---|---|
| Socio-demographic characterization | Gender, age, academic background and housing situation |
| Enrollment in electricity management | Responsibility for the payment of the electricity bill; knowledge about contracted tariff and responsibility to choose the electricity tariff and supplier; monitoring habits of the electricity meter |
| Motivational factors to be flexible | Main motivations for engaging into time-differentiated pricing programs, including potential savings, savings-comfort trade-off and others considered relevant by respondents |
| Adoption of time-differentiated tariffs | Two exercises were designed to assess the willingness to participate in a time-differentiated scheme exploiting the format of the information provided (potential savings vs. increased costs). The way information about a tariff is presented triggering feelings of possible savings or potential losses, known as the framing effect, is presented as a feature to be taken into account in the promotion of those tariffs. In these exercises, respondents were asked to choose between maintaining a flat tariff or adopting a time-differentiated tariff. Graphical and numerical information was provided highlighting potential savings and increasing costs, distributed randomly in different versions among participants who were warned of potential changes to daily routines |

The survey was made available through a LimeSurvey platform to higher education students all over the country between March and May 2018.

## 5  Results

### 5.1  Case Study 1

The sample composed by 125 respondents consisted mainly of men (61.6%), mostly aged 18–24 (84.8%), with 8.8% being between the ages of 25 and 29 and the remaining more than 30 years old (Table 3). 59.2% are undergraduate students from different training areas and 40.80% are Master students. The majority are Portuguese (94.4%) and full-time students (88%). As for the number of residents in the housing, 9.6% live with only 1 or 2 members; 30.4% with 3 members; 44.4% of respondents with 4 members and 16% with 5 or more members.

**Table 3.** Socio-demographic characterization of case 1 sample

| Category | Variables | Level | Quantification |
|---|---|---|---|
| Personal | Gender | Female | 38.40% |
| | | Male | 61.60% |
| | Age | Between 18 and 24 | 84.80% |
| | | Between 25 and 29 | 8.80% |
| | | More than 30 | 6.40% |

(*continued*)

**Table 3.** (*continued*)

| Category | Variables | Level | Quantification |
|---|---|---|---|
| | Nationality | Portuguese | 99.40% |
| | | Other | 5.60% |
| | Course enrolment | Under-graduate | 59.20% |
| | | Master | 40.80% |
| | Student status | Student-worker | 12% |
| | | Full-time student | 88% |
| House | Number of residents | Between 1 and 2 members | 9.60% |
| | | 3 members | 30.40% |
| | | 4 members | 44.40% |
| | | 5 members or more | 16.00% |
| Energy management at home | Familiarity with time-differentiated tariffs | Yes | 67% |
| | | No | 33% |
| | Communicate energy consumption to supplier | Yes | 24% |
| | | No | 76% |
| | Electricity supplier change in the last 2 years | Yes | 9% |
| | | No | 91% |

Regarding the level of knowledge and the dynamism for participating in the electricity market, results show that over 67% of respondents reported to be familiar with time-differentiated tariffs and 24% regularly communicate electricity consumption to the supplier. However, students showed to be much less proactive on changing supplier, as only 9% have done it in the last 2 years, and on owning and using an electricity monitoring device. Declared motivations to defer electricity use were tested by asking respondents to give their opinion about several statements concerning the contribution towards the environment, fuel imports and electricity bill. The results indicate that all these factors can be assumed as relevant for the engagement on a DR program. In fact, 95% of the students would be willing to defer their electricity consumption if that would have a positive environmental impact, 89% if that would have a have a positive impact on the fuel imports, and 90% if that would have a positive impact on the electricity bill.

The large majority of the sample shows a real concern about the environment. This is an expected result as the Eurobarometer on Attitudes of European citizens towards the environment showed those with a higher education degree tend more likely to agree that they can play a role in protecting the environment [15]. However, the possibility of the cost reduction is still the most often motivation mentioned, being classified as "totally agree". Pearson's chi-square statistic tests indicate that younger respondents are more motivated to shift their electricity usage driven by economic ($p < 0.001$) and environmental factors ($p < 0.001$) and energy dependence ($p < 0.001$). The majority of students, who attend engineering courses, tend to be more sensitive to environmental factors than those enrolled in other fields. Recognizing the importance of the cost factor, the flexibility to postpone electricity usage was tested against different potential cost savings and considering different deferral periods for using electricity appliances such as the washing machine. Flexibility was assessed based on the respondents' willingness to defer the use of their domestic appliances for 1–2 h, 3–6 h or for more than 6 h. The results indicate that the willingness to defer electricity use tend to increase for higher potential cost savings (Fig. 1). However, flexibility is limited and the number of respondents willing to postpone their electricity use for more than 6 h (long-term) is considerably lower than the ones willing to delay it for 1–2 h (short-term), for all range of cost savings.

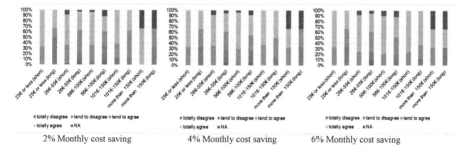

**Fig. 1.** Results regarding the willingness to defer electricity use according to potential monthly cost savings (2%, 4% and 6%, respectively)

The monthly electricity bill does not seem to play a major role on the overall assessment of the willingness to defer electricity use. Although the results indicate that consumers paying a high electricity bill (>150 €/month) tend to show a higher disagreement for both short-term and long-term flexibility, the number of participants included in this class is too low for considering the results as significant. As for consumers paying a low electricity bill (<25 €/month), the results also show a higher disagreement trend for long-term flexibility, comparatively to most of the other groups, for both the lowest and highest potential monthly cost saving cases. This can be explained by the lowest potential savings (in absolute terms) of respondents with lower electricity bills and by difficulties felt on changing electricity use patterns, or reduced interest on the topic in the case of respondents with higher electricity bills. It is worth noticing that this latter group is also the one showing more doubts for all the scenarios, as 33% of them selected the option "don't know". However, once more, this result must be looked with caution as the number of respondents in this group is very small. The middle groups (especially the ones 101–105 €/month) show a more stable pattern of responses with higher potential to participate in DR programs.

## 5.2   Case Study 2

Although case study 2 reached a total of 340 respondents, the sample was cut off at the age of 30 and the sample reduced to 270 respondents to ensure answers were only collected from the young adult segment. The sample is gender balanced (men 50%, women 50%) and respondents average age is around 22 years old (mean = 22.06; SD = 2.8) (Table 4). Most of them are students in Engineering and Exact Sciences (63.3%), while a small share is enrolled in Social Sciences and Humanities (28.9%),

**Table 4.** Socio-demographic characterization of case 2 sample

| Category | Variables | Level | Quantification |
|---|---|---|---|
| Personal | Gender | Female | 50% |
| | | Male | 50% |
| | Age | | Mean = 22.6 |
| | | | SD = 2.8 |
| | Academic background | Engineering | 63.3% |
| | | Social Sciences and Humanities | 28.9% |
| | | Life & Health Sciences | 6.3% |
| | | Non-specified | 1.5% |
| House | Ownership | Own | 6.3% |
| | | Owned by family | 33.0% |
| | | Rented | 56.7% |
| | | University facilities | 3.0% |
| | | Other | 1.1% |
| Energy management at home | Tariff | Flat | 37.8% |
| | | Time-differentiated | 23.0% |
| | | Unknown | 39.3% |
| | [If answer time-differentiated] Frequency of electric appliances usage only in the cheapest periods of the tariff | Valid = 56.45% Non-answers = 43.54% | Mean = 5.69 SD = 0.796 |
| | Responsibility for paying bills | Yes alone | 10.0% |
| | | Yes with other people | 51.1% |
| | | No | 38.9% |
| | Responsibility for decide contracted power/tariff | Yes alone | 7.4% |
| | | Yes with other people | 11.5% |
| | | No one else has decided | 37.4% |
| | | No, no one from the house decided | 43.7% |

Health and Life Sciences (6.3%) and other non-specified academic areas. Regarding housing, most of the surveyed sample rents a house with colleagues (56.7%), while 33% live with their own family, which may disclose that they typically do not make direct energy-related decisions (beyond the usage dimension).

As for electricity costs, 61.1% of the respondents are responsible for paying the electricity bills by themselves or with other people. Moreover, 30.7% of the respondents admit never, or very rarely, reading the invoice or online monitoring electricity consumption, but 61% state to know the contracted tariff. 37.8% still have a flat rate and, of these, 57.8% state that it is still the most advantageous solution given their consumption profile. However, respondents also presented other reasons to maintain this tariff, such as the landlord being the main energy decision maker. Similar results were found in the choice of the electricity supplier (81.1% of the respondents indicate that this choice lies on other residents or on the landlord). Respondents who already have a time-differentiated tariff (23%) were asked how often they turn on electric appliances only in the cheapest periods of the tariff. Most respondents seem to have adopted this practice and use some appliances at night when the price is cheaper (mean = 5.69, SD = 0.769). However, the high rate of non-responses to this question (43.5%) may indicate that even having a time-differentiated pricing mechanism some people do not take advantage of the lower priced periods. When asked about the likelihood of switching to a time-differentiated tariff (given a certain financial return), respondents were willing to adopt that type of tariff (Mean = 66.28, SD = 28.840). No statistically significant differences between information provided in the versions 'savings' and 'increased costs' were found (t = 0.443 p > 0.05), which means that, contrary to the framing effect theory, presenting information in terms of savings or increased costs seems not to be relevant to this population. When increasing the complexity of the time-differentiated tariff presented (from a daily to a weekly and monthly variation), results showed that the respondents' willingness to adopt the new tariff is affected by the framing formulation: 57.84% of the respondents who received the 'savings' version would be willing to adopt this rate (SD = 30.185) which is significantly different from the 37.23% of respondents who received the 'increased costs' version (SD = 31.057) (t = 0.000 p < 0.001). This result contradicts what has been reported in the literature and requires further attention [16, 17]. This outcome may have been generated by a respondents' misinterpretation of the question. While 30% of respondents who received the 'savings' version state that savings are attractive enough to change, 12.6% state they already turn on some appliances in cheaper periods. However, still 4.1% state that savings do not compensate the effort, 5.6% indicate day-to-day routine limitations do not enable taking advantage of a tariff with variable prices and 6.7% consider that the information presented during the survey was insufficient to decide. In the group of respondents that received the 'increased cost' version, 18.9% revealed that the added cost is significant and therefore the switch to the new pricing scheme is advantageous; 12.6% stated that daily routine requirements do not allow end-users to take advantage of a tariff with hourly price differentiations and 14.4% complained of insufficient information to decide. Respondents also pointed out other possible motives for not switching to the time-differentiated tariff, such as the fact that they are not responsible for this decision; the complexity of calculations to determine whether or not the change really pays off and the fact that the proposed tariff had higher prices during winter, when perceived heating needs are higher.

Results also showed correlations between age and the willingness to adopt the proposed tariffs (rho = 0.258 p < 0.001 and rho = 0.253 p < 0.001, respectively). However, contrary to what was initially expected, results did not confirm the influence of the academic background on the adoption of time-differentiated tariffs, which is generally associated with energy literacy. Moreover, those respondents already experiencing this type of tariff showed greater willingness to adopt the proposed one, thus indicating that experiencing different tariffs may be a positive decision factor.

## 6    Conclusions and Future Work

The results of both case studies showed that the next generation of Portuguese decision makers, namely young adults in higher education, are familiar with electricity tariffs and understand the implications and advantages of adopting DR schemes associated with time-differentiated tariffs. This segment of the population is available to adopt DR programs involving shifting the operation of some appliances such as the laundry machine and the dishwasher. However, this flexibility is limited to short-time shifting actions and influenced by sufficient, clear and attractive financial incentives and should not compromise the household activities. Cost savings and the contribution to environmental protection were found to be important motivating factors to enroll into DR programs. Moreover, the framing effect was also found to be a relevant feature to be considered when promoting time-differentiated tariffs and designing DR programs.

Future work should also address the integration of further issues arising in the realm of smart grid (e.g., willingness to accept automated decisions by energy management systems), as well as its adaptation to more representative target audiences.

**Acknowledgement.** This work was partially supported by project grants UID/MULTI/ 00308/2019 and UID/CEC/00319/2019 and by the European Regional Development Fund through the COMPETE 2020 Programme, FCT—Portuguese Foundation for Science and Technology within projects ESGRIDS (POCI-01-0145-FEDER-016434), Learn2Behave (02/SAICT/ 2016-023651), MAnAGER (POCI-01-0145-FEDER-028040), and POCI-01-0145-FEDER-007043, as well as by the Energy for Sustainability Initiative of the University of Coimbra.

# References

1. Ozaki, R.: Follow the price signal: people's willingness to shift household practices in a dynamic time-of-use tariff trial in the United Kingdom. Energy Res. Soc. Sci. **46**, 10–18 (2018)
2. Dütschke, E., Paetz, A.G.: Dynamic electricity pricing - which programs do consumers prefer? Energy Policy **59**, 226–234 (2013)
3. Herrmann, M.R., Brumby, D.P., Oreszczyn, T.: Watts your usage? A field study of householders' literacy for residential electricity data. Energy Effi. **11**, 1703–1719 (2017)
4. Faruqui, A., Sergici, S.: Household response to dynamic pricing of electricity: a survey of 15 experiments. J. Regul. Econ. **38**, 193–225 (2010)
5. Rae, C., Bradley, F.: Energy autonomy in sustainable communities - a review of key issues. Renew. Sustain. Energy Rev. **16**, 6497–6506 (2012)
6. Kessels, K., Kraan, C., Karg, L., Maggiore, S., Valkering, P., Laes, E.: Fostering residential demand response through dynamic pricing schemes: a behavioural review of smart grid pilots in Europe. Sustainability **8**, 1–21 (2016)
7. Yoon, J.H., Bladick, R., Novoselac, A.: Demand response for residential buildings based on dynamic price of electricity. Energy Build. **80**, 531–541 (2014)
8. Moghaddam, M.P., Abdollahi, A., Rashidinejad, M.: Flexible demand response programs modeling in competitive electricity markets. Appl. Energy **88**, 3257–3269 (2011)
9. Steriotis, K., Tsaousoglou, G., Efthymiopoulos, N., Makris, P., Varvarigos, E.: A novel behavioral real time pricing scheme for the active energy consumers' participation in emerging flexibility markets. Sustain. Energy Grids Netw. **16**, 14–27 (2018)
10. Li, R., Dane, G., Finck, C., Zeiler, W.: Are building users prepared for energy flexible buildings?—A large-scale survey in the Netherlands. Appl. Energy **203**, 623–634 (2017)
11. Lopes, M.A.R., Antunes, C.H., Janda, K.B., Peixoto, P., Martins, N.: The potential of energy behaviours in a smart(er) grid: policy implications from a Portuguese exploratory study. Energy Policy **90**, 233–245 (2016)

12. Layer, P., Feurer, S., Jochem, P.: Perceived price complexity of dynamic energy tariffs: an investigation of antecedents and consequences. Energy Policy **106**, 244–254 (2017)
13. Frederiks, E.R., Stenner, K., Hobman, E.V.: Household energy use: applying behavioural economics to understand consumer decision-making and behaviour. Renew. Sustain. Energy Rev. **41**, 1385–1394 (2015)
14. Darcy, S., Dudeney, C.: Tomorrow's world for energy and water - what will consumers and citizens want in 2030? A check-list for change. Sustainability first - Workshop report, United Kingdom (2017)
15. EC: Attitudes of European Citizens towards the Environment. Special Eurobarometer 416, European Commission (2014)
16. Thaler, R.H., Sunstein, C.R.: Nudge - Improving Decisions about Health, Wealth, and Happiness, 2nd edn. Yale University Press, London (2008)
17. Kahneman, D.: Thinking, Fast and Slow, 4th edn. Círculo de Leitores, Lisboa (2014)

# Optimizing the Train-Catenary Electrical Interface Through Control Reconfiguration

António Martins[1(✉)], Vítor Morais[1], Carlos Ramos[1], Adriano Carvalho[1], and João L. Afonso[2]

[1] Faculty of Engineering, University of Porto, Porto, Portugal
{ajm,v.morais,cjr,asc}@fe.up.pt
[2] Centro ALGORITMI, University of Minho, Guimarães, Portugal
jla@dei.uminho.pt

**Abstract.** Electric railway vehicles are supplied by substations and catenaries at increasingly high power levels being the interface between the traction motors and the overhead contact line based on power electronics converters. A large part of these are AC-DC four quadrant converters operating in parallel at relatively small switching frequencies but using the interleaving principle to reach a low harmonic distortion of the catenary current and imposing specific harmonic ranges in this current. However, the current is not a pure sinusoidal wave and its harmonics can excite unwanted resonances due to the combined effect of the catenary distributed parameters, the substation equivalent impedance and the current spectrum that can vary according to normal and abnormal operating conditions. This paper analyses this phenomenon and proposes a control strategy capable of minimizing the resonance effects.

**Keywords:** AC-DC converters · Electric railways ·
Interleaved converters · Resonance · Railway systems

## 1 Introduction

Across Europe, four major railway power supply systems exist: DC, with 1.5 kV and 3 kV voltage levels, and AC, with 50 Hz, 25 kV and 16.7 Hz, 15 kV. However, for mainlines, the most common supply is $1 \times 25$ kV and $2 \times 25$ kV, 50 Hz, and 15 kV, 16.7 Hz, [1]. Inside the traction vehicles one or more transformers, in case of AC supply, adapt the incoming high voltage to a lower one, more appropriate to feed the traction motors and the auxiliary equipment.

The interface between the intermediate DC-buses and the internal input AC voltage is made with different types of power electronics converters. These GTO or IGBT-based converters (single H-bridges, interleaved bridges or multilevel converters) operate under some kind of pulse-width modulation (PWM) method, are current-controlled ones and inject into the high-voltage catenary harmonics of different frequencies, magnitudes and time varying, [2–6]. These harmonics circulate in the catenary line and may originate network resonances. The resonance

J. L. Afonso et al. (Eds.): GreeNets 2018, LNICST 269, pp. 24–39, 2019.
https://doi.org/10.1007/978-3-030-12950-7_3

voltages cause different problems such as overheating, interference with communication lines, operating errors in protection equipment and zero crossing-based systems, etc. High-frequency resonances occur frequently and can severely disrupt the normal railway operation, [7–9]. These resonances in the supply line have been analysed in different works, and most studies gave attention to the influencing factors of resonance occurrence, such as the length of conductors, [4], the position of trains [10], and the terminal impedances of power-quality conditioners, [11]. This paper is organised as follows: Sect. 2 presents the frequency response analysis of the catenary/substation impedance while Sect. 3 studies the behaviour of the four-quadrant converter while operating in interleaving mode. Section 4 presents the main simulation results in different operating conditions and the method to avoid resonances. Finally, Sect. 5 discusses the obtained results and concludes the paper.

## 2   Catenary Interface

The catenary interface using pulse-width modulated converters with nearly unity power factor is the most widely used solution in modern locomotives (e.g., electric multiple unit locomotives) because these converters easily provide bidirectional power flow, are modular and have a reduced harmonic content at the AC output. However, the analysis of the harmonic/resonance problem continues to be very important due to the wide range of frequencies of the injected voltages/currents.

### 2.1   Impedance Estimation

Several studies analyse the parallel and series resonances of the equivalent impedance at the traction system pantograph terminals, [4,5,11–15]. Knowledge of the harmonic impedance of catenary line is important for designing effective harmonic resonance mitigation measures. This knowledge is used in the design of harmonics filters inside the vehicles, the verification of harmonic limit requirements and the prediction of system resonance, [6,13]. The frequency response of the catenary impedance can be, in some way, calculated using similar methods to those used in the estimation of the electric grid impedance.

A number of impedance measurement methods have been developed for this purpose: on-line and off-line methods, invasive or non-invasive, [16]. Although invasive methods give more accurate results (they achieve higher signal to noise ratio), in the context of catenary impedance estimation only on-line non-invasive methods should be considered. Nevertheless, the switching operation of PWM converters can also be considered an invasive method and thus a larger set of methods can be selected to estimate the catenary equivalent impedance. The complex impedance, in a specified range of frequencies, could be obtained by direct measurement of voltages and currents; frequency domain measurements constitute a direct means of measuring the frequency characteristics of system components. The measured voltages and currents can be used to calculate the equivalent impedance of the catenary and the connected converters at any frequency but the measurement of this impedance function has proved inaccurate at those specific frequencies where parallel resonances occur. Here, the pantograph current reduces to very small values, owing to the high impedance of the line, [12]. Also the method is affected by non-linearities, saturation and noise. Alternatively, spectral analysis of time domain data of system operation can be used to determine the frequency domain characteristics, [17]. A second frequency method employs correlation power spectral density (PSD) analysis on the time domain voltage and current waveforms to obtain a transfer function, which approximates the catenary impedance as a function of frequency; a coherence coefficient is used to give a confidence level of the frequency response. The power spectral density describes the contribution of each frequency to the energy of the signal and the correlational analysis reduces the effect of noise and accounts for coupling between different frequencies due to non-linearities, [17]. In the identification of a catenary impedance model, the presence of an intermediate filter between the catenary and the on-board converters can be used in order to employ the same PSD approach, [12].

The application of other impedance identification methods, essentially employed in grid networks, like the extended Kalman filter, [18], the chirp z-transform, [19], and the so-called Resonance Mode Analysis, [20], can also be used in on-line conditions. In any case, knowledge of the system resonant frequencies is obtained and can be used to modify the switching frequency or the level of interleaving of the on-board converters, [21].

In terms of power electronics based solutions, different approaches have been employed in the past to reduce the harmonic distortion of the current injected into the catenary and thus avoiding major resonances, [2, 3, 22, 23]:

- Tuned harmonic filters, inserted between the pantograph and the high-voltage winding of the input transformer;
- Three-level converters instead of two-level converters on the catenary interface;
- Adaptive pulse width modulation for the feeding power converters;
- Installation of active filters or power quality conditioners.

None solution is completely effective but the use of the architecture and control flexibility of the interleaved two-level converters and three-level converters provides one the best starting approaches to deal with the issue, [3, 23, 24]. Additionally, the modularity of these two types of converters, namely the two-level ones, allows for a smooth degradation of operation in case of some types of failures, [21]. This paper focus its attention in the first ones. Thus, in order to optimize the performance of the converter sets in relation to their control, the interaction with other converters, and their performance in the supply system, it is important to determine the catenary impedance during the converter operation.

## 2.2   Catenary Model

The harmonic currents and voltages occurring along the catenary give rise to travelling waves of various frequencies, which are partly reflected at the electrical line discontinuities caused by the presence of substations, [1]. The most common calculation method of the impedance seen by the pantograph consists in the replacement of a many wire catenary with a two wire transmission line, which is described by the well-known transmission line equations. Considering the simplified model in Fig. 1, the impedance of the left-side line section of length $x$, $Z_L$, is given by (1), [2,4,25]:

$$Z_L = Z_0 \frac{Z_{tL} \cosh(\gamma x) + Z_0 \sinh(\gamma x)}{Z_0 \cosh(\gamma x) + Z_{tL} \sinh(\gamma x)} \qquad (1)$$

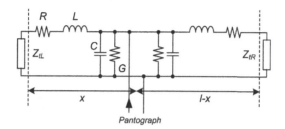

**Fig. 1.** Simplified model of the impedance seen by the train pantograph.

In Fig. 1, $R$, $L$, $G$ and $C$ correspond to series resistance and inductance, and parallel conductance and capacitance per unit length, respectively; $Z_{tL}$ and $Z_{tR}$ are the equivalent impedances of the left and right line section terminations, respectively. In (1), $Z_0$, $\gamma$ and $\lambda$ define the characteristic impedance, propagation constant, and wave speed respectively. They are given by:

$$Z_0 = \sqrt{\frac{R + j\omega L}{G + j\omega C}} \qquad (2)$$

$$\gamma = \sqrt{(R + j\omega L)(G + j\omega C)} \qquad (3)$$

$$\lambda = \frac{1}{\sqrt{LC}} \qquad (4)$$

The impedance of the right-side line section is obtained by substituting $l - x$ for $x$ in (1). In this set of parameters, the resistance $R$ and the inductance $L$ are frequency-dependent due to the skin effect in the soil underneath the railway track, while the capacitance $C$ can be considered constant and eventually the conductance $G$ can be neglected. The pantograph impedance is determined by the parallel of the two impedances: left and right sections, or

$$Z_P = Z_L // Z_L \qquad (5)$$

In Fig. 2 is represented a simplified model of the contribution of one interleaved converter to the pantograph voltage.

Using the equivalent circuit in Fig. 2, the $k^{th}$ harmonic voltage at the pantograph can be expressed in phasor notation as

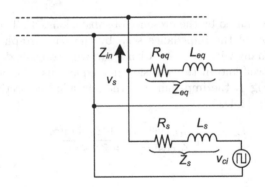

**Fig. 2.** Contribution of each converter voltage, $v_{ci}$, to the pantograph harmonics voltage.

$$V_{sk} = \sum_{i=1}^{N_T} V_{cik} \frac{Z_{pk}}{Z_{pk} + Z_{sk}} = V_{ck} \frac{Z_{pk}}{Z_{pk} + Z_{sk}} \qquad (6)$$

where

$$X_{pk} = \frac{Z_{ink} Z_{eqk}}{Z_{ink} + Z_{eqk}} \qquad (7)$$

and $V_{sk}$ is the $k^{th}$ harmonic root-mean-square (RMS) value of the pantograph voltage $v_s$, $V_{cik}$ is the $k^{th}$ harmonic RMS value of the AC pulse voltage $v_{ci}$, and $V_{ck}$ is the $k^{th}$ harmonic RMS value of the composite AC pulse voltage $v_c$ of the total converters. $Z_{sk}$ is the $k^{th}$ harmonic impedance of the leakage inductance and the internal resistance of the transformer, $Z_{ink}$ is the input impedance seen from the pantograph, which can be quite difficult to estimate, as (1) and (5) clearly indicate. If the connection to the catenary includes some kind of filters the expression for the harmonics voltages $V_{sk}$ becomes even more complex.

The resonant frequencies depend on the position of the vehicle, and are usually encountered between a few hundred Hz and several kHz, and above, depending on the circuit parameters. These frequencies are characterized by different damping coefficients which depend on: (i) the respective line distance, and (ii) the values of the electrical line parameters at the corresponding frequency. Typical parameters values of railway networks are presented in Table 1, [1,8,9,15].

As an example, Fig. 3 shows the magnitude-frequency responses of the catenary impedance, estimated at different points, using $R = 0.21$ $\Omega$/km, $L = 1.2$ mH/km, $G = 0$, $C = 11$ nF/km $L_{sub} = 2$ mH, and an open end at the other side;

**Table 1.** Typical parameters values of railway networks.

| Structure | R, [$\Omega$/km] | L, [mH/km] | G, [$\mu$S/km] | C, [nF/km] |
|---|---|---|---|---|
| One track, one catenary | 0.1 ... 0.3 | 1.2 ... 1.5 | 0.8 ... 1.0 | 11 ... 14 |
| Two tracks, two catenaries | 0.07 ... 0.1 | 0.75 ... 0.91 | 1.4 ... 1.8 | 18 ... 20 |

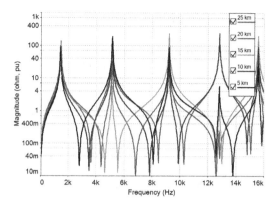

**Fig. 3.** Magnitude (in ohm, pu) of the impedance seen by the pantograph terminals as a function of the frequency and the distance of the train from the substation, with a section length of 30 km.

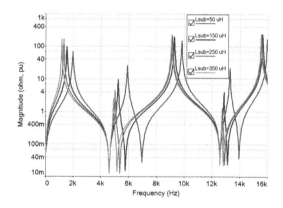

**Fig. 4.** Magnitude of the impedance seen by the pantograph terminals as a function of the substation impedance (in ohm, pu) with the train in the middle of a section with a length of 30 km.

parallel and series resonances are clearly exposed. The same parameters were used to evaluate the dependency of the catenary resonances according to the substation impedance and the results are shown in Fig. 4.

The low-frequency resonances are mainly affected by this uncertainty on the catenary and substation electrical parameters and, in order to assure a reliable operation, the relevant frequency ranges should be known. The harmonic excitation of the resonances is then suppressed if the specific frequencies, at which line resonances occur, are eliminated from the PWM spectrum. Of great importance is also the fact that in some frequency ranges the input admittance of the vehicle can exceed some critical negative real value so that the control may become unstable, [8,9,26,27]. Thus, an appropriate control strategy for the PWM converter(s) must be based on a prior identification of the harmonic conditions in the overhead supply system or on a real-time knowledge of the same conditions.

# 3    Interleaved PWM Converters

The two-level four-quadrant converter is one of the best choices to supply the internal DC-link from the AC catenary, [2, 3, 23]. The presence of more than one converter is required to guarantee a high redundancy in case of failure and gives the opportunity to interleave them in order to reduce the harmonic content of the absorbed current, as represented in Fig. 5, [1–3, 21, 24, 28].

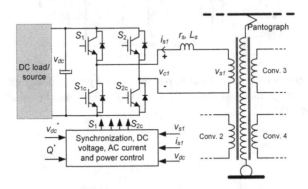

**Fig. 5.** Four interleaved four-quadrant converters and main control requirements.

Interleaving is achieved by phase shifting the carrier waveforms; for $N$ converters the carrier shift will be $\pi/N$. The four-quadrant converter constitutes a voltage source that generates higher-order line voltage harmonics. The levels and frequencies of these harmonics depend on several factors, [23, 27]:

- The switching frequency, $f_s$, per converter phase leg;
- The number of interleaved bridges; the operation point of the vehicle (actual voltage and power);
- The power unbalance between independent systems, e.g., for each bogie;
- The modulation strategy in the converter control.

In general ideal conditions, the first main burst of harmonics are located as side-bands to the resultant frequency:

$$F_{res} = 2f_sN \tag{8}$$

It can be easily demonstrated that perfect harmonic cancellation will only occur if all the interleaved PWM converters are operating under ideal symmetrical conditions. This means that the following conditions must be simultaneously fulfilled:

- The converter bridges parameters are perfectly balanced;
- The interleaved PWM converter bridges have equal load sharing;
- The phase shift angle of the PWM converters is symmetrical.

The converters use closed loop controllers to regulate the DC-link voltage as well as the AC current. The goal of the control system strategy is to ensure unity power factor operation and DC-link voltage regulation; however, some amount of reactive power can eventually be used to stabilize the catenary voltage, [29]. An external DC voltage control loop using a PI controller maintains the DC-link voltage equal to its reference, when the load current or grid voltage vary, and an inner loop controls the AC input current using some kind of controller in order to control the power factor and current magnitude.

The control system requires several current and voltage sensors and, as a consequence, wrong or degraded measurements due to sensor or communication failures, seriously perturb the performance of the converter and may cause system malfunction. In the specific configuration and operation mode of two or more converters some additional common blocks are required: a current sharing module in order to equalize the power in each converter, and a phase synchronization block for optimizing the current spectrum in the primary side of the transformer, as shown in Fig. 6.

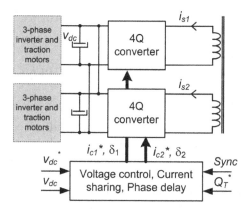

**Fig. 6.** Hierarchical control of the four-quadrant converters. $v_{dc}^*$ is the reference voltage for the common DC-bus; $i_{ci}^*$ is the total reference current for converter $i$; $\delta_i$ is the PWM phase for converter $i$; $Q_T^*$ is the reactive power reference.

Thus, a global control strategy for all PWM converters that eliminates the specific frequency bands from the harmonic spectrum of the pantograph should be devised in order to avoid the excitation of harmonic resonances under the actual conditions of the line. It involves the real-time identification of the resonance conditions (impedance), the estimation of the state of excitation of each actual resonant frequency and the generation of an appropriate switching strategy for the converters control. As more converters operate in interleaving mode and in balanced conditions, the equivalent harmonic voltages generated in the primary side of the transformer have lower magnitudes, higher frequencies and a wider spectrum. Thus, it is more difficult to excite resonances.

## 4    Simulation Results

A catenary with a length of 30 Km divided into 6 sections was used with the
parameters $R = 0.21$ $\Omega$/km, $L = 1.2$ mH/km, $G = 0$, $C = 11$ nF/km $L_{sub} = 2$ mH,
and an open end at the other side. With these parameters the first resonant
frequency is located between 1380 and 1400 Hz along the all catenary, as can be
concluded from Fig. 3. The other relevant parameters used in the simulations are
listed in Table 2. In order to achieve decoupled power control, a vector control
approach was used for the AC current controller using the 90° phase delay for
creating the beta component of the current.

**Table 2.** Parameters values used in the simulations.

| Parameter | Value/Type |
|---|---|
| Substation nominal power | 20 MVA |
| Substation impedance | $0.003 + i0.02$ p.u. |
| Transformer voltage: pr./sec | 25 kV/0.9 kV |
| Transformer impedance | $0.01 + i0.02$ p.u. |
| DC-bus voltage | 1.4 p.u. |
| Switching frequency | 600 Hz |
| AC current controller | dq-axes, PI-type |

The two relevant conditions related to the four-quadrant converters are exemplified in the next figures, where the train position is located 10 Km away from
the open end. Figure 7 shows two secondary currents and the primary current
(converter 1, which serves as phase reference, and converter 3, with a 90° shifted
PWM carrier; converters 2 and 4 have carriers phase shifted by 45° and 135°,
respectively) while Fig. 8 contains the spectrum of one secondary current and
of the primary current. It is clearly demonstrated the harmonic cancellation
occurring in the primary current.

### 4.1    Unbalanced Current

As referred before, two conditions negatively affect the harmonic cancellation
in the primary current and thus the avoidance of resonances can be no longer
possible: current unbalance and phase shift asymmetry. Figure 9 shows the result
of a malfunction in the current balancing module: at $t = 0.25$ s, converter 1 and
2 become not balanced (with $I_{s1} = 1.3$ p.u. and $I_{s2} = 0.7$ p.u.) while converters
3 and 4 are still balanced; also shown is the primary current.

The steady-state catenary voltage is shown in Fig. 10 and its harmonic spectrum in Fig. 11; in the two figures, and due to the appearance of harmonics
in the primary current centred at 1.2 kHz (twice the switching frequency) and
multiples, a small excitation of the resonance mode can be noticed.

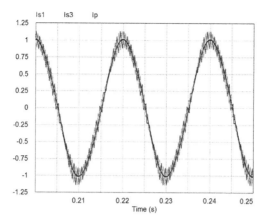

**Fig. 7.** Two secondary currents and the primary current in normal operation mode.

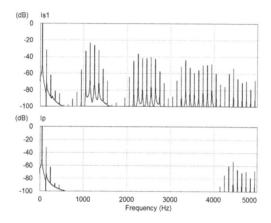

**Fig. 8.** Secondary and primary currents spectrum showing harmonic cancellation.

The steady-state catenary voltage is shown in Fig. 10 and its harmonic spectrum in Fig. 11; in the two figures, and due to the non-cancellation of harmonics in the primary current, components centred at multiples of 1.2 kHz (twice the switching frequency) have relevant magnitudes and a substantial excitation of the resonance mode is present (at around 1400 Hz, as referred above).

## 4.2  Loss of Synchronization

The potential occurrence of phase asymmetry is of more concern; harmonic cancellation is highly dependent on the fulfilment of this condition. Figure 12 shows the result of a loss of synchronization (starting at $t = 0.3$ s) between converters 1 and 2: converter 1 and 2 have in-phase PWM signals while converters 3 and 4 still have the correct phase shift. As can be seen, currents Is1 and Is2 are in phase and the primary current is more distorted.

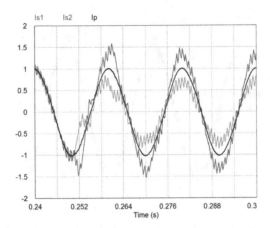

**Fig. 9.** Transient and steady-state current unbalance in converters 1 and 2.

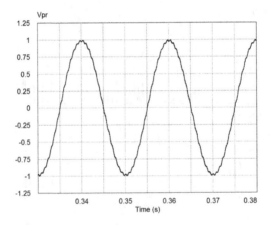

**Fig. 10.** Catenary voltage under current unbalance in the different converters.

The steady-state catenary voltage is shown in Fig. 13 and its harmonic spectrum in Fig. 14; in the two figures, and due to the non-cancellation of harmonics in the primary current, components centred at multiples of 1.2 kHz (twice the switching frequency) have relevant magnitudes and a substantial excitation of the first resonance mode is present (at around 1400 Hz, as referred above).

### 4.3   Proposed Method

The method proposed to avoid resonant conditions is based on the detection of the catenary resonant voltage made using fast Fourier transform analysis. When a resonant condition is detected the interleaved operation of the converters is lost and the current controller changes the PWM switching pattern in two ways: the switching frequency is changed to twice the normal value and there is no synchronization between any converter.

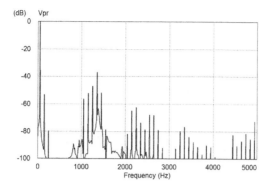

**Fig. 11.** Spectrum of the catenary voltage showing components around twice the switching frequency.

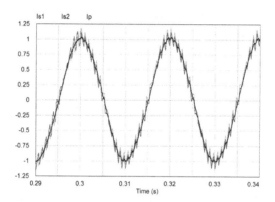

**Fig. 12.** Synchronization loss between converters 1 and 2, starting at $t = 0.3$ s.

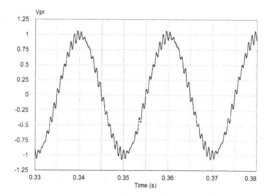

**Fig. 13.** Catenary voltage near resonance conditions.

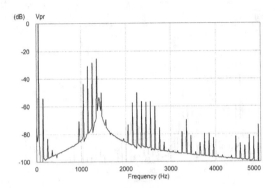

**Fig. 14.** Spectrum of the catenary voltage showing resonance conditions.

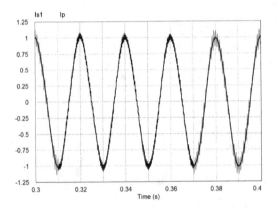

**Fig. 15.** One secondary current (Is1) and the primary current (Ip) in normal operation and when a resonance condition is detected (between $t = 0.31\,\text{s}$ and $t = 0.37\,\text{s}$).

This operation mode is a degraded one since the switching losses are increased and the catenary current is more distorted but the resonance condition is avoided. In Fig. 15 the resonance conditions occur between $t = 0.31\,\text{s}$ and $t = 0.37\,\text{s}$. After being detected the switching frequency is changed to twice the nominal one in all converters with any type of synchronization. As can be seen, during loss of synchronism the converter current becomes more sinusoidal but the primary current increases its distortion. On the other hand, as shown in Fig. 16, the catenary voltage slightly increases its distortion during that time interval but only in a small magnitude as quantified in Fig. 17.

Comparing the catenary voltage either in time domain (Figs. 13 and 16) and in frequency domain (Figs. 14 and 17) it is clear the avoidance of the resonance conditions. The approach requires the detection of the resonance occurrence, e.g. using a total harmonic distortion measurement, and knowledge of the equivalent characteristic impedance seen by the pantograph terminal in order to change the switching frequency. That impedance is mainly dependent on the catenary/rail

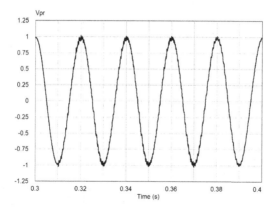

**Fig. 16.** Catenary voltage during loss of synchronism with different switching conditions (between $t = 0.31$ s and $t = 0.37$ s).

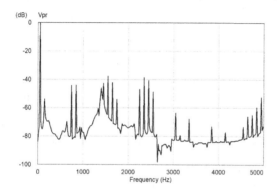

**Fig. 17.** Spectrum of the catenary voltage with different switching conditions.

distributed parameters and substation impedance and not on the train position or the number of trains in the track, as shown in Fig. 4 and also demonstrated in [2, 4, 7].

## 5   Conclusions

Modern electric traction systems employ four-quadrant converters operating in parallel with an interleaved switching strategy in order to achieve a very low current harmonic distortion. However, the existence of power unbalance between the converters or the loss of synchronism between the converters controllers originates resonance effects in the overhead contact line that can create high levels of harmonics voltages along the catenary. This paper presented a control reconfiguration approach capable of maintaining the converters operating in parallel without exciting relevant resonances.

**Acknowledgments.** The research has received funding from the FCT (Fundação para a Ciência e Tecnologia) under grant PD/BD/128051/2016. This work was partially supported by: FCT R&D Unit SYSTEC - POCI-01-0145-FEDER-006933/SYSTEC funded by FEDER funds through COMPETE 2020 and by national funds through the FCT/MEC, and co-funded by FEDER, in the scope of the PT2020 Partnership Agreement.

# References

1. Brenna, M., Foiadelli, F., Zaninelli, D.: Electrical Railway Transportation Systems, 1st edn. IEEE Press - Wiley, Hoboken (2018)
2. Holtz, J., Klein, H.-J.: The propagation of harmonic currents generated by inverter-fed locomotives in the distributed overhead supply system. IEEE Trans. Power Electron. **4**(2), 168–174 (1989)
3. Chang, G.W., Lin, H.-W., Chen, S.-K.: Modeling characteristics of harmonic currents generated by high-speed railway traction drive converters. IEEE Trans. Power Deliv. **19**(2), 766–773 (2004)
4. Zynovchenko, A., Xie, J., Jank, S., Klier, F.: Resonance phenomena and propagation of frequency converter harmonics in the catenary of railways with single-phase AC. In: Proceedings of the EPE 2005, 11–14 September, Dresden (2005)
5. Wang, B., Han, X., Gao, S., Huang, W., Jiang, X.: Harmonic power flow calculation for high-speed railway traction power supply system. In: Jia, L., Liu, Z., Qin, Y., Zhao, M., Diao, L. (eds.) EITRT 2013. LNEE, vol. 287, pp. 11–25. Springer, Heidelberg (2014). https://doi.org/10.1007/978-3-642-53778-3_2
6. Hu, H., He, Z., Gao, S.: Passive filter design for China high-speed railway with considering harmonic resonance and characteristic harmonics. IEEE Trans. Power Deliv. **30**(1), 505–514 (2015)
7. Janssen, M.F.P., Gonçalves, P.G., Santo, R.P., Smulders, H.W.M.: Simulations and measurements on electrical resonances on the Portuguese 25 kV network. In: Proceedings of the 8th World Congress on Railway Research, WCRR 2008, 18–22 May, Seoul, Korea (2008)
8. Suarez, J.: Étude et modélisation des intéractions électriques entre les engins et les installations fixes de traction électrique 25 kV–50 Hz. Ph.D. thesis, GEET-INP, Toulouse, France (2014)
9. Hu, H., Tao, H., Blaabjerg, F., Wang, X., He, Z., Gao, S.: Train-network interactions and stability evaluation in high-speed railways - part I: phenomena and modeling. IEEE Trans. Power Electron. **33**(6), 4627–4642 (2018)
10. Lee, H., Lee, C., Jang, G., Kwon, S.-H.: Harmonic analysis of the Korean high-speed railway using the eight-port representation model. IEEE Trans. Power Deliv. **21**(2), 979–986 (2006)
11. Brenna, M., Capasso, A., Falvo, M.C., Foiadelli, F., Lamedica, R., Zaninelli, D.: Investigation of resonance phenomena in high speed railway supply systems: theoretical and experimental analysis. Electric Power Syst. Res. **81**, 1915–1923 (2011)
12. Holtz, J., Krah, J.O.: On-line identification of the resonance conditions in the overhead supply line of electric railways. Electr. Eng. **74**(1), 99–106 (1990)
13. Mariscotti, A., Pozzobon, P.: Synthesis of line impedance expressions for railway traction systems. IEEE Trans. Veh. Technol. **52**(2), 420–430 (2003)
14. Dolara, A., Gualdoni, M., Leva, S.: Impact of high-voltage primary supply lines in the 2 × 25 kV–50 Hz railway system on the equivalent impedance at pantograph terminals. IEEE Trans. Power Deliv. **27**(1), 164–175 (2012)

15. Monjo, L., Sainz, L.: Study of resonances in $1 \times 25$ kV AC traction systems. Electr. Power Compon. Syst. **43**(15), 1771–1780 (2015)
16. Robert, A., Deflandre, T.: Guide for assessing the network harmonic impedance. In: Proceedings of the 14th International Conference and Exhibition on Electricity and Distribution, CIRED 1997, 2–5 June (IEEE Conference Publication No. 438) (1997)
17. Girgis, A., McManis, R.B.: Frequency domain techniques for modelling distribution or transmission networks using capacitor switching induced transients. IEEE Trans. Power Deliv. **4**(3), 1882–1890 (1989)
18. Hoffmann, N., Fuchs, F.W.: Minimal invasive equivalent grid impedance estimation in inductive-resistive power networks using extended Kalman filter. IEEE Trans. Power Electron. **29**(2), 164–175 (2014)
19. Duda, K., Borkowski, D., Bień, A.: Computation of the network harmonic impedance with chirp z-transform. Metrol. Measur. Syst. **16**(2), 299–312 (2009)
20. Xu, W., Huang, Z., Cui, Y., Wang, H.: Harmonic resonance mode analysis. IEEE Trans. Power Deliv. **20**(2), 1182–1190 (2005)
21. Perreault, D.J., Kassakian, J.G.: Distributed interleaving of paralleled power converters. IEEE Trans. Circ. Syst.-I: Fundam. Theor. Appl. **44**(8), 728–735 (1997)
22. Tan, P.-C., Loh, P.C., Holmes, D.G.: Optimal impedance termination of 25-kV electrified railway systems for improved power quality. IEEE Trans. Power Deliv. **20**(2), 1703–1710 (2005)
23. Zhang, R., Lin, F., Yang, Z., Cao, H., Liu, Y.: A harmonic resonance suppression strategy for a high-speed railway traction power supply system with a SHE-PWM four-quadrant converter based on active-set secondary optimization. Energies **10**, 1567–1589 (2017)
24. Holtz, J., Krah, J.O.: Suppression of time-varying resonances in the power supply line of AC locomotives by inverter control. IEEE Trans. Ind. Electron. **39**(3), 223–229 (1992)
25. Qiujiang, L., Mingli, W., Junki, Z., Kejian, S., Liran, W.: Resonant frequency identification based on harmonic injection measuring method for traction power supply systems. IET Power Electron. **11**(3), 585–592 (2018)
26. Sun, J.: Impedance-based stability criterion for grid-connected inverters. IEEE Trans. Power Electron. **26**(11), 3075–3078 (2011)
27. Cespedes, M., Sun, J.: Adaptive control of grid-connected inverters based on online grid impedance measurements. IEEE Trans. Sustain. Energy **5**(2), 516–523 (2014)
28. Youssef, A.B., El Khil, S.K., Slama-Belkhodja, I.: State observer-based sensor fault detection and isolation, and fault tolerant control of a single-phase PWM rectifier for electric railway traction. IEEE Trans. Power Electron. **28**(12), 5842–5853 (2013)
29. Bahrani, B., Rufer, A.: Optimization-based voltage support in traction networks using active line-side converters. IEEE Trans. Power Electron. **28**(2), 673–685 (2013)

# Home Energy Monitoring System Towards Smart Control of Energy Consumption

Zakariae Jebroni[1(✉)], Jose A. Afonso[2], and Belkassem Tidhaf[1]

[1] Laboratory of Embedded Electronics Systems and Renewable Energy
(SEEER), University Mohammed Premier, Oujda, Morocco
zakariae.jebroni@gmail.com
[2] CMEMS-Uminho Center, University of Minho, Guimarães, Portugal

**Abstract.** The need to manage, control and reduce energy consumption has led researchers to propose reliable solutions based on new technologies to achieve this goal. Our contribution in this subject is presented in this paper and consists of the design, implementation and testing of a home energy monitoring system. The presented system is dedicated for residential customers and allows the monitoring and control of the energy consumption, based on distributed and central processing. The system includes distributed monitoring devices, a gateway and a graphical user interface (GUI). To connect the all parts we use a hybrid wireless solution based on the Wi-Fi and Bluetooth Low Energy standards. We present the design and the implementation of the monitoring device hardware as well as the embedded software used to calculate the electrical quantities. We also present the calibration methodology used to eliminate gain and offset errors. In terms of performance test results, we have achieved voltage measurement accuracy below 0.2% and current measurement accuracy below 0.5%. A GUI was also developed for the user to visualize and control remotely the household appliances.

**Keywords:** Energy monitoring system · Home energy management system · Smart home · Smart metering

## 1 Introduction

The growing demand for electrical energy by customers has created new challenges in the management and control area. In the past, as the energy consumption was moderate, only basic equipment was needed to manage the electricity grid. Therefore, on the one hand, the electricity operators used basic measurement systems to control the energy consumption and, on the other hand, the customers did not pay attention to the control of the consumption. As the number of customers increased and the electricity grid became complicated, it was necessary to propose new solutions based on new technologies to better manage the electrical energy production-consumption chain [1].

Currently, the research in this area focuses on the management and control of electrical energy. Electricity operators are switching from static systems to Advanced Metering Infrastructures (AMI). This intelligent and real-time management is dedicated for energy theft detection, $CO_2$ emissions reduction, remote control and command of the electrical grid and to save energy production as much as possible [2]. The management

© ICST Institute for Computer Sciences, Social Informatics and Telecommunications Engineering 2019
Published by Springer Nature Switzerland AG 2019. All Rights Reserved
J. L. Afonso et al. (Eds.): GreeNets 2018, LNICST 269, pp. 40–53, 2019.
https://doi.org/10.1007/978-3-030-12950-7_4

of electrical energy on the production side was not enough to reduce its production. The population growth, urbanization as well as irrational use of electrical energy increase its consumption [3]. Therefore, to reduce the energy consumption and to shave the power demand, rational consumption on the demand side must be ensured by reducing energy consumption and eliminating peak power demand through the time shifting of the load. By managing and controlling energy consumption in demand side, satisfactory results may be achieved. Firstly, by reducing consumption on the consumer side, the bill will be reduced. Secondly, real-time management and forecasting through intelligent management systems in the production side will provide electricity operators a solid basis for balancing the production-to-consumption ratio over long term and, therefore, managing energy sources efficiently. Finally, on the environmental side, by reducing the energy consumption and losses, the $CO_2$ emissions will be reduced.

In order to manage and control energy consumption, it is necessary to introduce a reliable embedded system that can be integrated into the AMI, either directly or indirectly. That means, in the first case, the development of a Smart Home Energy Management System (SHEMS) connected to the Smart Grid Management System (SGMS), which is integrated directly into the AMI. The alternative is the development of this system but keeping it connectionless to the SGMS. In this case, the role of the system remains the same (reducing energy consumption and shaving power demand), but we keep independence between the customer and the electricity operator.

The embedded system contains two important parts: The monitoring system and the intelligent algorithm that manage the energy consumption. The monitoring system is the basis of the SHEMS [4] and consists mainly of several distributed wireless sensor devices, or Monitoring Devices (MDs), as well as a Graphical User Interface (GUI). A MD has the role of measuring the energy consumption of a household appliance, and then transmitting the measurement data to a local central device. In order to transmit the data, we may use a single wireless communication technology, such as Wi-Fi [5], Bluetooth, ZigBee [6] or GSM [7], or hybrid method, like Bluetooth/Wi-Fi [8], in the case where a gateway is used. In a house, several MDs form a Home Area Network (HAN). Regarding the data processing and calculation of electrical quantities, local processing and distributed calculation are more efficient in term of communication overhead and time calculation [9]. The GUI is used to monitor and control the monitoring system, and, therefore, the household appliances.

As related works, there are some publications in this area. Ahsan et al. [9] discuss the advantages of the distributed processing for home energy management system compared to centralized system. Their application is dedicated for smart grid, so it depends mainly of the electricity operator. The proposed system is tested in a mobile phone (Android app), but they did not propose a monitoring device hardware. In [10] Nesimi Ertugrul et al. propose a home energy management system for demand-based tariff, where they attempt to reduce the peak demand of household, but the system can create some inconvenience to the user, because it acts on any appliance without taking in consideration if the user uses this later. For that, they propose in the future to add a user priorities system to improve the old one. They also present the hardware of test, but they did not give information about the measurement reliability. In [4] the authors present a bill forecasting application for energy management based on an energy monitoring system. The authors assume that the monitoring system should be a learning tool and the user should make less effort to dealing with the system. In the end, they present an application of the monitoring system where they use Wi-Fi as the communication system. Afonso et al. [6] propose a monitoring system to monitor energy consumption and power quality. They presented the measurement accuracy of their designed monitoring device as well as the used GUI.

The aim of our contribution is to design and implement a SHEMS mainly adapted for use in the case of payment by consumption slices, like in Morocco. In this payment system, the price of one kWh is not related to the period of consumption (morning, afternoon or evening), but it is related to the amount of energy consumed, which means that when the monthly energy consumption increases, the price of energy increases. Table 1 shows the price per unit of electrical energy in Morocco.

Therefore, we propose a SHEMS that integrates an energy management algorithm. This, based on energy consumption, manages the operation of the household appliances. We distinguish between direct contact appliances with the user and indirect contact appliances, which was the issue of the proposition in [10]. For the first category, the system will not act on such this equipment, because maybe the user are using it. For example, if there is a visual interaction between the user and a television, the system will not turn off the appliance, it will just send notification for the customer in the case of an overuse. For the second category, the system can manage the appliances without notifying the user, like turning on/off a refrigerator, because there is no direct interaction between this later and the user. The proposed SHEMS is not totally connected to the electricity operator in order to keep some privacy for the customer.

In this paper, we present the first element of the whole system – the monitoring system. In the second section, we present the developed system, including the chosen communication technologies, the developed hardware, as well as the software of the monitoring device. In the third section, we present some experimental results of the measurement accuracy and the proper functioning of the measurement system. We present also, in the same section, the developed GUI dedicated to monitor and control the appliances. We finalize this paper with conclusions.

**Table 1.** Consumption slices per month and their price [11].

| Consumption slices per month | kWh price in Moroccan dirham (MAD) |
|---|---|
| 0 to 100 kWh | 0.9010 |
| 101 to 150 kWh | 1.0732 |
| 151 to 200 kWh | 1.0732 |
| 201 to 300 kWh | 1.1676 |
| 301 to 500 kWh | 1.3817 |
| >500kWh | 1.5958 |

## 2  System Development

### 2.1  Overview of the Communication Network

The main objective of the monitoring system is to make possible the remote monitoring and the remote control of the household appliances. To achieve this goal, we must implement a complete system consisting of embedded electronics and telecommunication module(s) working together. The proposed system consists of several connected parts. The connection between parts is guarantee by one or more wireless technologies. As mentioned before, several wireless communication technologies exist in the market. For this system, a low cost, low energy consumption wireless technology for the wireless sensor nodes is required and, for a future implementation, we have to guarantee the access from outside the home. According to these requirements and based on studies done on [12, 13], which discussed the benefits of Bluetooth Low Energy (BLE) for that kind of applications, we opted to use a hybrid communication solution to connect the whole system. Figure 1 shows the architecture of the monitoring system communication network. The system is composed by several elements connected to each other by wireless networks. The Monitoring Devices (MD1 to MDn) are connected to the BLE/Wi-Fi gateway via a BLE connection. We use the PSoC 4 BLE module from Cypress as processing and communication unit. This module is characterized by a 32-bit ARM Cortex-M0 processor core and an integrated Bluetooth 4.2 protocol stack. It also integrates programmable analog front ends used for measurements and a real time clock (RTC) used for time requirements.

As shown on Fig. 1, a user can view the power consumption, manage and control devices through the gateway using a client device (computer or phone). The connection between the client devices and the gateway is guaranteed by a Wi-Fi network through the Wi-Fi Access Point (Wi-Fi AP).

The gateway used in this system is a Raspberry Pi 3. This component has two roles. The first one is to ensure the connection between all devices. The second role is to collect, compute and store measurement data and to transmit control commands. In this case, this component presents itself as a local central device for the client.

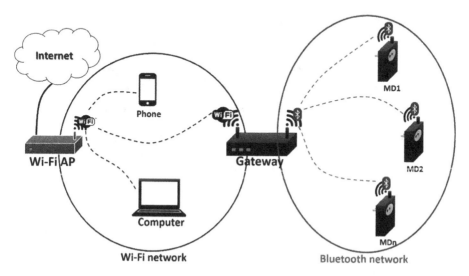

**Fig. 1.** Monitoring system communication network.

## 2.2  Developed Monitoring Device Hardware

The developed MD is shown in Figs. 2 and 3 presents its block diagram. It contains voltage and current sensors, signal conditioners and a processing and wireless communication unit. To calculate the power, and thus the energy consumption, we have to measure the instantaneous voltage and the instantaneous current. The MD was developed for a single-phase 230 V/50 Hz line.

Figure 4 presents the monitoring device board, whereas Fig. 5 presents its power supply board. Referring to Fig. 4, for the voltage chain we use as sensor a voltage divider based on resistors. The output-input ratio is 0.00057. The voltage sensor is following by the isolation amplifier AMC1100. This component ensure isolation between the grid and the application to secure the processing core from high voltage. The differential output voltage of the AMC1100 contains a negative part, but the Analog-to-Digital Converter (ADC) of the processing unit accepts only positive signals. For this reason, we added a signal conditioner based on operational amplifier TL082 (Fig. 6(a)) to add some offset and eliminate the negative part from the signal.

For the current chain, we use as sensor the TA12-100 current transformer. This component is characterized by a current ratio of 1000:1 and 1% accuracy. In its output, we placed a resistor to get a voltage proportional to the current. The resistor value (220 Ω) was chosen in such a way to have, for the maximum current, a maximum voltage equal to 1.5 V. To account for the negative part of the current, we added a fixed voltage as offset on one of output current sensor terminals as shown in Fig. 6(b).

**Fig. 2.**  Developed monitoring device prototype.

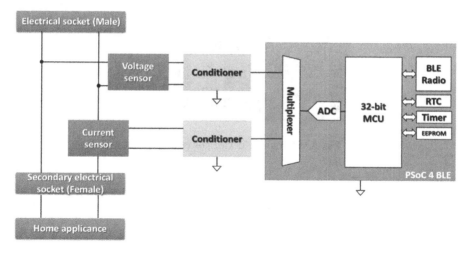

**Fig. 3.** Block diagram of the monitoring device.

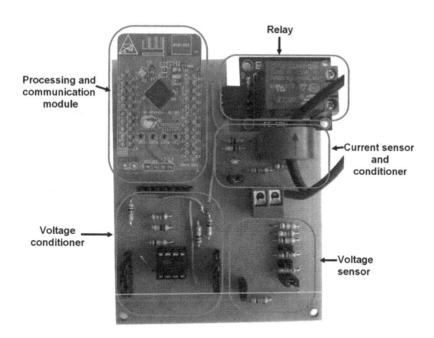

**Fig. 4.** Monitoring device circuit board.

**Fig. 5.** Monitoring device power supply.

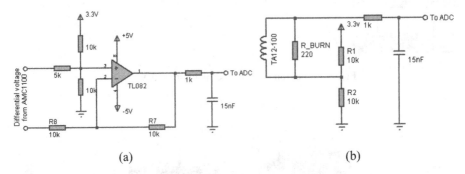

(a)                                     (b)

**Fig. 6.** (a) Voltage conditioner circuit and (b) current measurement and conditioner circuit.

In the developed monitoring device, we use the PSoC 4 BLE module as processing and communication unit. Therefore, after conditioning and filtering the signal from the two chains, we use the integrated ADC of the unit to convert the analog signal. The sampling frequency is 5000 samples per second. We note that the Shannon sampling criterion is widely respected. The electrical quantities computation is done in software inside the processing and communication unit, as explained in the next subsection.

### 2.3  Software Computation and System Calibration

As shown in Fig. 7, we use an interrupt mode in the ADC to detect an end of conversion. After the end of each conversion, we read the conversion register values for the voltage and the current. We use these values to calculate the instantaneous power in the ADC interrupt function. These three electrical quantities are calculated through Eqs. 1, 2 and 3, respectively.

$$V = G_v(k_v \cdot V_{REG} + V_{DCOFF})V_{REF} \tag{1}$$

where $G_v$ is the voltage gain used to calibrate the voltage chain gain, $k_v$ is a coefficient used to convert the value of the ADC register into a real value (equal to $\frac{1}{ADC\ resolution}$), $V_{REG}$ is the numerical value of the voltage stored into the corresponding register, $V_{DCOFF}$ is the voltage offset used to calibrate the offset into the voltage chain, if exists. And $V_{REF}$ is the voltage reference.

$$I = G_i(k_i \cdot I_{REG} + I_{DCOFF})I_{REF} \tag{2}$$

where each term is the same as the voltage equation, except that is used for the current chain.

$$P = V \cdot I \tag{3}$$

We add these values to temporary variables to calculate the RMS values and average values. After calculating and storing the new values, we raise a flag to notify that there is a new data.

In the infinite loop, we test if the new conversion flag is on. For each end conversion, we wait until reaching 5000 samples, which corresponds to a time interval of one second, and this represent the Low Rate Sampling Period (LRSP). When this condition is verified, we calculate the RMS values, active power, energy and others quantities with the equations presented in Table 2.

**Table 2.** Formulas used to calculate the RMS and average values.

| Electrical quantity | Formula | Description |
|---|---|---|
| RMS voltage | $V_{RMS} = \sqrt{\frac{1}{N}\sum_{i=1}^{N} V_i^2}$ | $N$ is the number of samples in one period |
| RMS current | $I_{RMS} = \sqrt{\frac{1}{N}\sum_{i=1}^{N} I_i^2}$ | $N$ is the number of samples in one period |
| Average power | $P_{AVG} = \frac{1}{N}\sum_{i=1}^{N} P_i$ | $N$ is the number of samples in one period |
| Power factor | $PF = \frac{P_{AVG}}{V_{RMS} \cdot I_{RMS}}$ | |
| Energy | $E_i = E_{i-1} + \frac{P_{AVG_i}}{N_s}$ | $E_i$ and $E_{i-1}$ present the current energy value and the previous energy value. The term $\frac{P_{AVG_i}}{N_s}$ presents the energy consumed in the last LRSP, where $N_s = \frac{3600}{LRSP}$. In this case the energy unit is Wh |

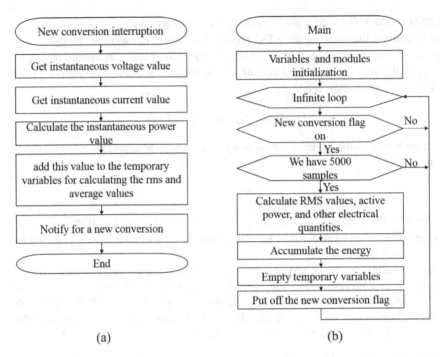

(a)                                    (b)

**Fig. 7.** (a) Flowchart of end of conversion interruption on ADC module. (b) Flowchart of main function including the calculation operation.

The voltage and current chains contain electronic components such as resistors, isolation amplifier, operational amplifier, and ADC. These components could create some measurement errors due to tolerance values, residual ADC offset, amplifiers offset and gain uncertainty. For this reason, the system must be calibrated to eliminate error and consequently to achieve a required accuracy. The calibration process could be performed analogically or numerically. In our case, we choose the numerical methodology to avoid hardware complications. As the measurement chains are linear, to adjust the measurement we have to calibrate the system for just one point of load.

To calibrate the DC offset, we put at the input measurement system a null signal and we measure several values of the instantaneous voltage and the instantaneous current. We note that in this operation the gain variable are initialized to 1. Then we calculate the average value for each chain. After that, we multiply the found values by $-1$ and store them into the corresponding variables (into $V_{DCOFF}$ variable in Eq. 1 and $I_{DCOFF}$ variable in Eq. 2). We store them into the EEPROM to avoid a system recalibration if the monitoring device is restarted.

For the gain calibration, we apply the reference signal (220 V and 5 A), then we calculate several RMS values of the voltage and the current. After that, we correct the gain value with Eq. 4:

$$G_x = \frac{Reference\ value}{The\ average\ of\ the\ measured\ values} \qquad (4)$$

where $x$ can be $v$ for the voltage gain or $i$ for the current gain. We store the values of the calculated gains into the corresponding variables as well as into the EEPROM to avoid a system recalibration.

## 3  Experimental Results and Discussion

### 3.1  Measurements Accuracy

We have put under evaluation our developed monitoring device to verify the measurement accuracy. We performed the accuracy tests for both RMS voltage and RMS current. For the RMS voltage we tested the accuracy in the interval of [176 V–253 V], because, according to [14], the RMS voltage value can vary between $0.8V_{REF}$ and $1.15V_{REF}$, knowing that the voltage reference value equals 220 V. For the RMS current, we tested the accuracy for the full-scale input range. Both measurement tests are compared with a precision power measurement device. The relative error of measurement is calculated with formula 5:

$$Error(\%) = \frac{Measured\ value - reference\ value}{reference\ value} \times 100 \qquad (5)$$

Figure 8 presents the voltage error of the measurements performed by the developed monitoring device. We notice that the maximum relative error is below 0.2%. Likewise, for the current relative error, seen in Fig. 9, the maximum relative error is below 1% for a RMS current less than 0.5 A, and for the other values this error do not exceed 0.5%.

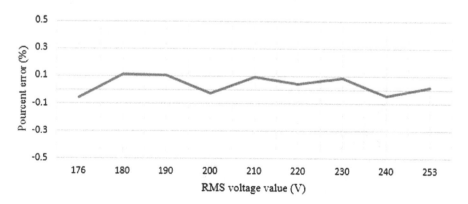

**Fig. 8.**  Voltage variation performance.

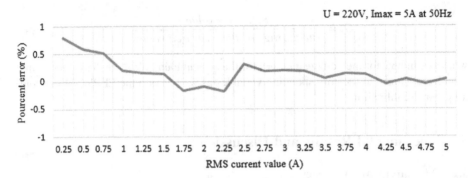

Fig. 9. RMS current performance.

## 3.2  Data Displaying on the GUI

To monitor and control the household appliances, we developed a GUI (Fig. 10) for the customer. This interface offers the possibility to add a new monitoring device to the monitoring system network, configure edit or delete a device, etc. Furthermore, as presented in Figs. 11 and 12, the user can visualize the power consumption per day, as well as the energy consumption per month and per year. Real time power consumption visualization is also offered (Fig. 13). Moreover, the user has the possibility to import or export data, to activate or disable the monitoring device, to turn on/off the household appliance and to define a turning on/off schedule, as seen in the menu at the left side of the GUI in Figs. 11, 12 and 13.

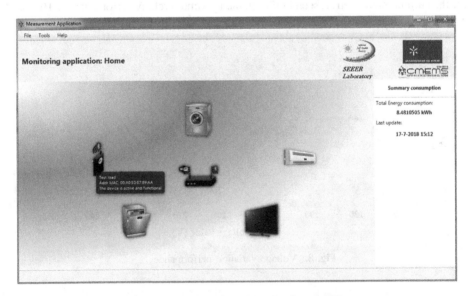

Fig. 10. Home screen of the developed GUI.

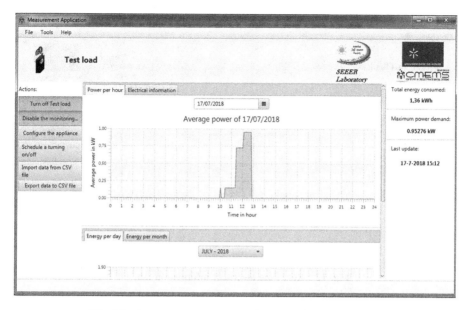

**Fig. 11.** Average power consumption chart for the test load.

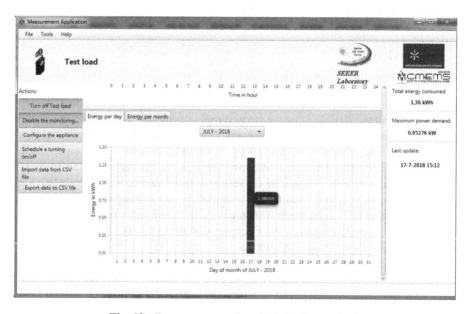

**Fig. 12.** Energy consumption chart for the test load.

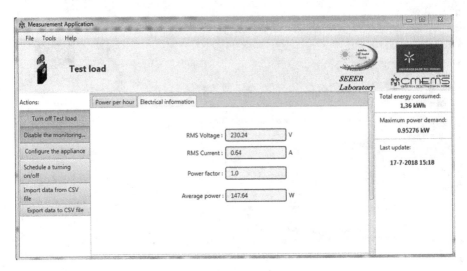

**Fig. 13.** Real time electrical information tab.

These charts, as well as the electrical information presented, are for a test load of theoretical power equal to 150 W. As shown in Fig. 11, we started tests with this load at 10:25AM. At 11:25AM, we added a second load that consumes 2.5 A. Later, we increased the current consumption until 4.15 A by increasing the second load.

## 4    Conclusions

The monitoring system proposed in this paper to visualize and control the energy consumption of household appliances forms the basis of the smart home energy management system (SHEMS) that we are developing currently. This system meets the needs of residential consumers to monitor and control household appliances.

This monitoring system is composed by monitoring devices, the gateway (local central device) and the GUI. The monitoring devices are connected to the gateway through a BLE connection. The gateway is responsible for data consumption collection from the monitoring devices, storing this information and making it available to the user. The presented GUI application, which can be installed into a personal computer, connects to the gateway through a Wi-Fi connection using the TCP/IP (Transmission Control Protocol/Internet Protocol) protocols.

The proposed monitoring system was validated through measurement accuracy tests for the developed monitoring device, where we obtained an accuracy below 0.2% for the voltage and below 0.5% for the current. We presented also the developed GUI to monitor and control the household appliances.

As future work, we will implement a home energy management algorithm to manage energy consumption automatically and help the user to control his energy consumption.

**Acknowledgments.** This work is supported by FCT with the reference project UID/EEA/04436/2013, COMPETE 2020 with the code POCI-01-0145-FEDER-006941.

# References

1. Rashed Mohassel, R., Fung, A., Mohammadi, F., Raahemifar, K.: A survey on advanced metering infrastructure. Int. J. Electr. Power Energy Syst. **63**, 473–484 (2014)
2. van der Spoel, E., et al.: New Technologies, Mobility and Security (2015)
3. Nejat, P., Jomehzadeh, F., Taheri, M., Gohari, M.: A global review of energy consumption, $CO_2$ emissions and policy in the residential sector (with an overview of the top ten $CO_2$ emitting countries). Renew. Sustain. Energy Rev. **43**, 843–862 (2015)
4. Chupong, C., Plangklang, B.: Electricity bill forecasting application by home energy monitoring system. In: 2017 International Electrical Engineering Congress, iEECON 2017 (2017)
5. Sharma, A., Bhalla, M.: WiFi home energy monitoring system. In: 2016 International Conference on Information Technology - Next Generation, IT Summit, pp. 6–8 (2016)
6. Afonso, J.A., Rodrigues, F., Pereira, P., Gonçalves, H., Afonso, J.L.: Wireless monitoring and management of energy consumption and power quality events. In: World Congress on Engineering (2015)
7. Rashdi, A., Malik, R., Rashid, S., Ajmal, A., Sadiq, S.: Remote energy monitoring, profiling and control through GSM network. Arab. J. Sci. Eng. **38**, 3249–3257 (2013)
8. Bikrat, Y., Moussaid, D., Benali, A., Benlghazi, A.: Electronic and computer system for monitoring a photovoltaic station. In: International Conference on Intelligent Systems and Computer Vision (ISCV). (2018)
9. Ahsan, U., Bais, A.: Distributed smart home architecture for data handling in smart grid. Can. J. Electr. Comput. Eng. Can. Genie Electr. Inform. **41**, 17–27 (2018)
10. Ertugrul, N., McDonald, C.E., Makestas, J.: Home energy management system for demand-based tariff towards smart applicances in smart grids. In: IEEE 12th International Conference on Power Electronics and Drive Systems (PEDS), pp. 511–517 (2017)
11. www.one.org.ma
12. Afonso, J.A., Maio, A.J.F., Simoes, R.: Performance evaluation of bluetooth low energy for high data rate body area networks. Wirel. Pers. Commun. **90**, 121–141 (2016)
13. Silva, R.B.C., Afonso, J.A., Afonso, J.L.: Development and test of an intra-vehicular network based on bluetooth low energy. In: World Congress on Engineering, pp. 5–9 (2017)
14. ONE-BE: Technical specification - electronics energy meter for low voltage customers (2014)

# Performance Comparison of a Typical Nonlinear Load Connected to Ac and Dc Power Grids

Tiago J. C. Sousa[✉], Vítor Monteiro, J. G. Pinto, and João L. Afonso

Centro ALGORITMI, University of Minho,
Campus de Azurém, Guimarães, Portugal
tsousa@dei.uminho.pt

**Abstract.** This paper presents a performance comparison of a typical nonlinear load used in domestic appliances (electronic load), when supplied by an ac and a dc voltage of the same rms value. The performance of the nonlinear load towards its connection to ac and dc power grids is accomplished in terms of the waveforms which are registered in the consumed current, internal dc-link voltage and output voltage. A simulation model was developed using realistic database models of the power semiconductors comprising a nonlinear load with input ac-dc converter, so that the efficiency can be calculated and compared for three distinct cases: (1) load supplied by an ac voltage; (2) load supplied by a dc voltage; (3) load without the input ac-dc converter supplied by a dc voltage. Thus, besides the comparison between the ac and dc power grids supplying the same nonlinear load (cases 1 and 2), a third case is considered, which consists of removing the input ac-dc converter (eliminating needless components of the nonlinear load when supplied by a dc voltage). The obtained results show that supplying nonlinear loads with dc power grids is advantageous in relation to the ac power grid, and therefore it can be beneficial to adapt nonlinear loads to be powered by dc power grids.

**Keywords:** Dc grids · Dc smart homes · Nonlinear loads · Efficiency

## 1 Introduction

Dc power transmission and dc grids have gained attention over the past few years. In the last century, ac power transmission was preferred due to transformers, which allow the changing of voltage and current levels in a reliable and efficient manner. Despite being heavy and bulky, transformers were a more suitable solution than power electronics-based converters towards the advent of power transmission, more than one hundred years ago. However, power electronics has been undergoing a significant development since the second half of the last century. This led to the establishment of the high voltage dc (HVDC) transmission systems, which was not only a research target at that time [1–9], but with real applications in the recent years [10–17]. In HVDC transmission systems, skin effect and voltage drops due to the conductors' reactance are inexistent when compared to ac power transmission. Moreover, HVDC

© ICST Institute for Computer Sciences, Social Informatics and Telecommunications Engineering 2019
Published by Springer Nature Switzerland AG 2019. All Rights Reserved
J. L. Afonso et al. (Eds.): GreeNets 2018, LNICST 269, pp. 54–63, 2019.
https://doi.org/10.1007/978-3-030-12950-7_5

power transmission can reduce power transmission losses even further with the appliance of superconductivity [18–24].

Besides the advent of HVDC transmission systems, the development of power electronics contributed to the implementation of more efficient and lower power demanding electrical loads. These loads are named nonlinear loads, i.e., the relation between the supplied voltage and the consumed current is not linear. This phenomenon gave rise to the widely known harmonic currents issue [25–29], as well as the respective proposed compensation techniques [30–34].

From the power grid point of view, nonlinear loads are comprised by a diode full-bridge ac-dc converter in the input, therefore operating in dc power at the output. In fact, this type of connection is present in the vast majority of domestic appliances, such as computers, televisions, modern refrigerators and modern lighting equipment such as compact fluorescent and light emitting diode (LED) lamps. Accordingly, the operation of nonlinear loads, both from the power grid and from the load point of view, can be improved if the traditional ac voltage supply is replaced by a dc voltage supply with equivalent rms value. Besides the electrical loads, the paradigm of dc grids is also more suitable than ac grids, which is proved by the dc systems based on photovoltaics, fuel cells and batteries. Dc microgrids are also an attractive asset for future power systems [35, 36] and can also be used for wind and wave power generation [37]. With the dc approach, power conversions can be reduced and the efficiency can be improved, whereby dc smart homes represent a viable alternative in the near future [38–41].

In this context, this paper presents a study about the performance of a typical nonlinear load connected to ac and dc power grids. The differences between the two types of power grids are analyzed in terms of consumed current, dc-link voltage and output voltage. A comparison is also made in terms of efficiency and a third case is considered, aiming to improve the efficiency of the type of nonlinear load under study in dc power grids. The analyses are based on simulation results using realistic database models of the power semiconductors comprising the load.

The paper is structured as follows: Sect. 2 presents the nonlinear load under analysis; Sect. 3 presents the developed simulation model and the obtained results in terms of waveforms and efficiency comparison. Section 4 finalizes the paper with the conclusions.

## 2 Load Analysis: Electrical Model

This section presents the electrical model of the load under analysis in this paper. As aforementioned, the typical loads used in domestic appliances are nonlinear loads. These loads are mainly comprised by an ac-dc converter, typically a diode full-bridge ac-dc converter with a filter capacitor, which converts the input ac voltage into an unregulated dc voltage. A dc-dc converter is connected downstream the filter capacitor in order to adjust the rectified voltage to the desired value, as well as to minimize its ripple. This load is basically a power supply that can be found in computers, televisions, modern refrigerators and battery chargers, for instance. Figure 1 depicts this type of load, where the aforementioned elements can be seen. The ac-dc converter is comprised by diodes $D_1$ to $D_4$ and contains a filter capacitor ($C_{dc}$) in order to smooth the dc-link voltage ($v_{dc}$) and an input inductive filter ($L_g$) in order to smooth the absorbed grid current ($i_g$). The dc-dc converter ($S_1$, $D_5$, $L_o$ and $C_o$) is a buck converter, whose function is to step-down the dc-link voltage ($v_{dc}$) into a controlled output voltage ($v_o$) with low ripple. Additionally, a resistor is connected in the output ($R_o$) to emulate the power consumption of the load.

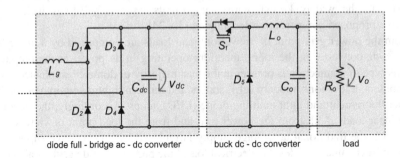

diode full - bridge ac - dc converter         buck dc - dc converter         load

**Fig. 1.** Nonlinear load under analysis.

## 3   Simulation Model and Results

This section presents the simulation model developed in the software PSIM v9.1 and the subsequent performed analysis for the nonlinear load described in the previous section when fed by ac and dc power. Three different cases are considered: (1) load supplied by an ac voltage (Fig. 2 (a)); (2) load supplied by a dc voltage (Fig. 2 (b)); (3) load without the input ac-dc converter supplied by a dc voltage (Fig. 2 (c)). Case 1 represents the traditional connection of the considered nonlinear load to an ac power grid. Case 2 represents the same load connected to a dc power grid instead, meaning the case of a traditional nonlinear load connected in a possible dc home that can also be connected in a regular ac power grid. On the other hand, case 3 represents a possible evolution suffered by the considered type of load, being possible to discard the diode full-bridge ac-dc converter since both the input and the output are dc. However, this type of load can operate only in a dc power grid, whereby this scenario is only feasible when dc smart homes and dc grids would be widespread. Furthermore, case 3 is more prone to failure, as the input terminals of the load are polarized; an input voltage with a reverse polarity cannot supply the load properly and even can destroy the electronic components, while a diode full-bridge ac-dc converter assures a fixed polarity in the dc-link voltage.

The parameters considered in the simulation model for the ac and dc power grids and the loads are listed in Table 1. It should be mentioned that the value of 24 V used in the ac power grid refers to the secondary side of a 230 V/24 V transformer, typically included in this type of loads, whereby the transformer is excluded from the analysis in order to compare the same load being supplied with ac and dc power.

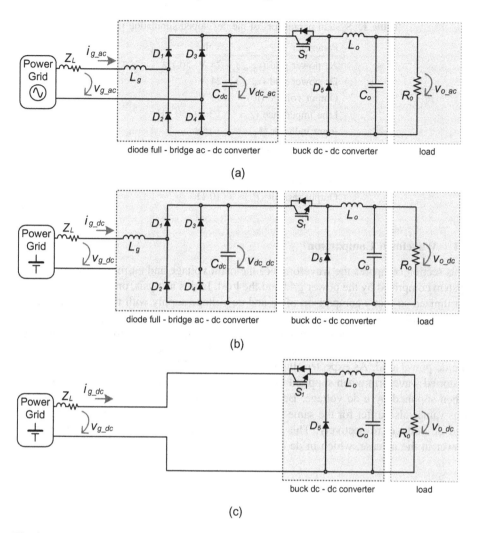

**Fig. 2.** Considered cases for the analyzed nonlinear load: (a) Load supplied by an ac voltage; (b) Load supplied by a dc voltage; (c) Load without the input ac-dc converter supplied by a dc voltage.

In order to perform an efficiency evaluation for the three cases, realistic database models of diodes and MOSFETs were used. The diodes used in both ac-dc and dc-dc converters are ST Microelectronics STTA206S (600 V, 8 A), and the MOSFET used in the dc-dc converter is International Rectifier IRF1010EZ (60 V, 75 A) switched at 20 kHz. It should be referred that the focus of analysis is the efficiency comparison between the cases and not the efficiency values per se.

**Table 1.** System parameters of the developed simulation model.

| Parameter | Value |
|---|---|
| Ac power grid ($v_{g\_ac}$) | 24 V, 50 Hz |
| Dc power grid ($v_{g\_dc}$) | 24 V |
| Output voltage ($v_o$) | 12 V |
| Line impedance ($Z_L$) | 1 mΩ, 50 µH |
| Input inductor ($L_g$) | 1 mH |
| Dc-link capacitor ($C_{dc}$) | 1 mF |
| Output inductor ($L_o$) | 2 mH |
| Output capacitor ($C_o$) | 470 µF |
| Output resistor ($R_o$) | 10 Ω |

### 3.1 Waveform Comparison

This section compares the waveforms of the main voltage and current quantities of the system comprised by the power grid and the load. In this analysis, only case 1 and 2 are scrutinized so that a comparison of ac and dc voltage supply with the same rms value for the same connected load is performed.

The waveforms of the current consumed by the nonlinear load from the power grid point of view can be seen in Fig. 3, where $i_{g\_ac}$ relates to the ac power grid and $i_{g\_dc}$ to the dc power grid. As expected, the current consumed by this type of load presents a distorted waveform when supplied by an ac voltage, while presenting a constant value when supplied by a dc voltage. Besides the difference in the waveforms, the current rms values also differ for the same rms supply voltage, being 1.1 A and 0.75 A for ac and dc voltage, respectively. This can be explained by the consumption of reactive power in the ac case, which in dc does not exist.

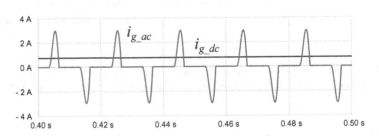

**Fig. 3.** Current consumed by the load when supplied by ac voltage ($i_{g\_ac}$) and when supplied by dc voltage ($i_{g\_dc}$).

Besides the differences in the grid current, the connection of this type of load to ac or dc power grids also results in differences in the dc-link voltage, i.e., the voltage rectified by the diode full-bridge ac-dc converter and the input voltage of the buck dc-dc converter. Figure 4 shows the waveforms of the dc-link voltage for the same load when supplied by an ac power grid ($v_{dc\_ac}$) and when supplied by a dc power grid

($v_{dc\_dc}$). As expected, the dc-link voltage in the ac power grid case exhibits a double grid frequency ripple (100 Hz) resultant from the ac-dc power conversion, while the ripple in the dc power grid case is negligible. Besides, the average value of the dc-link voltage is higher in the first case (29.5 V) because the 24 V rms sinusoidal voltage has a peak value of 34 V. Nevertheless, in the ac case occurs a voltage drop in the load input inductor ($L_g$), which is inexistent in dc. The average value of the dc-link voltage in the dc case is 20.9 V, with the diodes voltage drop being the main source of voltage decrease with respect to the power grid voltage.

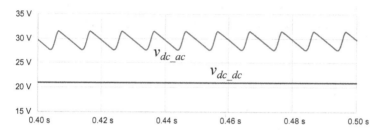

**Fig. 4.** Dc-link voltage of the load when supplied by ac voltage ($v_{dc\_ac}$) and when supplied by dc voltage ($v_{dc\_dc}$).

Figure 5 shows the waveforms of the output voltage of the load for the ac case ($v_{o\_ac}$) and the dc case ($v_{o\_dc}$). The buck dc-dc converter is responsible for the synthetization of this voltage, in both cases controlling its value to 12 V. Although the ripple is small in both cases, it is even smaller in the dc case, since the constant dc-link voltage facilitates the control of the output voltage. Consequently, the ripple component of the output voltage in the dc case consists of switching ripple only. It should be noted that the same control strategy was applied in both cases.

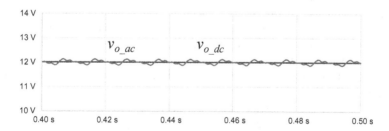

**Fig. 5.** Output voltage of the load when supplied by ac voltage ($v_{o\_ac}$) and when supplied by dc voltage ($v_{o\_dc}$).

## 3.2 Efficiency Comparison

The previous results compared the voltage and current waveforms of the power grid and the load for the same load being supplied with ac and dc voltages. In this section, case 3 (load without input ac-dc converter supplied by a dc voltage) is also analyzed and compared with the other two cases in terms of efficiency.

Table 2 presents a comparison in terms of input power, output power and efficiency for the three designed cases. Since the load output voltage is the same for the three cases (12 V), as well as the output resistor (10 Ω), the output power is 14.4 W for all the cases. In terms of input active power, i.e., the active power absorbed from the power grid, it should be noted that case 1 presents a lower value than case 2 (17.9 W against 18.1 W) and, consequently, a higher efficiency (80.4% against 79.6%). This is justified by the fact that the power losses in the diodes of the ac-dc converter are 1.92 W in case 1 and 2.32 W in case 2. However, in case 1 there is an apparent power of 26.7 VA, corresponding to a power factor of 0.67, which does not exist in cases 2 and 3, since these are related to dc grids. Nonetheless, the highest efficiency is attained by removing the ac-dc converter (case 3), resulting in a 96% efficiency for the same load supplied by a dc power grid.

**Table 2.** Power and efficiency comparison for the three cases.

| Case | 1 (ac grid with ac-dc converter) | 2 (dc grid with ac-dc converter) | 3 (dc grid without ac-dc converter) |
| --- | --- | --- | --- |
| Input active power | 17.9 W | 18.1 W | 15.0 W |
| Output active power | 14.4 W | 14.4 W | 14.4 W |
| Efficiency | 80.4% | 79.6% | 96.0% |

## 4 Conclusions

This paper presented an analysis of a typical nonlinear load used in domestic appliances and its behavior when connected to an ac power grid and to a dc power grid, both with the same rms voltage value. The considered load was a diode full-bridge ac-dc converter followed by a buck dc-dc converter, representing a typical power supply that can be found in computers, phone battery chargers, among other domestic appliances. Three distinct cases were considered, namely: (1) load supplied by an ac voltage; (2) load supplied by a dc voltage; (3) load without the input ac-dc converter supplied by a dc voltage. A simulation model was developed considering realistic database models of the power semiconductors used in this type of load, i.e., diodes and an MOSFET. The attained simulation results aimed to perform a comparison in terms of waveforms and efficiency, which was feasible due to the database model of the power semiconductors. It was seen that efficiency can be significantly improved (from 80% to 96%) in a dc power grid by simply removing the input ac-dc converter of the analyzed type of nonlinear load. This fact corroborates the feasibility of dc smart homes and dc grids, making them more suitable, not only from the renewable energy generation and from energy storage systems point of view, but also from the perspective of the vast majority of electrical appliances.

**Acknowledgments.** This work has been supported by COMPETE: POCI-01-0145–FEDER–007043 and FCT – Fundação para a Ciência e Tecnologia within the Project Scope: UID/CEC/00319/2013. This work is financed by the ERDF – European Regional Development

Fund through the Operational Programme for Competitiveness and Internationalisation – COMPETE 2020 Programme, and by National Funds through the Portuguese funding agency, FCT – Fundação para a Ciência e a Tecnologia, within project SAICTPAC/0004/2015 – POCI – 01–0145–FEDER–016434. Mr. Tiago Sousa is supported by the doctoral scholarship SFRH/BD/134353/2017 granted by the Portuguese FCT agency.

# References

1. Foerst, R., Heyner, G., Kanngiesser, K.W., Waldmann, H.: Multiterminal operation of HVDC converter stations. IEEE Trans. Power Appar. Syst. **PAS-88**(7), 1042–1052 (1969)
2. Dewey, C., Ellert, F., Lee, T., Titus, C.: Development of experimental 20-kY, 36-MW solid-state converters for HVDC systems. IEEE Trans. Power Appar.Syst. **PAS-87**(4), 1058–1066 (1968)
3. Hirsch, F., Schafer, E.: Progress report on the HVDC test line of the 400 kV-Forschungsgemeinschaft: corona losses and radio interference. IEEE Trans. Power Appar. Syst. **PAS-88**(7), 1061–1069 (1969)
4. Hingorani, N.: Transient overvoltage on a bipolar HVDC overhead line caused by DC line faults. IEEE Trans. Power Appar.Syst. **PAS-89**(4), 592–610 (1970)
5. Reeve, J., Baron, J., Krishnayya, P.: A general approach to harmonic current generation by HVDC converters. IEEE Trans. Power Appar.Syst. **PAS-88**(7), 989–995 (1969)
6. Hess, J.S., Rice, L.R.: Three megawatt HVDC transmission simulator. IEEE Trans. Ind. Gen. Appl. **IGA-3**(6), 531–537 (1967)
7. Ekstrom, A., Liss, G.: A refined HVDC control system. IEEE Trans. Power Appar.Syst. **PAS-89**(5), 723–732 (1970)
8. Horigome, T., Kurokawa, K., Kishi, K., Ozu, K.: A 100-kV thyristor converter for high-voltage dc transmission. IEEE Trans. Electron Devices **17**(9), 809–815 (1970)
9. Heising, C., Ringlee, R.: Prediction of reliability and availability of HVDC valve and HVDC terminal. IEEE Trans. Power Appar.Syst. **PAS-89**(4), 619–624 (1970)
10. Hingorani, N.G.: High-voltage DC transmission: a power electronics workhorse. IEEE Spectr. **33**(4), 63–72 (1996)
11. Hammons, T.J., et al.: Role of HVDC transmission in future energy development. IEEE Power Eng. Rev. **20**(2), 10–25 (2000)
12. Belda, N.A., Plet, C.A., Smeets, R.P.P.: Analysis of faults in multiterminal HVDC grid for definition of test requirements of HVDC circuit breakers. IEEE Trans. Power Deliv. **33**(1), 403–411 (2018)
13. Flourentzou, N., Agelidis, V.G., Demetriades, G.D.: VSC-based HVDC power transmission systems: an overview. IEEE Trans. Power Electron. **24**(3), 592–602 (2009)
14. Franck, C.M.: HVDC circuit breakers: a review identifying future research needs. IEEE Trans. Power Deliv. **26**(2), 998–1007 (2011)
15. Guo, C., Zhang, Y., Gole, A.M., Zhao, C.: Analysis of dual-infeed HVDC With LCC-HVDC and VSC-HVDC. IEEE Trans. Power Deliv. **27**(3), 1529–1537 (2012)
16. Liu, G., Xu, F., Xu, Z., Zhang, Z., Tang, G.: Assembly HVDC breaker for HVDC grids with modular multilevel converters. IEEE Trans. Power Electron. **32**(2), 931–941 (2017)
17. Liu, Y., Chen, Z.: A flexible power control method of VSC-HVDC link for the enhancement of effective short-circuit ratio in a hybrid multi-infeed HVDC system. IEEE Trans. Power Syst. **28**(2), 1568–1581 (2013)

18. Baek, S.-M., Kim, H.-J., Cho, J.-W., Ryoo, H.-S.: Cryogenic electrical insulation characteristics of solid insulator for the HVDC HTS cable. IEEE Trans. Appl. Supercond. **28**(4), 1–4 (2018)
19. Nam, T., Shim, J.W., Hur, K.: Design and operation of double SMES coils for variable power system through VSC-HVDC connections. IEEE Trans. Appl. Supercond. **23**(3), 5701004 (2013)
20. Kim, J.G., et al.: Loss characteristic analysis of HTS DC power cable using LCC based DC transmission system. IEEE Trans. Appl. Supercond. **22**(3), 3–6 (2012)
21. Malek, B., Johnson, B.K.: Branch current control on a superconducting DC grid. IEEE Trans. Appl. Supercond. **23**(3), 5401005 (2013)
22. Yang, Q., Le Blond, S., Liang, F., Yuan, W., Zhang, M., Li, J.: Design and application of superconducting fault current limiter in a multiterminal HVDC system. IEEE Trans. Appl. Supercond. **27**(4), 1–5 (2017)
23. Xiang, B., Liu, Z., Geng, Y., Yanabu, S.: DC circuit breaker using superconductor for current limiting. IEEE Trans. Appl. Supercond. **25**(2), 1–7 (2015)
24. Marian, A., Holé, S., Lesur, F., Tropeano, M., Bruzek, C.E.: Validation of the superconducting and insulating components of a high-power HVDC cable. IEEE Electr. Insul. Mag. **34**(1), 26–36 (2018)
25. IEEE Standards Association: IEEE recommended practice and requirements for harmonic control in electric power systems. In: IEEE Std 519-2014 (Revision of IEEE Std 519-1992), vol. 2014, pp. 1–29 (2014)
26. Enslin, J.H.R., Heskes, P.J.M.: Harmonic interaction between a large number of distributed power inverters and the distribution network. IEEE Trans. Power Electron. **19**(6), 1586–1593 (2004)
27. Goncalves, W.K.A., De Oliveira, J.C., Franco, V.L.S.: Harmonics produced by advanced static VAr compensator under electric power supply conditions with loss of quality. In: Proceedings of International Conference on Electric Utility Deregulation and Restructuring and Power Technologies, pp. 660–665 (2000)
28. Blanco, A.M., Stiegler, R., Meyer, J.: Power quality disturbances caused by modern lighting equipment (CFL and LED). In: 2013 IEEE Grenoble Conference, pp. 1–6 (2013)
29. Dugan, R.C., McGranaghan, M.F., Beaty, H.W., Santoso, S.: Electrical Power Systems Quality, 3rd edn. McGraw-Hill, New York (2004)
30. Grady, W.M., Samotyj, M.J., Noyola, A.H.: Survey of active power line conditioning methodologies. IEEE Trans. Power Deliv. **5**(3), 1536–1542 (1990)
31. Taylor, G.A.: Power quality hardware solutions for distribution systems: custom power. In: IEEE North Eastern Centre Power Section Symposium on the Reliability, Security and Power Quality of Distribution Systems, vol. 1995, pp. 1–9 (1995)
32. Singh, B., Al-Haddad, K., Chandra, A.: A review of active filters for power quality improvement. IEEE Trans. Ind. Electron. **46**(5), 960–971 (1999)
33. Morcos, M.M., Gomez, J.C.: Electric power quality - the strong connection with power electronics. IEEE Power Energy Mag. **1**(5), 18–25 (2003)
34. Khadkikar, V.: Enhancing electric power quality using UPQC: a comprehensive overview. IEEE Trans. Power Electron. **27**(5), 2284–2297 (2012)
35. Dragicevic, T., Vasquez, J.C., Guerrero, J.M., Skrlec, D.: Advanced LVDC electrical power architectures and microgrids: a step toward a new generation of power distribution networks. IEEE Electr. Mag. **2**(1), 54–65 (2014)
36. Kwasinski, A.: Quantitative evaluation of DC microgrids availability: effects of system architecture and converter topology design choices. IEEE Trans. Power Electron. **26**(3), 835–851 (2011)

37. Lu, S., Wang, L., Lo, T.-M., Prokhorov, A.V.: Integration of wind power and wave power generation systems using a DC microgrid. IEEE Trans. Ind. Appl. **51**(4), 2753–2761 (2015)
38. Patterson, B.T.: DC, come home: DC microgrids and the birth of the 'Enernet'. IEEE Power Energy Mag. **10**(6), 60–69 (2012)
39. Rodriguez-Diaz, E., Vasquez, J.C., Guerrero, J.M.: Intelligent DC homes in future sustainable energy systems: when efficiency and intelligence work together. IEEE Consum. Electron. Mag. **5**(1), 74–80 (2016)
40. Ghazanfari, A., Mohamed, Y.A.-R.I.: Decentralized cooperative control for smart DC home with DC fault handling Capability. IEEE Trans. Smart Grid **9**(5), 1 (2017)
41. Fairley, P.: DC versus AC: the second war of currents has already begun [In My View]. IEEE Power and Energy Mag. **10**(6), 103–104 (2012)

# How Much are Portuguese Residential Consumers Willing to Invest in Photovoltaic Systems?

Joana Figueira[1], Dulce Coelho[1,2], and Fernando Lopes[1,3(✉)]

[1] Coimbra Polytechnic - ISEC, Coimbra, Portugal
joanafigueira2@gmail.com, {dcoelho,flopes}@isec.pt
[2] INESC-Coimbra, Coimbra, Portugal
[3] Instituto de Telecomunicações - Coimbra, Coimbra, Portugal

**Abstract.** This paper presents the main results of a survey conducted aiming at analysing and evaluating the citizen's perceptions and willingness to invest in the installation of residential photovoltaic systems. Data has been collected in Coimbra, an urban municipality of Portugal, through a questionnaire involving three groups of questions related to socio-economic characterization of the household and building characteristics, ownership of any type of renewable energy system and willingness to invest in residential photovoltaic systems. Regarding the investment cost of the different photovoltaic systems considered, and according to the type of housing, an individual technical and economic evaluation was performed. Most of the 88 respondents have a positive attitude towards the integration of renewable energy systems in the residential sector and some of them have good knowledge of these systems. However, only a few of the respondents own a solar system and about two-thirds of respondents expressed no interest in investing in PV systems. The study served as a starting point for the assessment of the integration of renewable energies in an urban context and the obtained results will serve as the basis for the definition of scenarios related to the penetration of solar photovoltaic systems in the residential sector. This type of results can also be considered by Policy-makers in defining future measures to support the installation of residential renewable energy systems.

**Keywords:** Photovoltaic systems · Renewable energy systems ·
Residential sector · Willingness to invest

## 1 Introduction

Renewable energies, being of infinite supply, decentralized, and uniquely suited to their location, are the solution for cleaner and safer energy production. Increasing the generation of electricity from renewable energies can contribute to reduce greenhouse gas emissions, to decrease dependence from fossil fuels and fuel imports, to increase the safety of energy supplies and to meet sustainable energy development targets.

Portugal has privileged natural conditions for the generation of renewable energy. However, most of the energy from renewable sources is nowadays generated from

J. L. Afonso et al. (Eds.): GreeNets 2018, LNICST 269, pp. 64–75, 2019.
https://doi.org/10.1007/978-3-030-12950-7_6

large wind and photovoltaic farms, despite the fact that the potential for new small-scale installations for the distributed production of electricity, namely in the residential sector, using endogenous renewable sources, is very considerable. Among the various renewable technologies, solar Photovoltaic, or (PV)-based electricity, is dubbed as the most environmentally friendly and sustainable technology for electricity production and it is believed to have the largest potential for the residential sector [1].

Although the Portuguese positive attitude towards investments in innovative renewable energy systems (RES), namely solar projects and new hydropower units is high [2], the number of residential consumers adopting solar PV technologies is still relatively low, despite the fact that this activity is licensed through specific laws and there may be support measures.

Increasing the installation of photovoltaic solar systems in the residential sector could contribute to the compliance with European Union (EU) legislation on the energy performance of buildings (Energy Performance of Building Directive, 2010/31/EU). According to this Directive, Member States shall ensure that from the year 2020 all new buildings will have to be 'Nearly Zero Energy Buildings' (NZEB), which means, "a building that has a very high energy performance, as determined in accordance with Annex I. The nearly zero or very low amount of energy required should be covered to a very significant extent by energy from renewable sources, including energy from renewable sources produced on-site or nearby".

However, despite the potential of PV systems as an energy option in the urban energy system, several factors affect PV deployment [3, 4]. Based on an extensive range of literature in the broader field of renewable energy, five main types of barriers that limit site suitability, economic viability, and social acceptance of large-scale deployment of the solar option are identified in [3]: (1) technical barriers – space constraints, intermittency, and grid connection limitations; (2) economic considerations – high investment costs and long payback period; (3) market factors – misplaced incentives, unpriced costs, insufficient information and difficulty in accessing reliable information; (4) access to finance and institutional regulations – the existence of vested interests against new energy options, difficulties in dealing with permission require-ments; (5) social barriers – lack of public acceptance of new energy technologies and low perceived usefulness of a new energy technology.

The Feed-in-tariffs (FITs) scheme is the most common market driven instrument that governments, including the Portuguese Government, have been using to facilitate RES market development [5–7]. The central principle of FITs policies is to offer guaranteed prices for fixed periods, to enable a greater number of investors [8]. The scheme has rapidly increased the deployment of (PV) technologies at small scale since its introduction in 2008 (Portuguese Ministerial Order 201/2008). However, some researchers criticize the solar PV FITs used to incentivize consumers to acquire solar PV, because they are funded through increased electricity prices affecting lower income groups who are less capable of investing in solar technology [5]. The decline of the feed-in tariff rates is increasing the interest in self-consumption of PV electricity from residential systems (defined as the share of the total PV production directly consumed by the PV system owner) among PV system owners and in the scientific community [6, 9]. Moreover, the success of policies that encourage the uptake of solar PV in the residential sector requires consumer acceptance and engagement with new and emerging energy technologies, and their role is crucial to the implementation of energy policies [5].

In this context, the main objective of this paper is to analyse and evaluate the residential consumer's perceptions and willingness to invest in the installation of photovoltaic systems. The study is based on a survey of residential consumers conducted in a Portuguese city, used for this purpose. The paper is organised as follows: After the introduction the second section gives a brief overview of the evolution of photovoltaic systems' legislation and support measures. The third section presents the methodological framework and questionnaire design, while the main results are presented in the fourth section. Finally, some conclusions are drawn, including expected future developments in this field of research.

## 2 Residential PV Systems - The Portuguese Legal Framework and Support Measures

Some key findings of a study focused on residential prosumers in the European Energy Union [10], with prosumers as "energy consumers who also produce their own energy from a range of different onsite generators", using small scale solar PV to generate electricity, reveal that there is no harmonised regulatory framework for residential prosumers in the EU. Member States take different approaches, have simplified procedures for setting up residential prosumer installations and differ in terms of the financial incentives given to prosumers. Furthermore, in most Member States, the regulatory framework has evolved rapidly over time. The study also concludes that incentives have played an important role in promoting the development of self-generation, especially in the more mature solar PV markets.

In Portugal, renewable energy policy is in line with EU 2020 targets and Portuguese targets on renewable energy, that is, 31% of renewable energy in gross final energy consumption. The policies and measures to meet the targets were set out in the Portuguese National Renewable Energy Action Plan (NREAP) in July 2010. The Cabinet Resolution 20/2013 approved the new NREAP 2020, aiming to adjust the energy supply to the demand and to review the objective of each RES in the national energy mix, taking into account, namely, the maturity of the technology and its competitiveness [11].

Regarding electricity generation with residential PV in Portugal, Decree-Law 68/2002 initially regulated microgeneration: installations that use a single production technology and have a single-phase or three-phase load operating at a Low Voltage, and with a capacity of no more than 5.75 kW for single houses and 11.04 kW for condominiums. According to this law, at least 50% of the electricity produced by generators and solar panels should be consumed by the producer or by connected third parties. A Ministerial Order established the method for calculating the payment due for energy produced by microgeneration units. After five years of coming into effect, the number of microgeneration units did not achieve an expressive number.

In the end of 2007, a new law promoting the microgeneration of electricity was approved. Decree-Law 363/2007 defined a special and fast process of licensing where producers could register their installations via an electronic platform or SRM - System for the Registration of Minigeneration, and an interesting tariff - initial tariff of 650€/MWh for PV systems. The Ministerial Order 201/2008 introduced the FITs scheme and rapidly increased the deployment of PV technologies at small scale. As of October 2010, Decree Law 118-A/2010 modifies some aspects of the Microgeneration Law by simplifying the application procedure and by streamlining the access to the micro-generation regime for public, social, education, defence and local institutions. More-over, access to the benefits regime was adjusted to the cost of the equipment used in the microgeneration and subject to certain conditions, namely the compliance with energy efficiency rules and the use of solar thermal collectors or biomass boilers. Decree Law 34/2011 and Decree-Law 25/2013 complement the microgeneration regime. This new regulation simplifies the licensing regime through the new SRM electronic platform managed by the Directorate-General for Energy and Geology (DGEG).

At this time, the microgeneration law defines two regimes: the general regime, applicable to any type of microgeneration up to a limit of 5.75 kW and the special regime, applicable to renewable electricity production up to a limit of 3.68 kW. For the special regime, a reference FIT was established and applied to each technology according to a different percentage. The reference FIT for new producers reduces each year and, once defined, is valid for 15 years divided into two periods, one period of eight years and another for the remaining seven years with different tariffs for each. In 2010, the tariffs were 400€/MWh for the first period and 240€/MWh for the second. The mechanism includes an annual reduction rate of 20€/MWh. In 2014, the reference FIT was 66€/145€ per MWh for PV technologies. By mid-2014, there were 25000 installations in the special regime and 900 in the general regime, delivering a total capacity of 93 MW and 4.0 MW, respectively [11].

The more recent legislation in Portugal, Decree-Law 153/2014, was designed to streamline distributed electricity production, ensuring the technical and economic sustainability of the electric grid, simplifying the old model of microproduction and miniproduction and enabling entities with less constant consumption profiles, to be also included in this scheme.

The new Portuguese legal framework is applicable to the installation of a genera-tion unit (UP), which may take the form of a small-scale generation unit (UPP) or a generation unit for self-consumption (UPAC). It provides for the same simplified licensing procedures as the previous legislation and the potential producers could conduct their licensing using the Electronic System of Registration of Generation Units (SERUP). The procedure is similar for both generation units – UPP or UPAC. The producer must submit a request to the SERUP and pay the registration fee to the DGEG. Once the generation unit has been registered, the producer must install it using an authorised installation entity and submit a request for the inspection of the unit. If the unit has no defects nor irregularities, the exploitation certificate will be issued, the unit will be definitively registered and the generation unit can be connected to the grid – UPP or to the producer installation – UPAC.

However, there are different rules according to the type of generation unit. A UPP is applicable to any type of RES up to a limit of 250 kW, with grid injection and with a FIT for each primary energy used, according to a different percentage contained in Ministerial Order 15/2015. The reference FIT for new producers in 2015 is valid for 15 years, and has a value of 95€/MWh, to which 5.0€/MWh are added if there is 2 m$^2$ of solar thermal panels in the consumer's installation or of 10€/MWh if there is an electric vehicle charging power outlet connected to the mobility grid in the consumer facility [11]. A UPAC is applicable to any kind of source since it does not benefit from a FIT, and has the possibility of injecting the surplus into the grid, which if paid by the last-resort supplier at 90% of the average monthly market price. Optionally, a UPAC, either grid connected or off-grid, can also trade the electricity surplus or the generated electricity by green certificates [11].

## 3   The Methodological Framework and Questionnaire Design

Based on a survey supported in a questionnaire, our study proposes the analysis and evaluation of the consumers' willingness to invest in photovoltaic systems in the residential sector. As referred in [12], although there are several studies in the scientific literature on the estimation of the consumers' willingness to pay (WTP) for renewable energies, only a few of them focused on WTP for renewable energy technologies that may be installed in households. In [13] a survey of 200 Greek consumers was carried out, from December 2009 to January 2010, aiming to examine the determinants that affect consumers' intention towards the adoption of renewable energy sources in the residential sector in Greece. The work in [14] takes a closer look at the awareness regarding microgeneration and presents the results from a nationally representative study conducted in the Republic of Ireland. A survey was developed in March 2009 to identify the level of awareness for microgeneration technologies in Ireland, accessed a sample of 1010 adults aged above 15 years, and ensured representativeness by setting strict quotas for age, gender, social class and region. In this context, [12] also presents the results of a questionnaire survey carried out in order to identify the preferences on renewable microgeneration technologies in Lithuanian households and sharing thereof. Respondents were individual house owners living in Kaunas or in the Kaunas region and completed questionnaires in the period of April-June 2016. The study in [15] aims to do an in-depth analysis on how Swedish households search for and interpret information about PVs, as well as to discuss how to reach different groups with this information. The results of this work are based on three interview studies made between autumn 2013 and autumn 2016. The work in [16] presents a study aiming to explore how to motivate homeowners to adopt residential solar electric technology. This study is based on semi-structured interviews with homeowners throughout the state of Wisconsin, who have installed PV technology. Interviews were conducted between April and November 2011 and involved 48 individuals in 36 households.

### 3.1   Questionnaire Design and Respondents Profile

The questionnaire survey was made short (an expected total time of completion of 5 min maximum) and relatively simple, to increase the probability of receiving a higher number of respondents. It was prepared considering three groups of questions, all of multiple choice: the first group is related to the socio-economic characterization of the household; the second group deals with building characteristics; the third and last group considers the ownership of any type of residential renewable energy system and the willingness to invest in residential PV systems. We carried out the survey from July to September 2018. The questionnaire was made anonymous, distributed through Google Forms to a universe of 110 residential consumers and had 80% of the sent requests successfully answered.

All the 88 respondents to the online survey are residents of Coimbra, the Portuguese city chosen for this study. The average age of the respondents is 52, and their ages range from 25 to 78 years. Most respondents are between the ages of 25 and 40 years old (55.7%), 33% are between 40 and 60 years old, and only 11.7% above 70 years old. Regarding the educational level of respondents, the majority are university-educated where 68.2% hold a Bachelor's or a Master's Degree and 20.5% hold a PhD Degree. Only 11.4% have graduation from a secondary school as educational level.

Besides the age and educational level, residents have been questioned about the number of persons per household, net household income and house type. Almost half of the interviewed, 48.9% live in a three or four-person household. Another large share, 43.2%, live in a one or two-person household. Only for about 8% of the answers, the household composition is higher than 4 people. Half of the households have an income between 1,000 and 2,500 EUR/month, 11% have an income lower than 1,000 EUR/month and only 39% of households have an income higher than 2,500 EUR/month. The great majority of the respondents, 80.1%, own their house, 29.5% live in a single-family house, 12.5% live in a condominium with more than eighteen households and the majority, 58%, live in a condominium with a number of households between three and eighteen. Almost all the buildings in the sample are exclusively used for housing (85.2%).

## 3.2  Economic Analysis of Different Residential PV Systems

To support the questions related to residential consumers willing to invest in photovoltaic systems, as for example when defining the limits for the total investment costs, an economic analysis of different PV systems that can be installed in the residential sector had been conducted. This analysis took into account the local availability of solar radiation, existing market technologies and the new Portuguese legislation

**Table 1.** Economic analysis of different UPP units.

|  |  |  | UPP |  |
|---|---|---|---|---|
| Installed capacity | 500 W | 1500 W | 3000 W | 5000 W |
| Total investment cost (€) | 725.00 | 1923.00 | 5247.00 | 9517.00 |
| Annually electricity production (kWh) | 825.00 | 2475.00 | 4952.00 | 8251.00 |
| Net Present Value (€) | −102.98 | 1161.99 | 1535.42 | 2189.86 |
| Internal rate of return | 1.55% | 8.12% | 5.59% | 5.06% |
| Payback (years) | 19.93 | 10.13 | 12.84 | 13.56 |
| O&M costs (€) | 35.00 | 35.00 | 35.00 | 35.00 |
| Discount rate | 3.00% | 3.00% | 3.00% | 3.00% |
| Reference tariff (€/kWh) | 0.095 | 0.095 | 0.095 | 0.095 |

concerning the promotion of renewable energy sources in households [17–19]. The PVSYST® software has been used for the simulation of electricity production from the different PV systems considered.

The main results of the economic analysis for the different small-scale PV generation units, including the profitability of a PV system (see Net Present Value), are presented in Table 1.

According to the results presented in Table 1, one main conclusion is that the investment in a 500 W UPP is very appealing from the prosumer point of view, in what concerns the total investment cost. However, this system presents a negative NPV, meaning that it will be a non-economically viable project.

For UPAC units, the installed capacity considered for evaluation was decided according to the most frequent registrations in Portugal, in the SERUP platform, from March 2015 to July 2017. Table 2 presents the main results of the economic analysis for different PV generation units, for self-consumption.

**Table 2.** Economic analysis of different UPAC units.

|  |  |  |  | UPAC |
|---|---|---|---|---|
| Installed capacity | 500 W | 1500 W | 3000 W | 5000 W |
| Total investment cost (€) | 1025 | 4189 | 9294 | 15111 |
| Annually electricity production (kWh) | 825 | 2475 | 4952 | 8251 |
| Net Present Value (€) | 499.25 | 1602.66 | 2903.95 | 5619.19 |
| Internal rate of return | 7.25% | 6.34 | 5.75 | 6.24 |
| Payback (years) | 10.87 | 11.94 | 12.66 | 12.08 |
| O&M costs (€) | 35 | 35 | 35 | 35 |
| Discount rate | 3% | 3% | 3% | 3% |

An economic analysis for UPAC systems selling the surplus produced electricity to the national grid was not performed. This was because, for those cases, detailed knowledge is needed on the energy consumed in the dwelling and on the energy that is sold or not sold to the public grid.

## 4   Consumers Willing to Invest in PV Systems – Results and Discussion

To analyse and evaluate the residential consumer's perceptions and willingness to invest in the installation of photovoltaic systems, the focus of the results herein presented, additional questions were included in the questionnaire, regarding the ownership of renewable energy systems, renewable energy awareness, interest in investing in renewable energy systems and how much the household would be willing to invest in a PV system.

Only 31% of the houses surveyed here have a renewable energy system installed. Of these, 7% correspond to PV systems for electricity production, 6% to biomass units

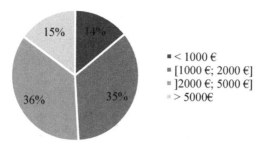

**Fig. 1.** Percentage of residential consumers willing to invest, by investment value range.

for heating and 18% to solar thermal systems for hot water production. Concerning these houses that already have a renewable energy system installed, 24 of the total enquires have confirmed energy related savings in their electric bill, corresponding to 89% of the consumers with an installed renewable energy system.

When questioned about the interest in investing in PV systems, about two-thirds of respondents (67%) expressed no interest in this investment. Figure 1 illustrates the results obtained regarding how many residential consumers are willing to invest in a PV system, expressed as a percentage, by investment value range considered. As it could be expected, the percentage of consumers willing to invest more than 5000 € is low. However, the percentage of consumers willing to invest up to 1000 € is the lowest. This result may be related to the pre-conceived idea of the cost associated with a photovoltaic system, together with the net household income of inquired consumers.

Figure 2a–d, depict how much residential consumers are willing to invest in a PV system according to the buildings' characteristics and according to their socio-economic characterization.

From the analysis of the results presented in the graphs of Fig. 2, as expected, there is a direct relationship between net monthly household income and investment in PV systems. 75% of respondents willing to invest more than 5000 € have a net monthly income of more than 2500 €. This percentage decreases as the income decreases reaching no responses to incomes less than 1000 €. Moreover, given the data on the economic evaluation of different PV systems, presented in Tables 1 and 2, the number of options for consumers who are willing to invest up to 1000 € is reduced. Of course, the options will increase as the amount the consumer is willing to invest increases. The same direct relationship exists regarding educational level. The totality of respondents who are willing to invest more than 5000 € are university-educated.

The younger respondents are more willing to invest. This is not surprising, as this group will correspond to consumers with greater knowledge regarding renewable energy and environmental concerns. The respondents aged over 60 represent the largest percentage of consumers willing to invest more than 5000 €.

There is no direct relationship between the amount of the monthly electricity bill and the amount willing to invest. The majority of respondents indicate a monthly electricity bill less than 75 €. Those with the highest monthly electricity bill (higher than 100 €) correspond to the highest percentage of respondents in the investment range between 1000 € and 2000 €. For consumers with monthly electricity bill between

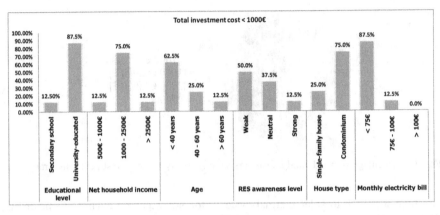

a)

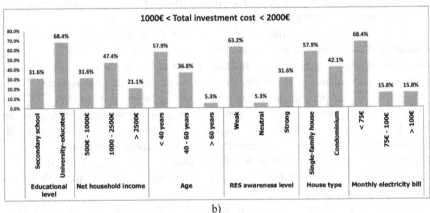

b)

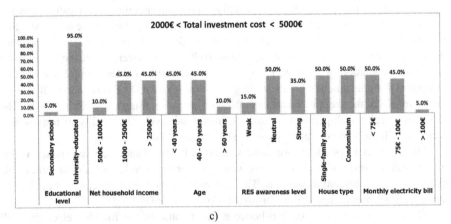

c)

**Fig. 2.** How much are residential consumers willing to invest in a PV system.

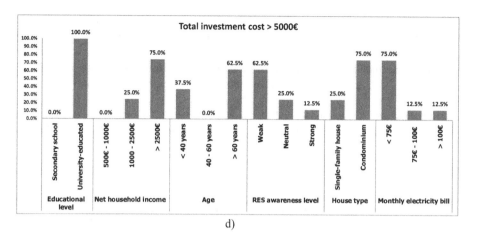

d)

**Fig. 2.** (*continued*)

75 € and 100 €, the largest number of responses (45%) corresponds to the investment range between 2000 € and 5000 €. Regarding the type of household involved in the survey, we can observe that, except for the investment range between 1000 € and 2000 €, the majority of respondents live in condominiums, where the installation of a PV system may be more difficult, requiring the acceptance of all condominium owners.

## 5  Conclusions

The main objective of the present study was to analyse and evaluate the residential consumer's perceptions and how much they are willing to invest in photovoltaic systems. This study is the starting point for a wider study, aiming at the assessment of the economic, social and environmental impacts of the integration of renewable energies in an urban context. Information about consumers' socioeconomic profile and about their willingness to adopt and to invest in renewable energies, namely in the installation of PV systems, will serve as the basis for the definition of different scenarios related to the penetration of solar photovoltaic systems in the residential sector, according to the buildings' characteristics and according to the consumers' socioeconomic characterization and electricity consumption profile.

Data collected through an online questionnaire allowed to conclude that the willingness to adopt or invest in renewable energy systems in the residential sector is dependent on the consumer's age and knowledge about RES and, eventually, about existing legislation concerning RES. On the other hand, regarding the amount that consumers are willing to invest in residential RES, there is a strong relationship with the net monthly household income. This fact justifies some recommendations in line with [10]: an EU-level legal framework focused on the establishment of a portfolio of carefully designed incentives, tailored to the different situations and measures designed aiming at supporting the development and uptake of new technologies with an environmental objective.

Although the presented methodology has been developed in a national context, using a medium-sized Portuguese city as a decision-making scenario, and considering the applicable national and international legislation and support programs, it can be applied to other national municipalities, or in other countries, taking into account the specificities of each urban energy system and legal framework under analysis.

**Acknowledgments.** The authors would like to acknowledge FCT (Portuguese Foundation for Science and Technology) support under project grant Learn2Behave (02/SAICT/2016-023651).

# References

1. Ahmad, S., Tahar, R.M., Cheng, J.K., Yao, L.: Public acceptance of residential solar photovoltaic technology in Malaysia. PSU Res. Rev. **1**(3), 242–254 (2017)
2. Ribeiro, F., Ferreira, P., Araújo, M., Braga, A.C.: Public opinion on renewable energy technologies in Portugal. Energy **69**, 39–50 (2014)
3. Mah, D.N., Wang, G., Loa, K., Leung, M.K.H., Hills, P., Lo, A.Y.: Barriers and policy enablers for solar photovoltaics (PV) in cities: perspectives of potential adopters in Hong Kong. Renew. Sustain. Energy Rev. **92**, 921–936 (2018)
4. Rai, V., Reeve, D.C., Margolis, R.: Overcoming barriers and uncertainties in the adoption of residential solar PV. Renew. Energy **89**, 498–505 (2016)
5. Sommerfeld, J., Buys, L., Vine, D.: Residential consumers' experiences in the adoption and use of solar PV. Energy Policy **105**, 10–16 (2017)
6. McKenna, E., Pless, J., Darby, S.J.: Solar photovoltaic self-consumption in the UK residential sector: new estimates from a smart grid demonstration project. Energy Policy **118**, 482–491 (2018)
7. Amorim, F., Vasconcelos, J., Abreu, I.C., Silva, P.P., Martins, V.: How much room for a competitive electricity generation market in Portugal? Renew. Sustain. Energy Rev. **18**, 103–118 (2013)
8. Cherrington, R., Goodship, V., Longfield, A., Kirwan, K.: The feed-in tariff in the UK: a case study focus on domestic photovoltaic systems. Renew. Energy **50**, 421–426 (2013)
9. Luthander, R., Widén, J., Nilsson, D., Palm, J.: Photovoltaic self-consumption in buildings: a review. Appl. Energy **142**, 80–94 (2015)
10. European Commission: Study on "Residential Prosumers in the European Energy Union". Framework Contract EAHC/2013/CP/04 (2017)
11. International Energy Agency: Energy Policies of IEA Countries. Portugal 2016 Review. OECD/IEA (2016)
12. Su, W., Liu, M., Zeng, S., Streimikien, D., Balezentis, T., Alisauskaite-Seskiene, I.: Valuating renewable microgeneration technologies in Lithuanian households: a study on willingness to pay. J. Clean. Prod. **191**, 318–329 (2018)
13. Sardianou, E., Genoudi, P.: Which factors affect the willingness of consumers to adopt renewable energies? Renew. Energy **57**, 1–4 (2013)
14. Claudy, M.C., Michelsen, C., O'Driscoll, A., Mullen, M.R.: Consumer awareness in the adoption of microgeneration technologies. Renew. Sustain. Energy Rev. **14**, 2154–2160 (2010)

15. Palm, J., Eriksson, E.: Residential solar electricity adoption: how households in Sweden search for and use information. Energy Sustain. Soc. **8**(14), 1–9 (2018)
16. Schelly, C.: Residential solar electricity adoption: what motivates, and what matters? A case study of early adopters. Energy Res. Soc. Sci. **2**, 183–191 (2014)
17. Decree-Law No. 153/2014, 20 October 2014
18. Ministerial Order No. 15/2015, 23 January 2015
19. Ministerial Order No. 60-E/2015, 2 March 2015

# Sustainability Assessment of High Voltage Transmission Lines

Paula Ferreira[1](✉) 🆔, Glaucivan da Cunha[2], and Madalena Araújo[1] 🆔

[1] ALGORITMI Research Centre, University of Minho, Campus Azurém,
4800-058 Guimarães, Portugal
paulaf@dps.uminho.pt
[2] Coordination of Electrical Engineering,
FAMETRO - Faculdade Metropolitana de Manaus, Manaus, Brazil

**Abstract.** This work aims to contribute to the proposal of a multi-criteria based methodology for sustainability evaluation of impacts from high voltage transmission lines integrating indicators reflecting environmental and socio-economic criteria. The proposed methodology was applied to a transmission grid project in Manaus/Amazonas, Brazil, evaluating its sustainability. From the analysis, it can be observed that the implementation of the project tends to have a significant impact during the construction phase. The most important indexes come from the environmental dimension resulting from a proximity to environmental protected areas and reduction of vegetation both during implementation and operation phases, which is particularly important for the case of Amazonia forest. As for the socio-economic index, this reflects an optimistic expectation of the population towards the arrival of electricity to communities that can lead to the creation of more jobs and improvement of cities infrastructures along with the low expected impact on local protected communities, given the previous studies addressing these concerns during the design phase. Based on the results achieved, avenues for future research are proposed.

**Keywords:** Transmission line · Impact evaluation · Sustainability

## 1  Introduction

The analysis of future electricity needs for different economic agents and society, represents the technical priority for the planning of the electricity sector in Brazil. The definition of the transmission layout is part of this planning requiring the identification of the impacts related to the construction and operation of electricity transmission projects, targeting its minimization and the mitigation of negative effects to the population and to the environment.

Sustainability evaluation can be understood as a multi-criteria problem that should include technical, economic, environmental and social aspects. This way, multi-criteria techniques have been applied for the evaluation of impacts of complex problems such as the expansion of the electric system including production, transmission and distribution. In the case of ecological impacts, which are still the major focus of sustainability evaluation, the situation is particularly complex, as the electricity transmission

J. L. Afonso et al. (Eds.): GreeNets 2018, LNICST 269, pp. 76–85, 2019.
https://doi.org/10.1007/978-3-030-12950-7_7

lines can have negative and positive impacts. However, the perception of negative impacts on the environment prevails among residents as is the case of visual pollution [1]. Positive aspects were associated with the perception that electricity transmission lines are necessary for modern life with gains of a socioeconomic nature [2]. Analyzing environmental, economic and social sustainability of the electricity projects along the whole value chain, will open the routes to reach social responsibility for the entire electricity system. As [3] highlighted energy use and availability are central issues in sustainable development. Participatory approaches and policy formulation at the local level can also facilitate these discussions, providing a valuable approach to understanding perceptions and possible conflicts over electricity transmission lines [4]. However, the studies related to the sustainability assessment of high voltage projects are still scarce, particularly in the case of Brazil. Given the expected development of the transmission grid for the next few years in the country [5] it becomes thus highly relevant to address this issue. It is then required to perform a detailed analysis of such large projects that are expected to have a major impact on the economic development of the local populations, having also positive impacts on the overall costs of the Brazilian electrical system.

This work addresses the segment of transmission grids aiming to contribute to demonstrate the use of a methodology for the evaluation of impacts integrating indicators reflecting environmental and socio-economic criteria. High Voltage (HV) grids (500 kV) are extensive and cover large portions of land with different characteristics resulting in significant impacts from the use of the land, from the intrusion caused by the required infrastructures and foundations and even for the opening of new roads and increasing traffic during the construction phase.

The proposed methodology was applied to evaluate the sustainability of the transmission grid project 500 kV Tucuruí - Manaus: Lot C, SE Oriximiná (Oriximiná/Pará) - SE Cariri (Manaus/Amazonas). The electricity system in Amazonia is the only non-interconnected one in Brazil and the size of the region represents a major challenge for its modernization. These characteristics demonstrate the relevance of the transmission line for the region and for the communities, but also put in evidence the importance of evaluating impacts and mitigate negative social and environmental effects.

The structure of the paper is as follows. Section 2 addresses the electrical system of Manaus, given the focus of the paper on this region. Section 3 presents the methodology for analyzing the sustainability of the transmission line project. In Sect. 4 the results are described. The main conclusions are summarized at the end.

## 2  Electrical System of Manaus

The state of Amazonas, despite having great hydroelectric potential, has always had difficulties in the supply of electricity, despite the permanent contribution of government investments. The long distance of the large consumer centers has contributed to the situation, forcing the exploitation of the isolated own generation, supplied in almost 90% by thermal generation in the capital, Manaus, and 10% by hydraulic generation.

The Amazonian electrical system is the only one in the country totally unconnected, where the extension of the region seems to multiply the challenges to make it part of the modern world. The development of the transmission grid is then considered an essential step to reach universalization of the access to electric energy in Brazil, along with renewable decentralized power generation [6].

The Tucuruí - Macapá - Manaus interconnection project was established on the Brazilian Transmission Expansion Program - PET 2008 to 2012. The Ministry of Mines and Energy - MME was responsible for the preparation of studies and planning of the project, through the Energy Research Company - EPE [7]. The Tucuruí Inter-connection - Macapá - Manaus has a total extension of 1811 km and crosses 29 municipalities in 3 Brazilian States, namely Amapá, Pará and Amazonas. It was auc-tioned on June 27, 2008 [8] and the bidding of the project took place in three lots (A, B and C), thus increasing the attractiveness and reducing the risks to the investors. The integration of the Amazon state on the Intergated Electricity System through Tucuruí - Macapá - Manaus line occurred in June 2013 [9].

Figure 1 presents a map of Brazil highlighting the three states crossed by the transmission line and Fig. 2 shows a scheme of the 3 lots considered. At an initial design stage different alternatives for the route and layout of the line were analyzed taking into account expected environmental impacts and effect on local population which allowed to select the preferential layout described in Fig. 2 [10].

**Fig. 1.** States crossed by Tucuruí - Macapá - Manaus transmission line.

The study presented in this paper focuses on the analysis of the Oriximiná-Cariri transmission line (Lot C), which will be the one ensuring the connection of the capital of the State of Amazonas to the Brazilian electricity grid.

The 500 km Oriximiná Cariri (Lot C) transmission line will pass through the states of Pará and Amazonas, along the left bank of the Amazon River, passing through 12 municipalities: 3 of them located in Pará (Oriximiná, Terra Santa and Faro) and 9 of

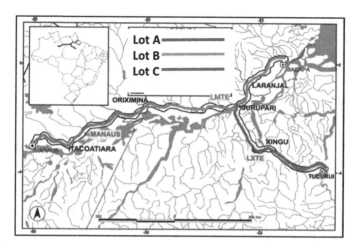

**Fig. 2.** Schematic representation of the 3 lots of the Tucuruí - Macapá - Manaus transmission line [10].

them located in Amazonas (Nhamundá, Parintins, Urucará, São Sebastião do Uatumã, Itapiranga, Silves, Itacoatiara, Rio Preta da Eva and Manaus) [10].

The justification for the construction of the 500 kV line Tucuruí - Macapá - Manaus is based on different studies considering different aspects [10].

- interconnection of the isolated systems of Manaus and Macapá to the Brazilian transmission network;
- possibility of replacing the oil-based thermal generation of existing systems in these cities with a reduction in the associated negative environmental impacts;
- possibility of increasing sustainable regional development;
- contribution to improving the quality of life of the population to be served.

## 3   Methodology

With the ultimate objective of analyzing the sustainability of the Tucuruí-Manaus transmission line project in relation to economic, environmental and social factors, the following specific research steps were defined:

- Investigate and characterize the Tucuruí-Manaus transmission line project;
- Investigate and select a set of social, environmental and economic criteria and indicators for the evaluation of transmission line projects;
- Evaluate the line design of 500 kV Tucuruí – Manaus (Lot C) in accordance with the selected criteria.

The process of evaluating the sustainability of a transmission project should aim to provide information on the set of impacts or interferences caused by the transmission system including transmission line and substations. In the evaluation of sustainability, there are usually methods that allow for the association of several indicators with their respective dimensions (e.g. social, economic, environmental, cultural). Sustainability is thus perceived as a multi-criteria problem, which should include widely accepted technical, economic, and environmental assessment criteria allowing to evaluate both the positive impact and the negative impact of the enterprise.

In this work, the methodology proposed in the Technical Note DEA - 21/10 [11] for the sustainability evaluation of hydroelectric power plants and HV transmission lines was followed. Based on sustainability criteria and considering that the indicators should necessarily comprise the evaluation of both the positive impacts and the negative impacts caused, a list of indicators was then defined to make up the sustainability index. This list has been reduced according to the availability of information, its accuracy and relevance for the case of HV transmission lined. According to the EPE [11], 11 indicators were then defined, six of them in the environmental dimension and five in the socioeconomic dimension, as presented in Table 1.

As different scales are used for each criterion their conversion in a common scale was required. The approach proposed by [12] was used and the conversion was then based on a simple ratio as indicated by Eq. (1) for positive impacts and by Eq. (2) for negative impacts.

$$I = (x - m)/(M - m) \tag{1}$$

$$I = (M - x)/(M - m) \tag{2}$$

where I is the value of the index (0–1 scale) to be calculated, x is the value obtained in the initial scale, m is the minimum value and M is the maximum value. As such each indicator represents the sustainability index of the project comparatively to the worst possible situation, with $I = 0$ representing the worst possible case (minimum sustainability) and $I = 1$ representing the best possible case (maximum sustainability).

Each one of the dimensions is then computed by calculating a simple arithmetic mean of all corresponding indicators, from which a classification is derived. Given the scarcity of information in what concerns impact assessment for transmission grids, the model assumes the independence of each indicator and equal weights assigned to each of them following the insufficient reason Principle (interested readers can see the principle [13]) and also the [11] proposal.

The HV sustainability indicator (I) assumes values between "0" and "1", assigning to "0" - "Very low sustainability" and to value "1" - "Very high sustainability", as shown in Table 2.

The criteria used to select the indicators were not limited to their importance, but considered also the existence of data and the quality of the information in order to be possible a judicious and reliable evaluation [11]. A Global Sustainability Index – GSI was obtained from the aggregation of indices obtained for each dimension, following the approach proposed by [12].

The proposed methodology was applied in the analysis of the sustainability of the 500 kV Tucuruí - Manaus transmission line project: Lot C, SE Oriximiná (Oriximiná/ Pará) - SE Cariri (Manaus/Amazonas) and the main results are presented in the following sections.

**Table 1.** Environmental and socioeconomic dimension (Source: adapted from [11])

| Dimension | Indicator | Notes | Description |
|---|---|---|---|
| Environmental | Corridor extension | Related to the required land for LT use Land use factor | Corridor extension (km) |
| | Presence and/or proximity to protected areas (PA) in the HV corridor | PA include lands and regions for which the natural conditions require special protection measures Biodiversity factor | Identification and positioning of PA near or within the corridor by PA category (%) |
| | Presence of biodiversity protection areas (BPA) in the corridor | BPA include lands and regions which can become in the future PA Biodiversity factor | Identification and positioning of BPA in the corridor (km$^2$) |
| | Presence of forest areas in the corridor | Potential for deforestation Biodiversity factor | Identification and quantification of the forest areas in the corridor (km$^2$) |
| | Presence of secondary vegetation areas in the corridor | Potential negative effects over local vegetation Biodiversity factor | Identification and quantification of secondary vegetation areas in the corridor (km$^2$) |
| | Presence of savannah and/or steppe areas in the corridor | Potential negative effects over savanna and steppe areas Biodiversity factor | Identification and quantification of savanna areas in the corridor (km$^2$) |
| Socio-economic | Presence and/or proximity of Indigenous Land (s) in the corridor | Living conditions factor/protection of vulnerable population | Identification and distance to Indigenous Lands near or within the corridor (km) |
| | Presence of classified/protected rural land (s) in the corridor | Living conditions factor/protection of vulnerable population | Identification and distance to the classified rural lands in the corridor (km) |
| | Presence of urban areas in the corridor | Living conditions factor | Identification and quantification of urban areas in the corridor (%) |
| | Presence of agriculture and forestry areas in the corridor | Living conditions factor | Identification and quantification of areas of agricultural and forestry areas in the corridor (km$^2$) |
| | Direct jobs to be generated in the line deployment phase | Living conditions factor | Number of direct jobs to be generated in the line deployment phase |

**Table 2.** Classification of Sustainability Indicators (Source: adapted from [11])

| Indicator (I) | Ranking |
|---|---|
| I < 0.2 | Very low |
| 0.2 < I < 0.4 | Low |
| 0.4 < I < 0.6 | Average |
| 0.6 < I < 0.8 | High |
| 0.8 < I < 1.0 | Very high |

## 4 Results

Table 3 presents the results of the environmental and socio-economic assessment, including the partial values obtained for each indicator and the aggregated environmental indicator (EI) and socio-economic indicator (SEI). Data for each one of the proposed indicators were obtained from [10] for the case of the selected transmission lined. The values were then converted into a dimensionless scale (0–1) obtained from [12] method. In order to obtain the Global Sustainability Index (GSI), the simple arithmetic mean between EI and SEI was calculated.

The results indicate a high sustainability index (GSI) for the transmission line, as follows from the scale proposed in Table 2.

It is observed that the implementation of the transmission line produced greater impacts during its construction phase. The Environmental Index - EI 0.38, reflects a low sustainability level which comes from the combination of several factors, namely the extension of the corridor, the proximity to protected environmental areas and expected high impacts on the vegetation. These results are particularly remarkable given that the region involved is the Amazon rainforest.

Regarding the Socioeconomic Index (ISE), it reached a quite high value of 0.84 which can be classified as very high according to Table 2. This high value comes mainly from the ensured minimum distance to lands with special classification because of their relation to vulnerable population. In fact, the effect on the reduction of agricultural and forestry areas in the corridor is considered to be low as less than 20% of these areas will be crossed by the corridor. This corridor is expected also to be more than 10 km away from Indigenous communities and from protected rural land (s) in the corridor, which once again result on high sustainability indicators.

However, it should be highlighted that these values are mainly based on the scale proposed in [11] and if more conservative values were to be considered, the resulting sustainability index can be significantly affected.

**Table 3.** Environmental and socio-economic assessment

| Dimension | Indicator | Value (0–1) |
|---|---|---|
| Environmental | Corridor extension | 0.07 |
| | Presence and/or proximity to protected areas (PA) in the HV corridor | 0.00 |
| | Presence of biodiversity protection areas (BPA) in the corridor | 0.84 |
| | Presence of forest areas in the corridor | 0.45 |
| | Presence of secondary vegetation areas in the corridor | 0.00 |
| | Presence of savannah and/or steppe areas in the corridor | 0.93 |
| **EI** | **Environmental Indicator** | **0.38** |
| Socio-economic | Presence and/or proximity of Indigenous Land (s) in the corridor | 1.00 |
| | Presence of classified/protected rural land (s) in the corridor | 1.00 |
| | Presence of urban areas in the corridor | 1.00 |
| | Presence of agriculture and forestry areas in the corridor | 0.83 |
| | Direct jobs to be generated in the line deployment phase | 0.36 |
| **SEI** | **Socio-Economic Indicator** | **0.84** |
| **GSI** | **Global Sustainability Index** | **0.61** |

## 5   Conclusions

With the implementation of the Tucuruí - Macapá - Manaus transmission line, several benefits can be enumerated: reduction of thermoelectric plants; improvement of the quality of life of the inhabitants, especially those who live in the interior, far from the capital; improvement in electricity supply and promotion of economic development in the city. But there will be major socio-environmental challenges in a region that has a rich biodiversity and the traditional culture of the people of the Amazon.

The advantages obtained from the interconnection of the city of Manaus to the other regions of the country by the National Interconnection System - SIN are significant in the drastic reduction of carbon dioxide released into the atmosphere, elimination of oil spills in rivers and related taxes. But there is the other side of the coin, which are particular remarkable for the case of the environmental aspects. The negative impact of "suppression of native vegetation" and the positive impact of "supplying electric power to communities" are highlighted as being of a high degree of significance.

The achieved Global Sustainability Index classified as High (GSI - 0.61), reflects the balance between the socio-economic and the environmental aspects and results also from the pre-selection stage for the layout of the line which already took into account these sustainability concerns. Even so, from the analysis it can be observed that the implementation of this portion of the line (Lot C) led to a significant impact during the construction phase. The most important negative indexes come from the environmental dimension as results of the reduction of vegetation both during implementation and operation phases. Recognizing that sustainability levels should be analyzed taking into account the region, and considering that this case includes the sensitive region and biome of Amazonia forest, the question of vegetation turns to be particularly important.

This research opens important avenues for future research on the need to adapt the methodology to the specificities of the region under analysis. As for the socioeconomic index, the results reflect an optimistic expectation of the population towards the arrival of electricity to communities which can lead to the creation of more jobs and improvement of cities infrastructures. However, some concerns about the impact on the availability of rural lands to be used mainly for agriculture purpose in the region should also be highlighted.

From the study, it becomes obvious that although a common framework can be envisaged, sustainability evaluation must reflect the characteristics of each case under analysis. The proper selection of specific indicators relevant for the case is required along with the definition of a well-suited scale, for the final integration in an overall index for which different weights may be considered. In this study, and for the sake of simplicity, equal weights were assumed for each factor. Future work may address weight differentiation or may even consider a change on the structure of the problem using a more complex multi-criteria model able to deal with different scales and weights.

**Acknowledgement.** This work is financed by the ERDF – European Regional Development Fund through the Operational Programme for Competitiveness and Internationalisation COMPETE 2020 Programme; by National Funds through the Portuguese funding agency, FCT Fundação para a Ciência e a Tecnologia, within project SAICTPAC/0004/2015-POCI/01/0145/FEDER/01643 and by the ALGORITMI research and FCT within the Project Scope: UID/CEC/00319/2019.

# References

1. Kaltenborn, B., Bjerke, T.: Associations between environmental value orientations and landscape preference. Landscape Urban Plan **59**, 1–11 (2002)
2. Soini, K., Pouta, E., Salmiovirta, M., Usitalo, M., Kivinen, T.: Local residents' perceptions of energy landscape: the case of transmission line. Land Policy **28**, 294–305 (2011)
3. Ferreira, P., Araújo, M., O'Kelly, M.E.J.: The integration of social concerns into electricity power planning: a combined Delphi and AHP approach. In: Rebennack, S., Pardalos, P.M., Pereira, M.V.F., Iliadis, N.A. (eds.) Handbook of Power Systems, pp. 323–364. Springer, Heidelberg (2010). https://doi.org/10.1007/978-3-642-02493-1_15
4. Soini, K., Aakkula, J.: Framing the biodiversity of agricultural landscape: the essence of local conceptions and constructions. Land Use Policy **24**, 311–321 (2007)
5. EPE – Empresa de Pesquisa Energética: Plano Decenal de Expansão de Energia 2026 - PDE 2026, July 2017. Ministério de Minas e Energia, Rio de Janeiro (2017)
6. Pereira, M.G., Freitas, M.A.V., da Silva, N.F.: Rural electrification and energy poverty: empirical evidences from Brazil. Renew. Sustain. Energy Rev. **14**(4), 1229–1240 (2010)
7. EPE – Empresa de Pesquisa Energética. Estudos para licitação da expansão da transmissão. Consolidação das analyes e pareceres técnicos. Programa de Expansão da Transmissão – PET 2008–2012, January 2008. Ministério de Minas e Energia, Rio de Janeiro (2008)
8. ANEEL: Edital 004/2008, de março de 2008, March 2008 (2008)
9. ONS: Necessidade de permanência das usinas térmicas de Manaus em 2015, Nota Técnica 0011/2015, January 2015, Rio de Janeiro (2015)

10. Biodinâmica Rio: Relatório de Impacto Ambiental/Rima – Linha de Transmissão 500 kV Oriximiná-Cariri, June 2009, Rio de Janeiro (2009)
11. EPE – Empresa de Pesquisa Energética: Metodologia para avaliação da Sustentabilidade socioeconômica e ambiental de UHE e LT, Série Estudos do Meio Ambiente, Nota Técnica DEA 21/10, November 2010. Ministério de Minas e Energia, Rio de Janeiro (2010)
12. Martins, M.F., Cândido, G.A.: Índices de desenvolvimento sustentável para localidades: uma proposta metodológica de construção e análise. Revista de Gestão Social e Ambiental **6**(1), 3–19 (2012)
13. Sinn, H.-W.: A rehabilitation of the principle of insufficient reason. Q. J. Econ. **94**(3), 493–506 (1980)

# Voltage Distortion Minimization
# in Cascaded H-Bridge Inverters

António Martins[1]([✉]), João Faria[1], and Abel Ferreira[2]

[1] Faculty of Engineering, University of Porto, Porto, Portugal
ajm@fe.up.pt, jpc.faria@hotmail.com
[2] CINERGIA - Control Intelligent de l'Energia, Barcelona, Spain
abel.ferreira@cinergia.coop

**Abstract.** Multilevel inverters based on the series connection of H-bridges are the most modular multilevel inverter family. The use of a large number of these devices connected in series, controlled by modulation based on the fundamental frequency, allows to obtain an output voltage of the inverter with low harmonic distortion and low losses in the inverter. This paper analyses the main characteristics of a fundamental frequency modulation method applied to multilevel inverters based on cascaded H-bridges (CHB). Particular emphasis is given to the harmonic distortion of the output voltage and the range of variation of the amplitude of the fundamental component in static and dynamic conditions. It is also discussed the implementation of the algorithm in real-time and in an FPGA platform. Simulation and experimental results are presented with a different number of H-bridges.

**Keywords:** Cascaded H-bridge inverters · Multilevel inverters ·
Square-wave modulation · Total harmonic distortion

## 1 Introduction

Multilevel inverters are electronic power converters that output a voltage wave with more than two levels. This waveform is more similar to a sine wave than that generated by a conventional two-level converter, thus presenting a lower total harmonic distortion. As with any other type of DC/AC converter, the control of the semiconductors is the means to control the output voltage, either via modulation index, number of bridges in series or contribution to the total fundamental component of each individual bridge. In relation to conventional topologies, the different multilevel topologies allow to reduce some additional less desirable properties that characterize them such as the reduction of switching and conduction losses, use of semiconductors of lower controlled power, reduction of voltage gradients, reduction of common mode voltages as well as overall reduction of electromagnetic interference. Therefore, input and/or output filters can be reduced or even eliminated, contributing to the increase of energy efficiency, [1,2].

© ICST Institute for Computer Sciences, Social Informatics and Telecommunications Engineering 2019
Published by Springer Nature Switzerland AG 2019. All Rights Reserved
J. L. Afonso et al. (Eds.): GreeNets 2018, LNICST 269, pp. 86–102, 2019.
https://doi.org/10.1007/978-3-030-12950-7_8

The multilevel converter architectures have some specific properties that should be emphasized: an increase in the number of controlled semiconductors, diodes and capacitors, the need for more elaborate semiconductor control and selection algorithms. In any of the architectures (conventional or multilevel), the harmonic content of the output voltage is reduced by increasing the switching frequency; however, either the specific technology of the semiconductors or the increase in switching losses limits that degree of freedom. The fundamental concept of the multilevel structure allowed the development of quite distinct topological alternatives with different expressions in the market, [1].

In this context, there are three main topologies of multilevel converters: with diode-clamped voltages, intermediate voltages defined by floating capacitors and single-phase bridges in series. In recent years, the MMC (modular multilevel converter) based on half-bridge or full-bridge has emerged, mainly with applications in the field of power conditioning in electric power grids and in medium and high power systems. In any configuration, single-phase and three-phase solutions are available in the market.

This work studies the configuration based on the series connection of full single-phase bridges and their single-phase topology. As mentioned above, the topology is modular and is applicable in medium and high power situations, being able to control very high voltages and able to define waveforms with very low total harmonic distortion (THD). This low value is possible since the total output voltage is obtained from the sum of many individual low-amplitude voltages with quasi-square waveform, i.e. switching at fundamental frequency thus maintaining very low switching losses, [2].

This paper is organized as follows: Sect. 2 describes and analyzes modulation methods, both high frequency (pulse width modulation) and fundamental frequency, for inverters in series. In the same section, two command methods are also analyzed at fundamental frequency with respect to the specific objectives and their ease of implementation in real-time, and one of them is selected for demonstration. The following Sect. 3 shows simulation results and characterizes the output voltage waveform (low frequency harmonics and total harmonic distortion). Section 4 presents experimental results for two inverters: with three single-phase inverters in series and with five inverters and discusses the main properties of the control method for a larger number of inverters. Finally, Sect. 5 discusses the main conclusions of the study.

## 2    Cascaded H-Bridge Inverters

A multilevel inverter with bridges in series consists of several inverters (H-bridges), as shown in Fig. 1 for the three-phase topology. Each elementary inverter is powered by an isolated source (or a capacitor) and can set three voltage levels $(-E, 0$ and $+E)$ in the output. Thus, in order to obtain a greater number of levels in the overall output, more than one inverter is required to be connected in series provided that their individual voltages are not instantaneously equal. Thus, the resulting voltage may be more similar to a sine wave.

If the voltage values of the different sources are equal and if $S$ is the number of bridges, the number of output voltage levels, $N_L$, is given by (1):

$$N_L = 2S + 1 \qquad (1)$$

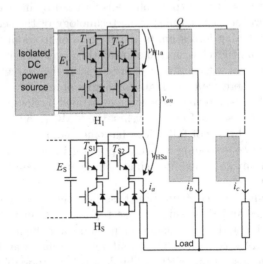

**Fig. 1.** Structure of a three-phase inverter based on series connection of single-phase full bridges.

If the inverters are fed by voltage sources of different value, a greater number of levels can be obtained in the global output, [1]. For two inverters, if the DC voltage values are, for example, $E_1 = E$ and $E_2 = 3E$, a 9-level waveform instead of 5 is obtained (when using the most common $E_1 = E_2 = E$). In principle, a high number of levels would produce a better waveform quality (i.e. a smaller THD) but, as will be demonstrated later, some important drawbacks occur in certain applications. Additionally, the semiconductors ($T_{1k}, T_{2k}, \ldots T_{Sk}$) are different and must be designed accordingly, therefore reducing the modularity of this converter.

The power structure of the inverter with cascaded bridges powered by regulated active power sources has several advantages and some specific aspects that must be considered within its application, [2]:

- Unlike other multilevel topologies, does not require balancing of DC voltages that feed the individual inverter
- Does not add diodes or capacitors to set the voltage levels
- Presents high modularity and is easily scalable in voltage and power.

The least favourable aspects identified in this topology are:

- It requires independent voltage sources for each bridge, which restricts the scope of its application
- Synchronous switching is required on bidirectional AC/DC/AC systems in order to avoid short circuits between isolated sources.

## 2.1   High-Frequency PWM

One of the main components of power losses in an inverter is the switching losses in the semiconductors which makes the switching frequency an important variable in the design; its impact should be considered and evaluated when it comes to defining the switching and modulation method.

For multilevel inverters, PWM-based switching methods are a generalization of the principle of operation for two-level inverters; multi-carrier PWM, [1,3]. For single-phase systems, PWM with level shift (LS-PWM) and PWM with phase shift (PS-PWM) can be used. However, the PS-PWM has a lower harmonic content, [3,4]. These methods have very good waveform quality (low THD of the voltage) and high bandwidth, which makes them preferable for low and medium power applications and high dynamic range. On the other hand, in high power applications, where switching losses are to be kept low, the fundamental frequency switching methods have specific advantages.

## 2.2   Low-Frequency Modulation Methods

Low-frequency modulation methods can be used in inverters with series bridges because of their specific configuration, [1]. In Fig. 2 the principle of operation of these methods is shown for an inverter with eleven levels (five bridges), where $\theta_k$ is the switching angle of the inverter $k$ and $E$ is the value of the DC voltage, common to all inverters.

The fundamental frequency modulation, or square wave modulation, is implemented to satisfy one of the possible objectives, [5–8]:

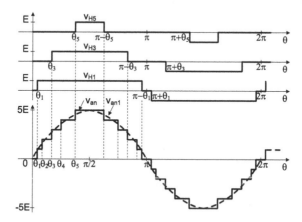

**Fig. 2.** Square-wave modulation: output voltage of three bridges and total output voltage when using five bridges.

- Minimizing the THD of the inverter output voltage
- Elimination of the main low-frequency harmonics of the output voltage, e.g. third, fifth, seventh, ...
- THD minimization of the output voltage of the inverter in three-phase systems (do not account for multiples of three)
- Elimination of the main low-frequency harmonics of the output voltage in three-phase systems, e.g. fifth, seventh, ....

As a first goal, in any method, one must have control of the magnitude of the fundamental component which is also done from the switching angles.

Analysing the output voltage, $v_{an}$, of a CHB inverter with $S$ bridges, as in Fig. 2, the Fourier coefficients, $C_h$, can be obtained as:

$$C_h = \frac{4E}{h\pi} \sum_{k=1}^{S} \cos\left(h\theta_k\right) \tag{2}$$

According to the Fourier coefficients and knowing that all harmonics are in phase with each other, the time evolution of the output voltage is given by

$$v_{an}(t) = \frac{4E}{\pi} \sum_{h=1}^{\infty} \{\frac{1}{h} \sum_{k=1}^{S} \cos\left(h\theta_k\right) \sin\left(h\omega t\right)\} \tag{3}$$

From (2), it can be easily obtained the expression for the peak amplitude of the fundamental component under controlled modulation index; it is given by (4):

$$V_{an1} = \frac{4E}{\pi} \sum_{k=1}^{S} \cos\left(\theta_k\right) \tag{4}$$

The expressions that relate the switching angles to a specific objective are obtained from the Fourier series. With five bridges, if it is desired to control the fundamental component and eliminate the first four odd harmonics, the following system of equations is obtained:

$$\begin{cases} \cos\left(\theta_1\right) + \cos\left(\theta_2\right) + \cos\left(\theta_3\right) + \cos\left(\theta_4\right) + \cos\left(\theta_5\right) = 5m_a \\ \cos\left(3\theta_1\right) + \cos\left(3\theta_2\right) + \cos\left(3\theta_3\right) + \cos\left(3\theta_4\right) + \cos\left(3\theta_5\right) = 0 \\ \cos\left(5\theta_1\right) + \cos\left(5\theta_2\right) + \cos\left(5\theta_3\right) + \cos\left(5\theta_4\right) + \cos\left(5\theta_5\right) = 0 \\ \cos\left(7\theta_1\right) + \cos\left(7\theta_2\right) + \cos\left(7\theta_3\right) + \cos\left(7\theta_4\right) + \cos\left(7\theta_5\right) = 0 \\ \cos\left(9\theta_1\right) + \cos\left(9\theta_2\right) + \cos\left(9\theta_3\right) + \cos\left(9\theta_4\right) + \cos\left(9\theta_5\right) = 0 \end{cases} \tag{5}$$

subjected to $0 < \theta_1 < \theta_2 < \theta_3 < \theta_4 < \theta_5 < \pi/2$.

For the fundamental component, the amplitude modulation index is defined as:

$$m_a = \frac{\pi}{4E} \frac{V_{an1}}{S} \tag{6}$$

The system of equations is non-linear and can be solved off-line or in real-time. In the first case, the system is solved and the results (switching angles) are stored in memory for use in controlling the various bridges. There are several numerical methods capable of solving the system of equations, [5,6]: Newton's method, method of the resulting polynomials, [4], among others. All of these iterative methods require large computation effort, both at runtime and in memory, which makes it difficult to implement them in real-time on digital platforms (e.g., microcontrollers or digital signal processors). On the other hand, as the number of levels increases (i.e. number of angles to be calculated), the nonlinearity of the system increases significantly, requiring much longer processing time. Thus, the angles are initially calculated for a wide range of modulation indices and stored in tables for later real-time use.

This procedure is extensible to DC sources of different value or variable in time in the various inverters, and the tables must contain all input voltage alternatives and the entire modulation index range. The size of the tables obviously depends on the resolution of the modulation index and the interpolation process defined to obtain the angles associated with intermediate modulation indices.

In the second case, real-time algorithms, several alternative methods are also available to obtain the switching angles: theory of balancing of the voltage-time area of the reference voltage in relation to the output voltage, [7]; by the analytical approximation of the THD expression of the output voltage, [8]. One of the characteristics common to all methods is that there is no control of the amplitude of harmonics not eliminated or not considered for minimization; its value depends on the point of operation and tends to be quite variable.

## 2.3   THD Minimization

In this work, the method that minimizes THD was selected for analysis and demonstration, [9]. In fact, the method minimizes $(THD)^2$; it is equivalent and simpler and exhibits faster procedures. The THD is given by:

$$THD = \frac{\sqrt{\sum_{h=2}^{\infty} V_h^2}}{V_1} \qquad (7)$$

It is difficult to achieve the minimization of THD directly because the numerator of (7) has an infinite number of terms. One solution is to eliminate only a finite number of harmonics. Generally, one eliminates a few low-order harmonics because they contribute more to THD, namely of the current. In a cascade multilevel inverter with $S$ H-bridges, only $(S - 1)$ low-order harmonics can be eliminated, which is done in selective harmonic elimination methods, [5].

In [8], through a deductive process, the minimization of $(THD)^2$ value for $S$ bridges is defined and an implicit expression is obtained for an auxiliary variable, $\rho$, on which all switching angles depend. The procedure, to run in real-time, uses the following two steps:

1. Determine $\rho$ by solving the equation:

$$0 = \sum_{k=1}^{S} \sqrt{1 - \left(\frac{k - 1/2}{S - 1/2}\rho\right)^2} - m_a S \tag{8}$$

2. Determine the switching angles by evaluating

$$\theta_k = \arcsin\left(\frac{k - 1/2}{S - 1/2}\rho\right), k = 1, 2, \ldots, S. \tag{9}$$

From the different possible alternatives it was used the method of Newton due to require a very low number of iterations to determine $\rho$ and a numerically efficient coding thus allowing the operation in real-time.

The factors that determine the speed of convergence of the method are: the initial angle, the evolution of the function (8) and its derivative around the solution. The limits where there is no solution for either $m_a$ or $S$ are easily determined from the analysis of (8): for $S = 3$, $m_a$ must be greater than 0.6; for $S = 5$, $m_a$ must be greater than 0.72. Restriction of the range of $m_a$ as $S$ increases may be a major drawback depending on the type of application.

## 3   Voltage Range and Distortion

Any inverter must be able to control both the fundamental component of the output voltage and its frequency. Frequency variation is an easy goal to meet; depends on the phase variation of an alternating quantity and is independent of the amplitude variation. Amplitude variation in both static and dynamic terms requires other procedures. According to the foregoing, the limits of the range of the fundamental component of the output voltage are a characteristic of the modulation method and the number of inverter bridges.

### 3.1   Switching Angles Dynamics

In this work, an inverter with different numbers of H-bridge was simulated. The first step was the validation of the real-time characteristics of the modulation method in the simulation environment using a fundamental frequency of 50 Hz and with $E = 50$ V for three and seven bridges and $E = 40$ V for five bridges. With three, five and seven H-bridges the control algorithm was tested in two conditions: slow and fast variation of the modulation index. For three bridges, $m_a$ varies between 0.67 and 0.98 in 40 ms (slow variation) and 2 ms (fast variation) as shown in Fig. 3. The same conditions were used to test the algorithm with five and seven bridges: amplitude variation from $m_a = 0.73$ to 0.98 in 40 ms (slow variation) and 2 ms (fast variation), and from $m_a = 0.98$ to 0.73 in 2 ms, as shown in Fig. 4, for five bridges, and from $m_a = 0.76$ to 0.98 in 40 ms and 2 ms, and from $m_a = 0.98$ to 0.73 in 2 ms, as shown in Fig. 5, for seven bridges.

The analysis of the three sets of results allows to conclude that the switching angles are updated almost instantaneously after four cycles of the iterative process. The maximum number of iterations depends on the utilized software/hardware platform and is discussed in the implementation and results section.

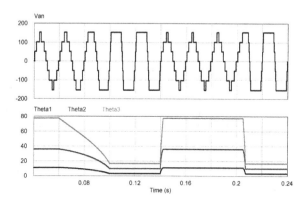

**Fig. 3.** Output voltage and switching angles for slow and fast changes of the modulation index with three H-bridges. ($V_{an}$: 100 V/div; $Theta_i$: 20 degrees/div).

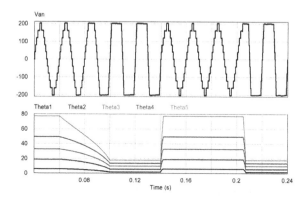

**Fig. 4.** Output voltage and switching angles for slow and fast changes of the modulation index with five H-bridges. ($V_{an}$: 100 V/div; $Theta_i$: 20 degrees/div).

A detail of Fig. 4, dynamic variation of the modulation index for five H-bridges, with $m_a$ increasing from 0.73 to 0.98 in 100 ms, is presented in Fig. 6.

The modulation method does not eliminate specific harmonics, but minimizes the voltage THD. Thus, it is important to verify the evolution of low-frequency harmonics, which contribute the most to distorting the output current in loads with inductive characteristics.

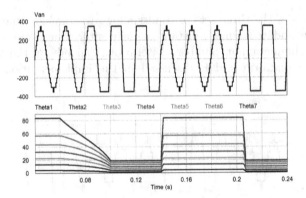

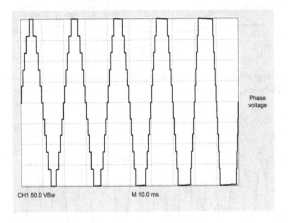

**Fig. 5.** Output voltage and switching angles for slow and fast changes of the modulation index with seven H-bridges. ($V_{an}$: 200 V/div; $Theta_i$: 20 degrees/div).

**Fig. 6.** Increasing modulation index with five bridges (50 V/div; 10 ms/div).

In this subsection it is focused only the five bridge inverter; the other configurations have the same qualitative behaviour and the differences will be discussed later.

Figure 7 shows the evolution of the amplitude of all odd harmonics multiples of 3 up to the 15th, in function of the modulation index; these harmonics are cancelled in a three-phase system. Figure 8 is similar to Fig. 7 but represents only harmonics non-multiples of 3 up to the 19th.

The output voltage THD, with and without harmonics multiples of three, is shown in Fig. 9 and clearly demonstrates the influence of the low-frequency harmonics, mainly the third, fifth and seventh.

The steady-state single-phase voltage is demonstrated in the next figures. For three bridges, it is shown in Fig. 10, for $E = 50$ V, $m_a = 0.75$ and $f = 50$ Hz; also presented is the voltage spectrum, showing the residual low-frequency components characterizing the method; THD is $\approx 15\%$. The topology considering

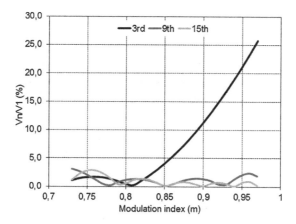

**Fig. 7.** Odd harmonics multiples of three for five H-bridges.

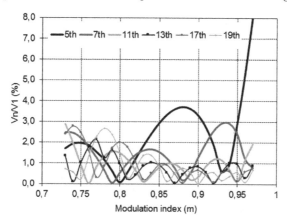

**Fig. 8.** Odd harmonics non-multiples of three for five H-bridges.

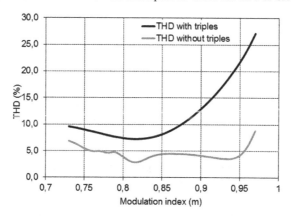

**Fig. 9.** THD of the output voltage for five H-bridges, with and without the triple harmonics.

five bridges was also simulated and the steady-state single-phase voltage is shown in Fig. 11, now with $E = 40$ V, $m_a = 0.8$ and $f = 50$ Hz. THD is $\approx 7.5\%$, much smaller than the one with three bridges. Finally, the seven bridges inverter is shown in Fig. 12, now with $E = 50$ V, $m_a = 0.83$ and $f = 50$ Hz; the THD is $\approx 6\%$, the smallest one. More comparative results, for the whole range of modulation index, will be shown later, in Figs. 19 and 20.

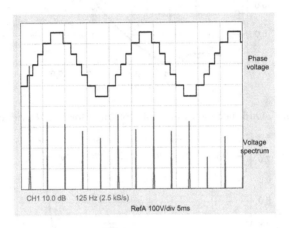

**Fig. 10.** Inverter output voltage with three H-bridges (100 V/div; 5 ms/div) and harmonic spectrum (10 dB/div; 125 Hz/div).

The method works well for a restricted range of modulation index values, not converging for other (smaller) values of $m_a$. On the other hand, in the upper range of modulation index values (e.g. greater than 0.87 for THD <10%, see Fig. 9) the THD value is quite high which may make it not feasible to use. It is therefore necessary to evaluate the range of operation of the inverter in terms of the amplitude of the fundamental component knowing that it decreases as the number of bridges constituting it increases.

## 4   Implementation and Results

A FGPA board, which incorporates a soft processor and peripheral analogue and digital I/O, was used to implement the complete process of calculating the switching angles for the inverters and transferring them to dedicated timers. The prototype of the developed CHB inverter has five bridges, each powered by an isolated DC voltage source of 40 V (experiments with three bridges were done using a DC voltage level of 50 V). The presented experimental results are focused on the characterization of the modulation method for a different number of levels. The features to be analysed are, as mentioned above, low order harmonics, THD and real-time dynamics.

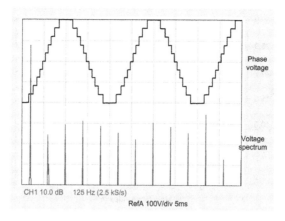

**Fig. 11.** Inverter output voltage with five H-bridges(100 V/div; 5 ms/div) and harmonic spectrum (10 dB/div; 125 Hz/div).

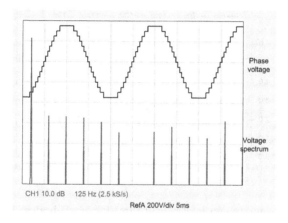

**Fig. 12.** Inverter output voltage with seven H-bridges (200 V/div; 5 ms/div) and harmonic spectrum (10 dB/div; 125 Hz/div).

## 4.1   Low-Frequency Harmonics and THD

The amplitude of the low-frequency harmonics, which is variable as a function of the modulation index, is shown in Figs. 13 and 14. The comparison with Figs. 7 and 8 (in the simulation environment) demonstrates the correct implementation of the command method.

The total harmonic distortion, shown in Fig. 15, has an absolute minimum value for small modulation indices and, as already obtained in simulation, increases rapidly for high modulation indices. The result has a good agreement with that obtained by simulation in Fig. 9.

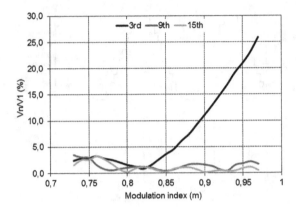

**Fig. 13.** Odd harmonics multiples of three for five H-bridges (experimental).

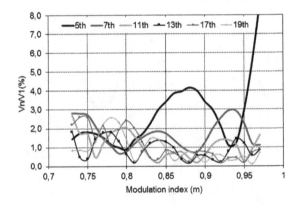

**Fig. 14.** Odd harmonics non-multiples of three for five H-bridges (experimental).

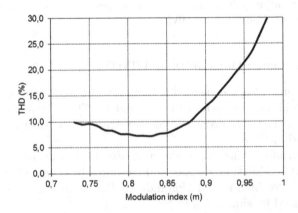

**Fig. 15.** THD of the output voltage for five H-bridges (experimental).

## 4.2 Voltage Dynamics

As an illustration of the variation of the modulation index, Fig. 16 shows the evolution of the output voltage when $m_a$ changes from 0.73 to 0.98 in 100 ms.

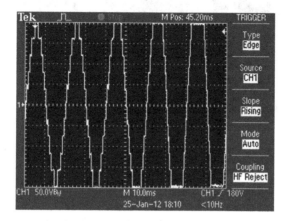

**Fig. 16.** Experimental dynamic variation of the modulation index.

The steady-state output voltage of the three-bridge inverter is shown in Fig. 17, using the same conditions as in Fig. ($V_{dc}$, $m_a$ and $f$) and one can verify a high degree of similarity between the experimental and simulated results.

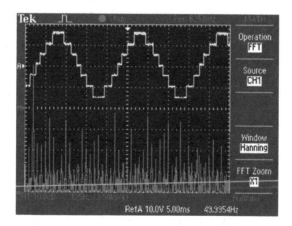

**Fig. 17.** Experimental output voltage and harmonic spectrum for three bridges.

In Fig. 18, for five bridges, is shown the steady-state AC voltage using $E = 40$ V, $m_a = 0.8$, with $f = 50$ Hz. It is also presented the harmonic spectrum of the voltage.

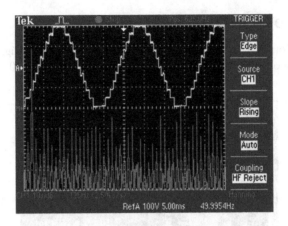

**Fig. 18.** Experimental output voltage and harmonic spectrum for five bridges.

As expected from the simulations, the spectrum is a widespread one, showing low-frequency components. The results in Figs. 17 and 18 compare with the ones in Figs. 10 and 11, respectively, and they are quite similar.

### 4.3  Discussion

For a global characterization, the method was simulated with three, five and seven bridges and was experimentally validated with three and five bridges. With respect to the fundamental component, the range of variation of $m_a$ is reduced with the increase of the number of bridges. It is also found that the limits of the range of modulation indices in which a relatively small THD occurs are reduced as the number of bridges increases.

In any configuration, the THD is high for high modulation indices. In this region, however, the voltage waveform is close to a square wave which is not desirable in any application. These conclusions are documented in Figs. 19 and 20. Generally, there is a contradiction with the high number of degrees of freedom in the inverter control (the switching angles).

There are other methods also with real-time capability that do not minimize THD, as the one developed in [10].

When compared to the expected dynamics at the output of a current controller, the analysed method provides sufficiently rapid changes in amplitude and phase although within a relatively small range. It thus enables effective control of a power converter provided that the variations occur in the vicinity of a given reference to the voltage output. Two classes of applications can therefore be distinguished: those relating to drives, where the frequency variation implies a wide variation of modulation indices, and those relating to applications where the converter is connected to the electric network, where the method operates with good characteristics.

The concept that supports the method is applicable to any number of bridges but the available range of variation of the fundamental component is decreasing.

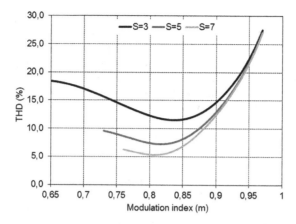

**Fig. 19.** THD of the output voltage for three, five and seven H-bridges (simulation).

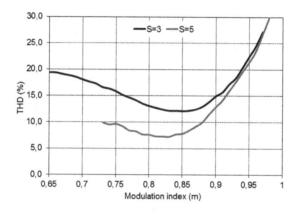

**Fig. 20.** THD of the output voltage for 3 and five H-bridges (experimental).

The question arises as to what is the number of bridges of an inverter from which it is no longer possible to apply it in converters connected to the electric grid.

## 5    Conclusion

The method described and implemented to determine the switching angles of each individual H-bridge requires a reduced number of iterations. Therefore, it can be easily implemented in a real-time control board, such as uP/DSP/FPGA. The experimental analysis of the characteristics of the method allows to conclude that it is compatible with the interface of power electronic converters with the electric network. The method can be applied to a larger number of H-bridges (7, 9, ... ) with similar characteristics.

**Acknowledgments.** This work was financially supported by: Project POCI-01-0145-FEDER-006933/SYSTEC - Research Center for Systems and Technologies funded by FEDER funds through COMPETE 2020 and by national funds through the FCT/MEC, and co-funded by FEDER, in the scope of the PT2020 Partnership Agreement. Abel A. Ferreira gratefully acknowledges the financial support from the People Programme (Marie Curie Actions) of the European Union's Seventh Framework Programme FP7/2007-2013/ (Grant Agreement no. 317221), project title MEDOW.

# References

1. Rodriguez, J., et al.: Multilevel converters: an enabling technology for high-power applications. Proc. IEEE **97**(11), 1786–1817 (2009)
2. Malinowski, M., Gopakumar, K., Rodriguez, J., Pérez, M.A.: A survey on cascaded multilevel inverters. IEEE Trans. Ind. Electron. **57**(7), 2197–2206 (2010)
3. Holmes, D.G., Lipo, T.: Pulse Width Modulation for Power Converters. Wiley/IEEE Press, New York (2003)
4. Chiasson, J.N., Tolbert, L.M., McKenzie, K.J., Du, Z.: A unified approach to solving the harmonic elimination equations in multilevel converters. IEEE Trans. Power Electron. **19**(2), 478–490 (2004)
5. Dahidah, M.S., Konstantinou, G., Agelidis, V.G.: A review of multilevel selective harmonic elimination PWM: formulations, solving algorithms, implementation and applications. IEEE Trans. Ind. Electron. **30**(8), 4091–4116 (2015)
6. Hong, D., Bai, S., Lukic, S.M.: Closed-form expressions for minimizing total harmonic distortion in three-phase multilevel converters. IEEE Trans. Power Electron. **29**(10), 5229–5241 (2014)
7. Rathore, A.K., Holtz, J., Boller, T.: Generalized optimal pulsewidth modulation of multilevel inverters for low-switching-frequency control of medium-voltage high-power industrial AC drives. IEEE Trans. Ind. Electron. **60**(10), 4215–4224 (2013)
8. Liu, Y., Hong, H., Huang, A.Q.: Real-time calculation of switching angles minimizing THD for multilevel inverters with step modulation. IEEE Trans. Ind. Electron. **56**(2), 285–293 (2009)
9. Faria, J., Martins, A.: Analysis and characterization of a square-wave modulation method for single-phase cascaded H-bridge multilevel inverters. In: Proceedings of the International Conference on Renewable Energies and Power Quality (ICREPQ 2012), 28–30 March 2012, Santiago de Compostela, Spain (2012)
10. Kang, D.-W., Kim, H.-V., Kim, T.-J., Hyun, D.-S.: A simple method for acquiring the conducting angle in a multilevel cascaded inverter using step pulse waves. IEE Proc.-Electr. Power Appl. **152**(1), 103–111 (2005)

# A Selective Harmonic Compensation with Current Limiting Algorithm

Nayara V. Oliveira$^{(\boxtimes)}$ , Cleiton M. Freitas , and Luis F. C. Monteiro

Rio de Janeiro State University, Campus Maracanã,
Rio de Janeiro, RJ 25550-000, Brazil
nayvillela@gmail.com, {cleiton.freitas,lmonteiro}@uerj.br

**Abstract.** This paper addresses a control algorithm to determine the reference currents indirectly from the grid voltages, taking into account the limited capacity of the power converter for compensating, entirely, the selected harmonic current. In previous works, the reference current was indirectly determined based on an average component correlated with the selected harmonic current. Thus, when the selected harmonic current was entirely compensated, that average value was decreased to zero. Now, this paper introduces a novel control algorithm considering the limited capacity of the power converter for producing the selected harmonic current. In this novel condition, the phase-angle of the reference current is dynamically modified while the minimum point of the cost function is not reached. The remaining parameters of the reference currents correspond to the harmonic frequency and amplitude as well. The harmonic frequency was identified through a PLL (Phase-Locked-Loop) circuit whereas the amplitude corresponds to a specific value of $10A$ to all of the developed test cases. Other aspects of the simulated power circuit, control algorithms, including the optimization methods, are described throughout the paper. Simulation results involving different test cases were implemented to verify the performance of the proposed algorithm compensating of the fifth-harmonic component under transient -and steady-state conditions.

**Keywords:** Active filtering · Real-time control algorithms · Optimization methods · Distribution power-grids

## 1 Introduction

Due to the proliferation of nonlinear loads, power quality has been compromised in distribution power grids [1,2]. Indeed, current harmonics cause undesirable effects as, for instance, over heating of cables and transformers, over current in neutral wires and electromagnetic interference (EMI) problems. As alternative to

"This study was financed in part by the Coordenação de Aperfeiçoamento de Pessoal de Nível Superior - Brasil (CAPES) - Finance Code 001".

© ICST Institute for Computer Sciences, Social Informatics and Telecommunications Engineering 2019
Published by Springer Nature Switzerland AG 2019. All Rights Reserved
J. L. Afonso et al. (Eds.): GreeNets 2018, LNICST 269, pp. 103–118, 2019.
https://doi.org/10.1007/978-3-030-12950-7_9

suppress current harmonics are the use of passive power filters, which has been a preferred solution by consumers once it is considered a low-cost solution in comparison to the existing ones. However, passive filters present several problems as, for example, the resonance phenomena, which leads to over current or over voltage on the grid. An enhanced solution corresponds to the active power filters as mentioned by [3]. Active filters are capable to compensate current harmonics generated by different types of nonlinear loads and power factor as well, with fast transient response.

Active power filters have been researched for decades and, even now, they are of great interest due to the their controlled harmonic mitigation [4–10]. In a general approach, the load currents are measured and their harmonic components are identified to compensated by the power converter [11]. In this context, the power converter behaves as a very-low impedance path to the harmonic currents produced by nonlinear loads, such that, considering an ideal situation, only the fundamental component flows throughout the grid.

Different current control strategies for active power filters have been reported in the literature, such as adaptive fuzzy control [12], linear feedback control [13] and adaptive observer [14]. As shown by [12], the load -and filter-currents are used as reference for the adaptive fuzzy control to generate the total compensation currents for a nonlinear load. Moreover, in [13] was proposed a linear feedback control based on an iterative learning control algorithm based on adaptive proportional–integral controller (PI) with load reference current and source of the algorithm. In [14] the proposed control was based on an adaptive observer without considering the voltage information at the Point of Common Coupling (PCC). Other possibility was to conceive the control algorithms based on the grid currents instead of the load currents, such that the grid currents are forced to track this fundamental positive-sequence component, with the load current harmonics provided by the active filter in an indirect way [15]. The main advantages of this approach are that only one low-bandwidth current sensor is required, and a faster transient response is achieved [11].

Nevertheless, one may see that all of these aforementioned solutions are based on the load -or grid-currents to determine the reference ones. Furthermore, in radial grids with widespread loads it is not feasible spreading large amount of current transducers so as to detect the variety of loads up and downstream from the active power filters. An alternative consists on swapping the measured-current compensation approach for one in which the compensation currents are computed from the harmonic voltage-drops caused by the harmonic currents flowing through the grid impedance, as proposed by [16–18]. In this approach, a specific harmonic component or even a symmetrical component of the harmonic current is compensated taking into consideration the corresponding harmonic voltage-drop, which is measured at the PCC voltage. Basically, it was calculated a cost function based on the harmonic voltage drop and the reference current was dynamically modified (phase-angle and magnitude) while the average component of this cost function was not decreased to zero. In this condition (average component of the cost function equal to zero) it was assured fully compensation of the selected harmonic current. However, to meet this condition, the active filter is forced to produce the selected harmonic current drawn by all of the non linear loads, which may become unfeasible once the limited capacity of the power converter was not taken into account. Thus, as a contribution of this paper, this issue was considered which leaded to a novel control algorithm. Other aspects of the proposed control algorithm are exploited and explained throughout this paper.

The article is organized into four sections. In Sect. 2 there is a general description of the simulated circuit. Sections 3 and 4 exploits the control algorithms and the simulation results, respectively. Finally, conclusions obtained through this work are described in Sect. 5.

## 2   General Circuit Description

In Fig. 1 a simplified electrical scheme of the simulated circuit is shown. It corresponds to a three phase radial grid, 220 V (line-line voltage) and 60 Hz, with the source voltage and the grid impedance labelled as $v_s$, and $Z_s$, respectively. In this work $Z_s$ was considered inductive and constant. Nevertheless, currently there is a new concept of the grid impedance being variable, and this issue will be taken into account in our future works. This grid supplies a linear load, $R_c$, and a set of unbalanced harmonic loads. Yet, a shunt active power filter is connected to the point of common coupling through a damped LCL circuit. For sake of simplicity the dc-link voltage, $v_{dc}$, was considered constant and equal to 1200 V, however, a voltage source was used as it was not the purpose of this paper to carry out the control of the dc-link voltage. Thus, a high voltage source was used for the study in question. Furthermore, as illustrated in Fig. 1 and summarized in Table 1, $L_1$ and $L_2$ are coupling inductors and $Z_c$ is the RC branch, composed by a capacitor $C_1$ and resistor $R_1$, to provide low-impedance path to switching-frequency components.

## 3   Control Algorithms

The simplified block diagrams as it is presented in Fig. 2 depicts the implemented algorithms to determine the reference currents and the produced voltages as well. It is composed by a synchronizing circuit Phase-Locked-Loop (PLL) to extract a control signal $(\omega t)$ synchronized with the fundamental positive-sequence component of the grid voltages $v_{ga}, v_{gb}$ and $v_{gc}$. Based on the PLL output signal, $5\omega t$, together with the grid voltages, the direct -and quadrature-components of the fifth-harmonic (negative-sequence) grid voltages ($vd_{5h}$ and $vq_{5h}$) are calculated through Park Transformation. In sequence, $vd_{5h}$ and $vq_{5h}$ are filtered through a $1^{st}$ order low-pass filter with cut-off frequency of 30 Hz. It is necessary once the grid voltages, in our case study, are comprehended by the fundamental -and fifth-harmonic components. Thus, $vd_{5h}$ and $vq_{5h}$ are composed by an average component plus oscillating components at $4\omega t$ and $6\omega t$.

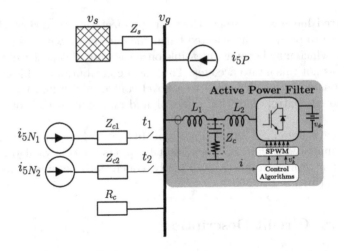

**Fig. 1.** Simplified electrical diagram of the simulated circuit.

**Table 1.** Summarized parameters of the simulated circuit - Fig. 1.

| Item | Symbol | Value |
|---|---|---|
| Grid impedance | $Z_S$ | $130\,\mu H$ |
| Converter-side filter inductor | $L_2$ | $250\,\mu H$ |
| Grid-side filter inductor | $L_1$ | $300\,\mu H$ |
| RC branch impedance | $Z_C$ | $R_1 = 5\,\Omega$ & $C_1 = 10\,\mu F$ |
| Harmonic load 1 | $Z_{c1}$ | $R_{c1} = 0.6\,\Omega$ & $L_{c1} = 3.7\,mH$ |
| Harmonic load 2 | $Z_{c2}$ | $R_{c2} = 1.4\,\Omega$ & $L_{c2} = 8.9\,mH$ |
| Three-phase load resistance | $R_c$ | $5\,\Omega$ |
| Harmonic current source 1 | $I5_P$ | $5\,A$ |
| Harmonic current source 2 | $I5_{N1}$ | $15\,A$ |
| Harmonic current source 3 | $I5_{N2}$ | $5\,A$ |

In sequence, the compensation algorithm determines the reference currents, $ia_{5h}^*, ib_{5h}^*, ic_{5h}^*$. Finally, there is a controller to ensure that the power-converter currents $(i_{fa}, i_{fb}, i_{fc})$ correspond to the reference ones, with $C_i(S)$ corresponding to a proportional gain and $v_a^*, v_b^*, v_c^*$ modulated through pulse width modulation (PWM) switching technique.

## 3.1 Proposed Compensation Algorithm

The proposed compensation algorithm can be divided into 2 stages, comprehended by the cost-function -and optimization-algorithms. The output of the cost-function corresponds to the control signal $|V_g|$ and it is determined as follows:

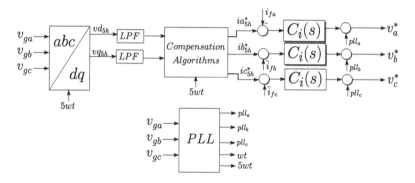

**Fig. 2.** Simplified block diagrams of the implemented algorithms.

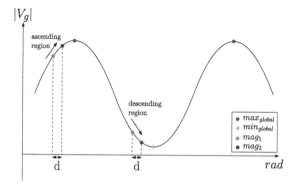

**Fig. 3.** Cost function for a cycle period of the phase angle $\delta$.

$$|V_g| = \sqrt{Vd_{5h}^2 + Vq_{5h}^2} \tag{1}$$

The control signals $Vd_{5h}$ and $Vq_{5h}$ are the average components of $vd_{5h}$ and $vq_{5h}$, respectively. As an example, $|V_g|$ is decreased to zero if fully compensation of the selected harmonic current was considered. Nevertheless, considering the limited capacity of the power converter to provide fully compensation, optimization algorithms were used to identify the phase-angle of the selected harmonic component that leads $|V_g|$ to its minimum value, being constant the magnitude of the reference currents. Figure 3 illustrates the cost function for a cycle period of $\delta$, being $\delta$ the phase angle of the reference currents. In this case, the angular frequency ($\omega t$) was previously determined by the PLL circuit whereas the magnitude was considered constant and equal to 10 A. Moreover, it was considered that the resultant amplitude of the fifth-harmonic components drawn by the non linear loads were always higher than 10 A. Taken into account these conditions, the optimization method was implemented.

According to the cost function illustrated in Fig. 3 one may note 2 critical points, corresponding to the maximum -and minimum-values of $|V_g|$. Our objective is to identify the phase-angle that leads $|V_g|$ to its minimum value. Thus,

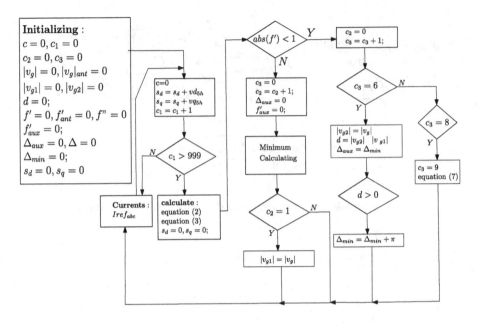

**Fig. 4.** Flow chart of the proposed algorithm.

to solve this problem an optimization method must consider the gradient signal of the cost function. Indeed, a positive gradient signal, or ascending region indicated in Fig. 3, indicates the cost function at its maximum. In sequence, further details of the implemented optimization method are explained with the help of a flowchart illustrated in Fig. 4.

The flow chart can be divided into three steps: initially, $|V_g|$ and its corresponding derivative signal $(f')$ were calculated as follows:

$$|V_g| = \sqrt[2]{(\frac{S_d}{1000})^2 + (\frac{S_q}{1000})^2};$$ (2)

$$S_d = \sum_{n=1}^{1000} Vd_{5h\_n};$$ (3)

$$S_q = \sum_{n=1}^{1000} Vq_{5h\_n};$$ (4)

$$f' = |V_g| - |V_{g\_ant}|$$ (5)

It is important to comment that 1000 samples correspond to a 1.5 cycle period of the fundamental frequency $(\omega t)$, or 9 cycle periods of 6 $\omega t$, which remains as the oscillating component in the control signals $vd_{5h}$ and $vq_{5h}$. In sequence the identification of the minimum region of the cost function was performed. It was done combining a minimization method with the corresponding gradient signal of the cost function. It was implemented 2 minimization methods (Newton-Raphson and secant) to evaluate the performance of the proposed algorithm. The gradient signal was determined based on the difference between 2 samples of $|V_g|$, one acquired at steady state condition and the other one corresponds to the first sample acquired. The steady state condition was assumed when the derivative signal remains inside a bandwidth region for a minimal time period, which corresponds to 9 cycle periods of the fundamental frequency. In this condition is assured that the cost function is at its minimum with the reference currents given by:

$$\begin{cases} ia_{5h}^* = 10sin(5wt + \Delta_{min}) \\ ib_{5h}^* = 10sin(5wt + 2\pi/3 + \Delta_{min}) \\ ic_{5h}^* = 10sin(5wt - 2\pi/3 + \Delta_{min}) \end{cases} \tag{6}$$

One may note that the steady state condition is remained while the derivative signal of the cost function is inside of the bandwidth region. Furthermore, it is important to comment that this method is able to identify the global minimum point or global maximum point, which could be applied to tracker of the Maximum Power Point (MPPT) algorithms for instance [19].

**Implementation of the Minimization Methods.** Essentially, the Newton-Raphson method is based on the simple idea of linear approximation, as described through Eqs. 7 and 8.

As explained in the previous sections, once determined a critical point of the cost function, is also possible to identify if the critical point corresponds to the maximum or minimum value of the cost function. Indeed, once the cost function is similar to the sine or cosine functions, if $f''(x_n) > 0$ then $f(x_n)$ is a local (or global) minimum. On the other hand, if $f''(x_n) < 0$ then $f(x_n)$ is a local maximum. This method is repeated while the absolute value of the cost function $(f'(x_n))$ remains higher than the stop criteria value.

$$f''(x_n) = f'(x_n) - f'(x_{n-1}) \tag{7}$$

$$x_{n+1} \approx x_n - \frac{f'(x_n)}{f''(x_n)} \tag{8}$$

The Secant Method starts with two estimates of the root, $x_0$ and $x_1$, and can be interpreted as a method in which the derivative is replaced by an approximation and is thus a quasi-Newton method. For $n \geq 1$, the iterative function is described in the Eq. 9 as follows.

For n $= 1, 2, \cdots$, until the stopping criteria is achieved,

1. Compute $f(x_n)$ and $f(x_{n-1})$
2. Compute the next approximation: $x_{k+1}$

3. Test for convergence or maximum number of iterations: If $|x_{k+1}x_k| <$ *tolerance* or if $k > N$

$$x_n = x_{n-1} - f(x_{n-1})\frac{x_{n-1} - x_{n-2}}{f(x_{n-1}) - f(x_{n-2})}$$
$$x_n = \frac{x_{n-2}f(x_{n-1}) - x_{n-1}f(x_{n-2})}{f(x_{n-1}) - f(x_{n-2})} \tag{9}$$

If we compare secant method with the Newton-Raphson, one may note that Newton-Raphson converges faster than secant method. However, secant method only requires the evaluation of $f$, while the Newton's method requires the evaluation of both $f$ and its derivative $f'$ at every step. Therefore, the secant method may occasionally be faster in practice (Fig. 5).

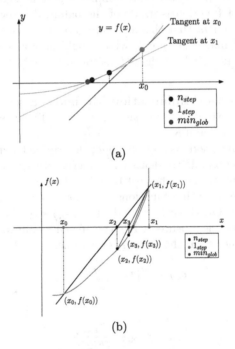

(a)

(b)

**Fig. 5.** (a) Geometric interpretation of the Newton-Raphson iteration, (b) Geometric interpretation of the Secant iteration.

## 4    Simulation Results

To verify the effectiveness of the controller with the proposed algorithm, test cases of the described circuit in Sect. 2 were carried out with PSIM simulator.

Basically, 2 test cases were performed considering the active filter performance with the control algorithms determining, dynamically, the reference currents. At each test case the reference currents were determined by a different minimization method, where the first one corresponds to Newton-Raphson, while the second corresponds to the Secant method.

In both test cases, the simulation starts with the active power filter (APF) turned-off, and all of the control algorithms disabled. At $t_1 = 0.5$ s and $t_2 = 2.0$ s, the first -and the second-loads were turned-on as follows. It is important to comment that the drawn currents by these loads are identified in Fig. 1 as $i_{5N1}$ and $i_{5N2}$, respectively. Moreover, $i_{5P}$ was not compensated once the control algorithm was configured to compensate only the negative-sequence fifth-harmonic currents. The active filter was turned-on at $t = 1.0$ s, and the algorithms of the reference currents were enabled.

Transient response of the control algorithm based on Newton-Raphson -and Secant-methods are shown from Figs. 6, 7, 8, 9, 10, 11, 12 and 13. Initially, the derivative waveform of the cost function with Newton-Raphson -and Sectant-methods are depicted at Fig. 6(a) and (b), respectively. One may note a smooth behavior at Fig. 6(a) with a faster convergence, indicating a better performance of the algorithm based on the Newton-Raphson method. Nevertheless, with both methods, the gradient of the cost function decreased to zero, indicating, initially, that a critical point was reached.

In sequence, the cost function waveform with the control algorithm based on the Newton-Raphson -and Secant-methods are shown in Fig. 7(a) and (b), respectively. Based on these results, the cost function was decreased to its minimum, with Fig. 7(a) presenting a smooth behavior and a faster convergence. Furthermore, one may note that, initially, the harmonic currents were entirely compensated once cost function was decreased close to zero. In sequence, when the second load was turned-on, it was no longer possible to provide fully compensation of the harmonic currents due to the limited capacity of the power converter. This condition leads to note a correct performance of the proposed algorithm. Next, the average components of direct -and quadrature-voltages with the control algorithm based on Newton-Raphson -and Secant-methods are illustrated in Fig. 8(a) and (b), respectively.

Figure 9 presents the grid current, $ia_{source}$, and the active filter current, $ia_{filter}$, during the entire simulation. Based on the previous results, both algorithms were capable to minimize the distorted load-currents and, as expected, one can see a decrement of $ia_{source}$ when both algorithms reached their steady-state condition. At $t = 2.0$ s, when the second harmonic turned-on, it was no possible to provide full compensation due to the limited capacity of the power converter and, therefore, $ia_{source}$ has increased. Moreover, as observed at the previous results, the algorithm based on the Newton-Rahpson method (Fig. 9(a)) presented a faster transient convergence reaching a steady-state condition at, approximately, $t = 1.4$ s whereas, with the Secant method (Fig. 9(b)) the steady-state condition was reached at $t = 1.5$ s. In the second transient, both methods presented a similar performance.

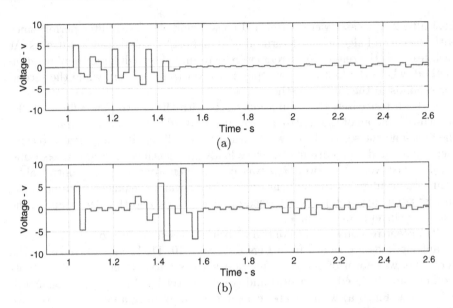

**Fig. 6.** Derivative waveform of the cost function with (a) Newton-Raphson method and (b) Secant method.

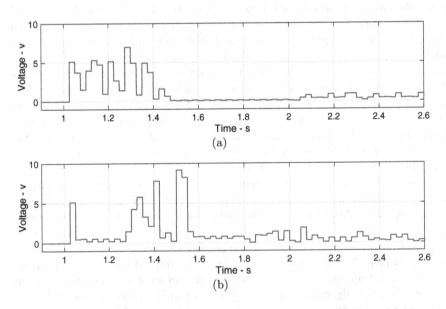

**Fig. 7.** Cost function waveform with minimization algorithms based on (a) Newton-Raphson method and (b) Secant method.

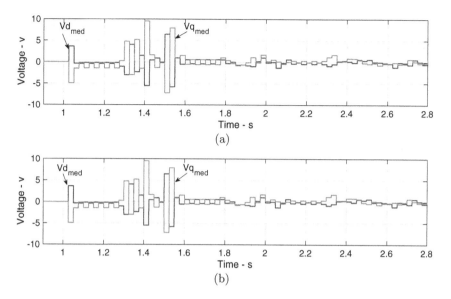

**Fig. 8.** Average components of the direct -and quadrature-voltages with (a) Newton-Raphson method and (b) Secant method.

Figure 10 illustrates the grid current, $ia_{source}$, active-filter current, $ia_{filter}$, and load current, $ia_{load}$, during the transient when the active filter was turned-on with Newton-Raphson method (Fig. 9(a)) and Secant method (Fig. 9(b)). In this transient $ia_{filter}$ was in phase with $ia_{load}$ and, as a consequence, $ia_{source}$ has increased. It is important to comment that $ia_{load}$ refers to the equivalent fifth-harmonic current drawn by the nonlinear loads.

Figure 11 illustrates the grid current, $ia_{source}$, active-filter current, $ia_{filter}$, and load current, $ia_{load}$, during the first steady-state condition with Newton-Raphson method (Fig. 11(a)) and Secant method (Fig. 11(b)). As expected, in this condition $ia_{filter}$ was in counter-phase with $ia_{load}$ and, as a consequence, $ia_{source}$ has decreased. Furthermore, once the amplitudes of $ia_{load}$ and $ia_{filter}$ are similar, the active filter was capable to compensate, practically, the entire harmonic content.

Figure 12 illustrates the grid current, $ia_{source}$, active-filter current, $ia_{filter}$, and load current, $ia_{load}$, during the transient when the second nonlinear load was turned-on. With both algorithms the active filter presented similar performance once the equivalent phase-angle of the nonlinear loads was not modified, as shown in Fig. 12(a) and (b). Nevertheless, even at this transient both algorithms were enabled once the cost-function gradient was no longer within the bandwidth region.

Finally, Fig. 13 illustrates the grid current, $ia_{source}$, active-filter current, $ia_{filter}$, and load current, $ia_{load}$, during the second steady-state condition with Newton-Raphson method (Fig. 13(a)) and Secant method (Fig. 13(b)). Again, as expected, in this condition $ia_{filter}$ was in counter-phase with $ia_{load}$, however,

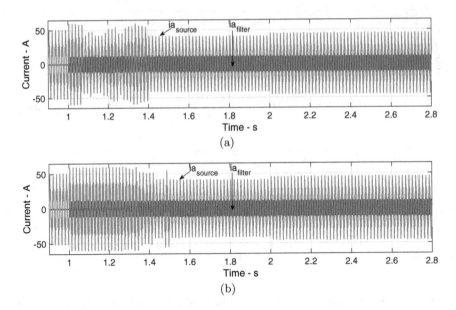

**Fig. 9.** Grid current, $ia_{source}$, and active-filter current, $ia_{filter}$, during the entire simulation with (a) Newton-Raphson method (b) Secant method.

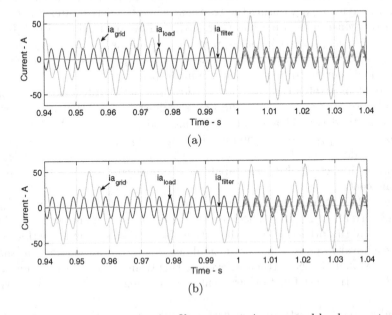

**Fig. 10.** Grid current, $ia_{source}$, active-filter current, $ia_{filter}$, and load current, $ia_{load}$, during the transient when the active filter was turned-on with (a) Newton-Raphson method (b) Secant method.

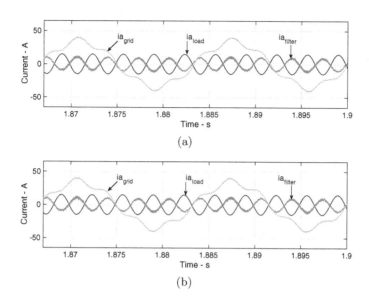

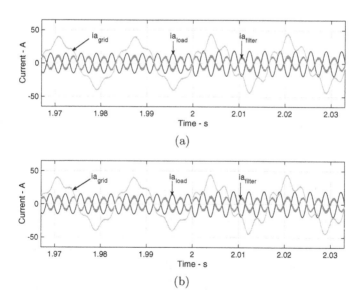

**Fig. 11.** Grid current, $ia_{source}$, active-filter current, $ia_{filter}$, and load current, $ia_{load}$, in the first steady-state condition with (a) Newton-Raphson method (b) Secant method.

**Fig. 12.** Grid current, $ia_{source}$, and active-filter current, $ia_{filter}$, and load current, $ia_{load}$, at the transient when the second nonlinear load was turned-on with (a) Newton-Raphson method (b) Secant method.

due to the limited capacity of the power converter for compensating the entire harmonic current, $ia_{source}$ has increased. Nevertheless, this result reinforces the correct operation of the proposed algorithm for providing the best harmonic filtering within its limitations.

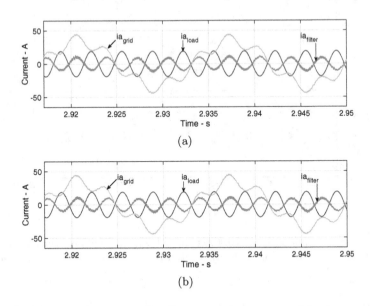

(a)

(b)

**Fig. 13.** Grid current, $ia_{source}$, active-filter current, $ia_{filter}$, and load current, $ia_{load}$, in the second steady-state condition with (a) Newton-Raphson method (b) Secant method.

## 5    Conclusions

It is important to note that there are other techniques that can identify the global minimum point and correctly trace the harmonic current, such as those presented by [12–14, 16, 18].

Based on the results of the simulation, the ability of the proposed algorithm to identify the global minimum point after a disturbance occurred and to maintain it at steady-state was verified, even after new disturbances. Thus, it is capable of correctly tracking the frequency and phase-angle of the selected harmonic current. Nevertheless, it is important to point out that we assumed that the produced current by the active filter was always lower than the selected harmonic currents and this condition is not necessarily true.

To the future works, other global optimization algorithms will be explored and compared with the algorithm introduced in this work, considering other test cases such as use of variable network impedance, harmonic current tracking when the harmonic current source is disconnected of the power grid. These questions will be explored in the future work, as well as the evaluation of the algorithm proposed through experimental results.

# References

1. Wu, C.H., et al.: Investigation and mitigation of harmonic amplification problems caused by single-tuned filters. IEEE Trans. Power Deliv. **13**(3), 800–806 (1998)
2. Dao, T., Phung, B.T.: Effects of voltage harmonic on losses and temperature rise in distribution transformers. IEE Proc. - IET Gener. Transm. Distrib. **12**(2), 347–354 (2017)
3. Nishida, K., Rukonuzzman, M., Nakaoka, M.: Advanced current control implementation with robust deadbeat algorithm for shunt single-phase voltage-source type active power filter. IEE Proc. - Electr. Power Appl. **151**(3), 283–288 (2004)
4. Akagi, H., Nabae, A., Atoh, S.: Control strategy of active power filters using multiple voltage-source PWM converters. IEEE Trans. Ind. Appl. **IA–22**(3), 460–465 (1986)
5. Aredes, M., Watanabe, E.H.: New control algorithms for series and shunt three-phase four-wire active power filters. IEEE Trans. Ind. Appl. **10**(3), 1649–1656 (1995)
6. Mattavelli, P.: A closed-loop selective harmonic compensation for active filters. IEEE Trans. Ind. Appl. **37**(1), 81–89 (2001)
7. Yuan, X., Merk, W., Stemmler, H., Allmeling, J.: Stationary-frame generalized integrators for current control of active power filters with zero steady-state error for current harmonics of concern under unbalanced and distorted operating conditions. IEEE Trans. Ind. Appl. **38**(2), 523–532 (2002)
8. Miret, J., Castilla, M., Matas, J., Guerrero, J.M., Vasquez, J.C.: Selective harmonic-compensation control for single-phase active power filter with high harmonic rejection. IEEE Trans. Ind. Electron. **56**(8), 3117–3127 (2009)
9. Trinh, Q., Lee, H.: An advanced current control strategy for three-phase shunt active power filters. IEEE Trans. Ind. Electron. **60**(12), 5400–5410 (2013)
10. Morales, J., et al.: Modeling and sliding mode control for three-phase active power filters using the vector operation technique. IEEE Trans. Ind. Electron. **65**(9), 6828–6838 (2018)
11. Akagi, H.: Active harmonic filters. Proc. IEEE **9312**, 2128–2141 (2005)
12. Lee, T., Tzeng, K., Chong, M.: Fuzzy iterative learning control for three-phase shunt active power filters. In: 2006 IEEE International Symposium on Industrial Electronics (2006)
13. Luo, A., et al.: Feedback-feedforward PI-type iterative learning control strategy for hybrid active power filter with injection circuit. IEEE Trans. Ind. Electron. **57**(11), 3767–3779 (2010)
14. Kukkola, J., Hinkkanen, M.: State observer for grid-voltage sensorless control of a converter under unbalanced conditions. IEEE Trans. Ind. Appl. **54**(1), 286–297 (2018)
15. Bai, H., Wang, X., Blaabjerg, F.: A grid-voltage-sensorless resistive-active power filter with series LC-filter. IEEE Trans. Power Eletronics **33**(5), 6828–6838 (2018)
16. Monteiro, L.F.C., Encarnação, L.F. Aredes, M.: A novel selective control algorithm for the shunt active filter. In: IEEE International Power Electronics Conference, pp. 2288–2293 (2010)
17. Freitas, C.M., Do Nascimento, C.R., Bellar, M.D., Monteiro, L.F.C.: Control algorithms for a transformerless hybrid active filter without current sensors. In: 40th Annual Conference of the IEEE Industrial Electronics Society, pp. 5163–5168 (2014)

18. Freitas, C.M., Monteiro, L.F., Watanabe, E.H.: A novel current harmonic compensation based on resonant controllers for a selective active filter. In: 42nd Annual Conference of the IEEE Industrial Electronics Society, pp. 3666–3671 (2016)
19. Macellari, M., Grasselli, U., Schirone, L.: Modular MPPT converter with series-connection for PV installations embedded in the urban environment. In: IECON 2013–39th Annual Conference of the IEEE Industrial Electronics Society, pp. 1755–1760 (2013)

# Power Electronics Converters for an Electric Vehicle Fast Charging Station with Storage Capability

J. G. Pinto[1(✉)], Vítor Monteiro[1], Bruno Exposto[1],
Luis A. M. Barros[1], Tiago J. C. Sousa[1], Luis F. C. Monteiro[2],
and João L. Afonso[1]

[1] Centro ALGORITMI, University of Minho, Campus de Azurém,
Guimarães, Portugal
gabriel.pinto@algoritmi.uminho.pt
[2] State University of Rio de Janeiro, Electronics Engineering Program,
Campus F. Negrão de Lima, 20559-900 Rio de Janeiro, Brazil

**Abstract.** Fast charging stations are a key element for the wide spreading of Electric Vehicles (EVs) by reducing the charging time to a range between 20 to 40 min. However, the integration of fast charging stations causes some adverse impacts on the Power Grid (PG), namely by the huge increase in the peak demand during short periods of time. This paper addresses the design of the power electronics converters for an EV DC fast charging station with local storage capability and easy interface of renewables. In the proposed topology, the energy storage capability is used to smooth the peak power demand, inherent to fast charging systems, and contributes to the stability of the PG. When integrated in a Smart Grid, the proposed topology may even return some of the stored energy back to the power grid, when necessary. The accomplishment of the aforementioned objectives requires a set of different power electronics converters that are described and discussed in this paper.

**Keywords:** Power electronics · Electric Vehicles · DC fast charging ·
Energy Storage System

## 1 Introduction

In recent years, a major concern with climatic changes and energy efficiency have made the electrification of the transport sector a major field of research. Although there are vehicles that are fed directly from the Power Grid (PG), as is the case of railway electric locomotives, a great number of Electric Vehicles (EVs) will be powered from batteries, motivating the research of battery charging systems for EVs [1, 2].

Worldwide, there are three organizations working in the standardization of electrical vehicle charging equipment, namely the Society of Automotive Engineering (SAE), the CHAdeMO association and the International Electrotechnical Commission (IEC). The IEC 61851 defines four different charging modes: Mode 1 refers to the slow charge in AC with a maximum current of 16 A per phase (3.7 kW–11 kW) and the EV connection to the AC PG uses standard power connections; Mode 2 refers to the slow

J. L. Afonso et al. (Eds.): GreeNets 2018, LNICST 269, pp. 119–130, 2019.
https://doi.org/10.1007/978-3-030-12950-7_10

charge in AC with a maximum current of 32 A per phase (3.7 kW–22 kW) and the EV connection to the AC PG requires a specific power connection with an intermediate electronic device with a pilot control function and protections; Mode 3 refers to the slow or semi-quick charge in AC with a maximum current of 63 A per phase (<43 kW) and the EV connection to the AC PG requires a specific device; Mode 4 refers to a DC charging, with a maximum DC current of 400 A (<240 kW), where an external charger is required [3]. However, the PGs were not prepared to withstand this new type of loads or the peaks of demand that they can cause, therefore the impact caused by the pro-liferation of EVs cannot be neglected [4, 5]. The integration of EVs in the PGs will be an interesting challenge to the future Smart Grids [6, 7].

In order to reduce the negative effects and to facilitate the integration of EVs, some authors propose the use of bidirectional on-board chargers, enabling the Vehicle-to-Grid (V2G) mode of operation, which allows returning part of the stored energy back to the PG [7, 8], and the Vehicle-to-Home (V2H), where the charging power of the EV is continuously adjusted as a function of the home electric appliances [9]. With respect to DC fast chargers (off-board chargers) the main concern is related with the impacts to the power grid in terms of harmonics and peak demand [10]. The time required for a fast EV battery charging depends on the battery capacity and on its State-of-Charge (SoC). However, usually it does not exceed 20 to 40 min considering a charging power of 50 kW [11]. Despite the relatively short charging times, in a station with several charging posts, there will be situations where several EVs are charging simultaneously and in other occasions no EV is charging, resulting in a highly intermittent power consumption from the power grid. In this way, the simultaneous fast charging of a large number of EVs represents a significant oscillation in the power demand that can be problematic, especially in weak power systems, like islands or remote villages [12]. To mitigate these negative impacts, several studies have been conducted. A concept of low voltages DC-Buses, including power buffers based in Battery Energy Storage Systems (BESS) is proposed in [13]. In [14], it is addressed the design of a DC fast charging station coupled with a local battery energy storage. In [15] is proposed an optimal EV fast charging infrastructure, where the EVs are connected to a DC-Bus, employing an individual control for the charging process in order to optimize the power transfer from the AC PG to the DC-Bus. Other studies propose the integration of renewables con-nected to DC fast charging stations [16, 17].

Due to the increasing number of EV charging and discharging cycles over time, the capacity of the EVs batteries reduces, and consequently the EV range decreases, thereby it is necessary to proceed with the replacement. However, these batteries can be used in applications where the charge density is not significant. Considering that the batteries of the EVs have a charge density of about 70% of the initial value after 10 years of use [18], the replaced batteries can be reused in stationary Energy Storage Systems (ESS) to smooth the peak demand of the EV fast charging stations. In [19] is presented a study demonstrating that the integration of BESS and renewables in DC charging stations can be also economically advantageous.

## 2   Power Converters for the Proposed Charging Station

The proposed topology for the EV fast charging station is presented in Fig. 1, which consists of a set of power converters sharing the same DC-Bus, including a high capacity ESS. The first converter interfaces the DC-Bus with the PG. To prevent power quality problems in the PG, this converter may operate with sinusoidal currents and unitary power factor from the PG side. Several converter topologies can be used to accomplish this task. In order to increase flexibility and taking into account the convergence for Smart Grids, it can be useful to allow a two-way energy flow. Therefore, taking into account the application and the required nominal power, a three-phase two-level interleaved converter can be a good solution.

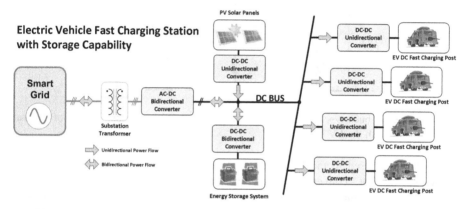

**Fig. 1.** Block diagram of the proposed topology for the EV fast charging station with storage capability.

Figure 2 presents the power circuit of the bidirectional AC-DC converter used to interface the PG with the DC-Bus. It consists of a three similar three-phase IGBT bridges sharing the same DC-Bus with a second order low-pass LC passive filter in the PG side.

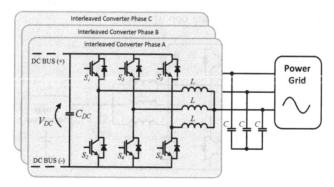

**Fig. 2.** Three-phase interleaved bidirectional AC-DC power converter used to interface the power grid with the DC-Bus of the EV fast charging station.

To charge the EVs batteries independently, it is necessary a DC-DC converter for each charging post. To accomplish with the usual battery charging recommendations, a possible solution for this task is a buck-type converter with constant current output.

Taking into account the application and the nominal power of the converter (50 kW), instead of a buck-type converter, it can be used an interleaved topology which allows to decrease the switching frequency and the power rating of each semiconductor, while maintaining a low battery current ripple. Figure 3 presents the power circuit of the interleaved buck-type constant output current converter.

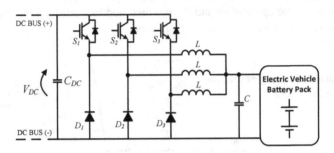

**Fig. 3.** Interleaved buck-type DC-DC power converter used to interface the DC-Bus of the fast charging station with the EV battery pack.

The batteries used to the load shift purposes must interface the DC-Bus with a bidirectional DC-DC converter. To prevent problems that may occur with parallel connection of individual battery cells it is recommendable that each pack of individual battery cells connected in series has its own DC-DC converter. The adoption of individual DC-DC converters for each battery pack also endows the system with fault tolerance capability. To preserve the batteries state of health, the DC-DC power converter should operate with constant current from the batteries side. A good solution to accomplish this task can be a buck-boost bidirectional converter. Taking into account the power rating of the converter, it can be used the interleaved bidirectional buck-boost DC-DC converter that is presented in Fig. 4. This converter operates as a buck-type converter to transfer energy from the DC-Bus to the BESS and operates as a boost-type converter to transfer energy in the opposite way.

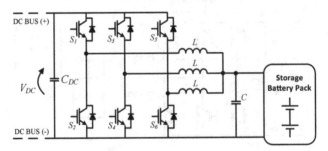

**Fig. 4.** Interleaved bidirectional buck-boost DC-DC converter used to interface the DC-Bus of the fast charging station with the BESS.

With the proposed topology for the DC fast charging station, the interface with renewable energy became simplified because it is possible to use a simple DC-DC converter. For example, to interface an array of photovoltaic solar panels, it can be used a boost-type converter with constant input current. In function of the maximum power from the photovoltaic solar panels, it can be adopted a simple boost-type or an inter-leaved converter with 2 or 3 legs, as represented in Fig. 5. However, the power available in the photovoltaic installation is not constant over timer, being necessary to implement a Maximum Power Point Tracker (MPPT) control algorithm in order to find the Max-imum Power Point (MPP) and force the power converter to operate at that point.

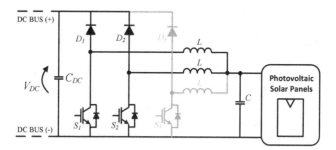

**Fig. 5.** Interleaved boost-type DC-DC converter used to interface an array of photovoltaic solar panels with the DC-Bus of the DC fast charging station.

## 3 Power Converters Control

The three-phase bidirectional AC-DC power converter used to interface the PG with the DC-Bus of the EV fast charging station is presented in Fig. 2. It should be controlled to absorb the required active power ($P*$), imposing sinusoidal currents and a unitary power factor, avoiding distortions in the PG voltages. To accomplish with this task, it is used a digital Phase-Locked Loop (PLL) algorithm implemented in the $\alpha$-$\beta$ coordinates to synchronize the controller with the positive sequence of the PG fundamental voltages [20]. From the PLL algorithm it results three sinusoidal signals with unitary amplitude, representing the positive sequence of the PG voltages. These signals are then multiplied by the reference current rms value to obtain the AC reference currents. The reference currents are then applied to a predictive current control that produces the reference voltages that the converter must produce [21]. The reference voltages are then compared with a triangular carrier to produce the gate signals to be applied to the IGBTs. To enhance the quality of the obtained currents, it is used a strategy to compensate the nonlinearities introduced by the dead-time [22]. The block diagram of the three-phase bidirectional AC-DC converter control system is presented in Fig. 6.

According to the majority of battery supplier's recommendations, the EV fast charging must be done with a constant current [23]. Therefore, the interleaved buck-type DC-DC power converter used to interface the DC-Bus with the EV battery pack is controlled to produce a constant output current ($I_{BAT}$). Usually, the maximum charging current is determined by the EV Battery Management System (BMS) and its value is transmitted to the fast charger controller [23].

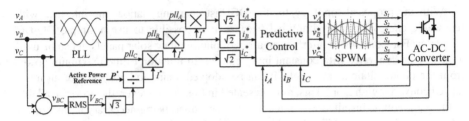

**Fig. 6.** Block diagram of the three-phase bidirectional AC-DC converter control system.

To accomplish with the fast charging it is used a Proportional Integral (PI) controller to ensure that the output current correctly follows the set points defined by the BMS. The output of the proportional integral controller is compared with three triangular carriers with the same amplitude and a phase-shift of 120° between them to generate the IGBTs pulse pattern for an interleaved operation. As mentioned above, the use of an interleaved converter allows to reduce the size of the passive output filter and to maintain a low value for the IGBTs switching frequency. The block diagram of the buck-type DC-DC converter control system is presented in Fig. 7.

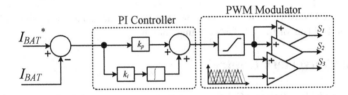

**Fig. 7.** Block diagram of the buck-type DC-DC converter control system.

The interleaved bidirectional DC-DC converter, used to interface the DC-Bus of the fast charging station with the storage battery pack, is controlled using a PI controller to maintain the voltage of the DC-Bus ($V_{DC}$) regulated. Since the converter is bidirectional, if the power absorbed from the PG is higher than the power used in the charging posts, the DC-Bus voltage tends to increase and the converter sends energy to the storage battery packs to maintain the DC-Bus voltage regulated. During this mode, the bottom IGBTs of each converter leg are kept open, while the top IGBTs are switched at a fixed frequency. If the power absorbed from the PG is lower than the power used in the charging posts, the converter gets energy from the BESS to maintain the DC-Bus voltage regulated. During this mode, the top IGBTs are kept open and the bottom IGBTs are switched. To control the IGBTs of the proposed converter, three triangular carriers are used with the same amplitude and a phase-shift of 120° between them. Due to the 120° phase-shift between the triangular carriers, the ripple frequency in the batteries current is three times higher than the ripple frequency in each output inductor. This allows to reduce the size of the passive filters, while keeping a low value of switching frequency. The total charging current is also divided by the three legs, allowing a reduction in the IGBTs power rating. The block diagram of the bidirectional DC-DC converter control system is presented in Fig. 8.

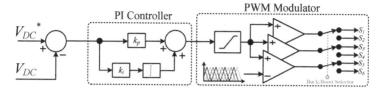

**Fig. 8.** Block diagram of the bidirectional DC-DC converter control system.

Currently, the vehicles filling stations always have some kind of protection for users against climatic phenomena, where it is usually used a roof to cover the entire area of the gas station. In many cases, this roof is an excellent location to install photovoltaic solar panels. In this case, it can be interesting to interface the solar panels directly to the DC-Bus of the fast charging station, avoiding the utilization of a DC-AC converter. Depending on the photovoltaic solar panels peak power, it can be advantageous to choose an interleaved converter instead of the simple boost-type converter. The controller of the interleaved boost-type DC-DC converter used to interface an array of photovoltaic solar panels with the DC-Bus should maximize the power extracted from the photovoltaic solar panels. Therefore, it is important to use a MPPT algorithm to control this converter. The main general characteristics that distinguish the MPPT algorithms are: panel independence, convergence speed, tracking efficiency, implementation complexity and robustness [24]. The panel independency is an important characteristic, because avoids the determination of some parameters of the PV array empirically, to different irradiance and temperature levels. Besides, if the parameters vary, the previous measurements can become outdated and, therefore, the MPPT will lose the convergence for the MPP. The convergence speed is important, because under sudden changes, if the MPPT is not able to a fast convergence, a considerable amount of energy can be lost in that transient. A good tracking performance ensures that the harvested energy is maximized. This is particularly important in situations when the solar radiation is minimal. Considering these premises, the incremental conductance algorithm can be a good choice. The incremental conductance algorithm works based on the fact that the slope of the photovoltaic solar panel power curve is zero at the MPP, positive on the left of the MPP, and negative on the right. Therefore, this method can determine that the MPP has been reached and interrupt the perturbing of the operating point. The advantages of the incremental conductance algorithm are the calculation of the direction to perturb the operating point to reach the MPP and the actual determination of the MPP reaching. Also, incremental conductance can track sudden increases or decreases of solar irradiance conditions with higher accuracy than algorithms based on perturb and observe [24]. The output of the MPPT algorithm is then compared with the triangular carriers to obtain the IGBTs pulse patterns. In the case of a single boost-type converter adoption, it must be used a single triangular carrier. In the case of a two-leg interleaved converter, two triangular carriers with a phase shift of 180° must be used. A three-leg interleaved converter requires three triangular carriers with a phase shift of 120° between them. The block diagram of the boost DC-DC converter control system is presented in Fig. 9.

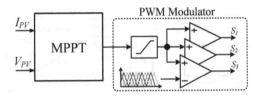

**Fig. 9.** Block diagram of the boost DC-DC converter control system.

## 4 Simulations of the Proposed System

In order to validate the hardware topologies and the control algorithms of the converters used in the fast DC fast charging stations, it was developed a simulation model using PSIM. PSIM is a simulation software from *Powersim Inc.* specially designed for power electronics.

The most common EVs are equipped with battery packs whose nominal voltage ranges between 300 V and 420 V. Therefore, the DC-Bus voltage was defined to 450 V. Thus, the individual converter of each charging post always operates in buck mode. In order to optimize the power converters in terms of efficiency, it was selected an AC phase to phase voltage around 300 V. As the service station connects to the PG in medium voltage, it is possible to choose a transformer with the required secondary voltage. In the simulation, it is used a transformer with a secondary voltage of 300 V. However, the system can be easily dimensioned to operate with different voltage levels, if required.

In Figs. 10 and 11 are presented some simulation results of the three-phase interleaved bidirectional AC-DC power converter used to interface the PG with the DC-Bus. Figure 10 presents the instantaneous power, the voltages and the currents in the AC side of this converter. As it is possible to see, although the voltages are distorted, the currents produced by the converter are sinusoidal as required. In consequence of the PG voltage distortions, the instantaneous power oscillates around 170 kVA, which corresponds to the absorbed active power.

Figure 11 shows in detail the interleaved effect in the produced currents. Figure 11(a) shows the current in each of the output inductors in the phase A, and Fig. 11(b) shows the total current of the phase A, which corresponds to the sum of the currents in the three inductors. As it is possible to see, the total output current presents a ripple frequency three times higher than the ripple frequency in each of the inductors, with a frequency three times greater. In the simulation, the IGBTs switching frequency was fixed in 10 kHz, and each of the three inductors presents a value of 750 μH. In combination with the inductor are also used three 20 μF capacitors, allowing a further reduction of the current ripple.

In Fig. 12 is presented a simulation result of the interleaved buck-type DC-DC power converter used to interface the DC-Bus of the fast charging station with an EV battery pack. Figure 12(a) shows the current in each of the output inductors of the converter, and Fig. 12(b) shows the total current, which corresponds to the sum of the currents in the three inductors. In the simulation, the switching frequency of the IGBTs was fixed in 15 kHz, and each of the three inductors presents a value of 500 μH. In combination with the inductors are also used three capacitors with a value of 100 μF to reduce the ripple in the battery current.

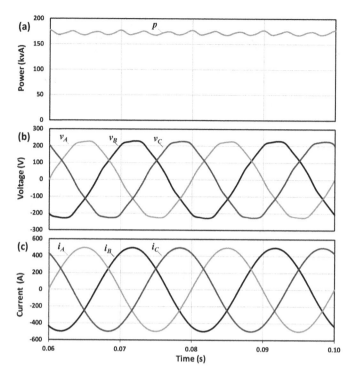

**Fig. 10.** Simulation results of the three-phase interleaved bidirectional AC-DC power converter used to interface the PG with the DC-Bus: (a) Instantaneous input power, $p$; (b) PG voltages, $v_A$, $v_B$ and $v_C$; (c) PG currents, $i_A$, $i_B$ and $i_C$.

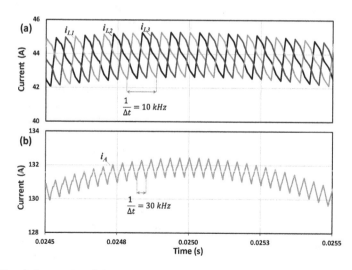

**Fig. 11.** Simulation results of the three-phase interleaved bidirectional AC-DC power converter used to interface the power grid with the DC-Bus: (a) Current in the *phase A* output inductors, $i_{L1}$, $i_{L2}$ and $i_{L3}$; (b) Total current of the *phase A*, $i_A$.

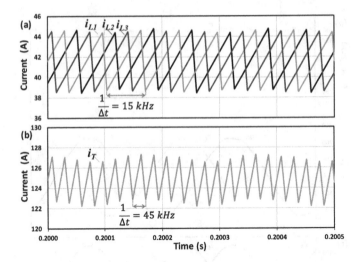

**Fig. 12.** Simulation results of the interleaved buck-type DC-DC power converter used to interface the DC-Bus of the DC fast charging station with the EV battery pack: (a) Current in the output inductors, $i_{L1}$, $i_{L2}$ and $i_{L3}$; (b) Total current, $i_T$.

## 5    Conclusion

In this paper, a new concept of a DC fast charging station for EVs is presented. The main advantages of the proposed topology are the storage capability and the easy integration of renewable energy sources. The ESS in this proposed charging station can be mainly composed by electrochemical batteries, reused from EVs. The system is composed by a set of power converters. One AC-DC bidirectional converter is used to interface the DC-Bus of the charging station with the PG. The interface with the storage batteries is done by means of bidirectional DC-DC converters, one converter for each battery pack. The charging posts are implemented by means of buck-type DC-DC converters, one for each individual charging point. The interface of renewables can be implemented by means of a simple DC-DC converter. In terms of performance, the proposed topology with the suggested storage system allows a significant reduction in the maximum power absorbed from the PG. The topology of the proposed solution was defined taking into account the required power for each one of the converters. The proposed topologies and control algorithms were validated through computer simulations developed with the software PSIM.

**Acknowledgement.** This work has been supported by COMPETE: POCI-01-0145-FEDER-007043 and by FCT within the Project Scope: UID/CEC/00319/2013. This work is financed by the ERDF – COMPETE 2020 Programme, and FCT within project SAICTPAC/0004/2015-POCI-01-0145–FEDER-016434 and FCT within project PTDC/EEI-EEE/28813/2017. Mr. Luis A. M. Barros is supported by the doctoral scholarship PD/BD/143006/2018 granted by the Portuguese FCT agency. Mr. Tiago Sousa is supported by the doctoral scholarship SFRH/BD/134353/2017 granted by the Portuguese FCT agency.

# References

1. Rajashekara, K.: Present status and future trends in electric vehicle propulsion technologies. IEEE J. Emerg. Sel. Top. Power Electron. **1**(1), 3–10 (2013)
2. Emadi, A., Lee, Y.J., Rajashekara, K.: Power electronics and motor drives in electric, hybrid electric, and plug-in hybrid electric vehicles. IEEE Trans. Ind. Electron. **55**, 2237–2245 (2008)
3. Gjelaj, M., Træholt, C., Hashemi Toghroljerdi, S., Andersen, P.B.: Optimal design of DC fast-charging stations for EVs in low voltage grids. In: Proceedings of 2017 IEEE Transportation Electrification Conference (2017). https://doi.org/10.1109/itec.2017.7993352
4. Raghavan, S.S., Khaligh, A.: Electrification potential factor: energy-based value proposition analysis of plug-in hybrid electric vehicles. IEEE Trans. Veh. Technol. **61**(3), 1052–1059 (2012)
5. Shao, S., Pipattanasomporn, M., Rahman, S.: Grid integration of electric vehicles and demand response with customer choice. IEEE Trans. Smart Grid **3**(1), 543–550 (2012)
6. Lopes, J.A.P., Soares, F., Almeida, P.M.R.: Integration of electric vehicles in the electric power systems. Proc. IEEE **99**(1), 168–183 (2011)
7. Güngör, V.C., et al.: Smart grid technologies: communication technologies and standards. IEEE Trans. Ind. Inform. **7**(4), 529–539 (2011)
8. Monteiro, V., Pinto, J.G., Afonso, J.L.: Operation modes for the electric vehicle in smart grids and smart homes: present and proposed modes. IEEE Trans. Veh. Technol. **65**(3), 1007–1020 (2016). https://doi.org/10.1109/tvt.2015.2481005. ISSN: 0018-9545
9. Pinto, J.G., Monteiro, V., Gonçalves, H., Afonso, J.L.: Onboard reconfigurable battery charger for electric vehicles with traction-to-auxiliary mode. IEEE Trans. Veh. Technol. **63**(3), 1104–1116 (2014). https://doi.org/10.1109/tvt.2013.2283531. ISSN 0018-9545
10. Bai, S., Lukic, S.M.: Unified active filter and energy storage system for an MW electric vehicle charging station. IEEE Trans. Power Electron. **28**(12), 5793–5803 (2013)
11. Efacec QC 50 Quick Charger: Efacec - Portfolio of Products (2008)
12. Monteiro, V., Sepúlveda, M.J., Aparício Fernandes, J.C., Pinto, J.G., Afonso, J.L.: Evaluation of the introduction of electric vehicles in the power grid—a study for the Island of Maio in Cape Verde. In: Garrido, P., Soares, F., Moreira, A.P. (eds.) CONTROLO 2016. LNEE, vol. 402, pp. 713–724. Springer, Cham (2017). https://doi.org/10.1007/978-3-319-43671-5_60
13. Vasiladiotis, M., Rufer, A., Béguin, A.: Modular converter architecture for medium voltage ultra fast EV charging stations: global system considerations. In: 2012 IEEE International Electric Vehicle Conference, Greenville, SC, pp. 1–7 (2012). https://doi.org/10.1109/ievc.2012.6183228
14. Gjelaj, M., Træholt, C., Hashemi, S., Andersen, P.B.: DC fast-charging stations for EVs controlled by a local battery storage in low voltage grids. In: 2017 IEEE Manchester PowerTech, Manchester, pp. 1–6 (2017). https://doi.org/10.1109/ptc.2017.7980985
15. Shariff, S., Alam, M.S., Ahmad, F., Khan, W.: Optimal electric vehicle fast charging infrastructure. In: Proceedings of the Intelligent Transportation Society of America 2018 Annual Meeting, Detroit, Michigan, 4–7 June 2018
16. Monteiro, V., Pinto, J.G., Afonso, J.L.: Experimental validation of a three-port integrated topology to interface electric vehicles and renewables with the electrical grid. IEEE Trans. Ind. Inform. **14**(6), 2364–2374 (2018). https://doi.org/10.1109/tii.2018.2818174
17. Youssef, C., Fatima, E., Najia, E., Chakib, A.: A technological review on electric vehicle DC charging stations using photovoltaic sources. In: IOP Conference Series: Materials Science and Engineering, vol. 353 (2018). https://doi.org/10.1088/1757-899x/353/1/012014

18. ABB: ABB and partners to evaluate the reuse of the Nissan LEAF battery for commercial purposes, Zurich, Switzerland, January 2012
19. Pinto, J.G., Monteiro, V., Pedrosa, D., Afonso, J.L.: Economic assessment of a public DC charging station for electric vehicles with load shift capability. In: Proceedings of the 3rd International Conference on Energy and Environment: Bringing Together Economics and Engineering – ICEE 2017, Porto, Portugal, 29–30 June 2017, pp. 460–466 (2017). ISBN:978-972-95396-9-5, ISSN:2183-3982
20. Rolim, L.G.B., Costa, D.R., Aredes, M.: Analysis and software implementation of a robust synchronizing PLL circuit based on the pq theory. IEEE Trans. Ind. Electron. **53**(6), 1919–1926 (2006)
21. Orts-Grau, S., Gimeno-Sales, F.J., Abellan-Garcia, A., Segui-Chilet, S., Alfonso-Gil, J.C.: Improved shunt active power compensator for IEEE Standard 1459 compliance. IEEE Trans. Power Deliv. **25**(4), 2692–2701 (2010)
22. Munoz, A.R., Lipo, T.A.: On-line dead-time compensation technique for open-loop PWM-VSI drives. IEEE Trans. Power Electron. **14**(4), 683–689 (1999)
23. Qiang, J., Yang, L., Ao, G., Zhong, H.: Battery management system for electric vehicle application. In: 2006 IEEE International Conference on Vehicular Electronics and Safety, Shanghai, pp. 134–138 (2006). https://doi.org/10.1109/icves.2006.371569
24. Esram, T., Chapman, P.L.: Comparison of photovoltaic array maximum power point tracking techniques. IEEE Trans. Energy Convers. **22**(2), 439–449 (2007)

# Experimental Evaluation of Magnetostrictive Strain of Electrical Steel

António Vieira, João Espírito Santo[✉], Cristiano P. Coutinho,
Sérgio M. O. Tavares, Marta Pinto, Cassiano C. Linhares, and Hélder Mendes

Efacec Energia, Máquinas e Equipamentos Eléctricos, S.A., S. Mamede de Infesta,
Porto, Portugal
{antonio.vieira,joao.espiritosanto}@efacec.com

**Abstract.** Environmental noise pollution has gained increasing importance, over the past few years. Due to population growth along with a rapid urbanization and the increasing power supply needs, more and more electrical power transformers are set near or inside of urban agglomerations. This fact has generated several complaints regarding the noise produced by this equipment, forcing manufacturers to develop low noise solutions. As it is known, magnetostriction is one of the main sources of electrical machines noise. This research presents an experimental study in which magnetostriction properties of electrical steel are evaluated and analyzed. The magnetic flux density influence on the hysteretic strain behavior of magnetostriction was addressed, as well as the effect of a clamping load on the core joints. This study was addressed by means of an Epstein frame and a data acquisition system, where strain, current and voltage data is obtained and then processed in a data logging software. These measurements gave essential inputs for numerical models which simulate the power transformer core behavior, allowing a faster evaluation of noise mitigation solutions.

**Keywords:** Magnetostriction · Epstein frame · Power transformer · Noise

## 1 Introduction

Nowadays, more importance is given to noise pollution [4], what has yielded several regulations and directives that specify the maximum noise levels in sensitive zones, such as urban areas. Hence, industry is now compelled to manufacture quieter equipment, in order to fulfil these requirements.

In spite of being stationary machines, the active part of power transformers is a source of noise due to mechanical vibrations resulting from electromagnetic forces and magnetomechanical effects. Due to the increasing demands on power supply, more and more transformers are set near the final consumer, subjecting manufacturers to more restrictive specifications regarding noise levels.

J. L. Afonso et al. (Eds.): GreeNets 2018, LNICST 269, pp. 131–141, 2019.
https://doi.org/10.1007/978-3-030-12950-7_11

Transformers noise can be classified according to its source: core noise, instigated by the magnetostriction of the transformer core and by the Maxwell forces; load noise, caused by the action of electromagnetic forces on the windings; cooling noise, which is due to auxiliary cooling equipment. According to several studies [3,5,7], core noise is the dominant source of noise for transformers whose rating is below 150 MVA. Since transformers rated power is usually lower near consumption, the mitigation of core noise has been the focus of many studies during the past years. Maxwell forces occur whenever magnetic flux changes medium, these forces act to minimize magnetic reluctance, reducing the gap between electrical steel sheets, causing adjacent sheets to attract and to repel. Magnetostriction is the mechanical deformation a ferromagnetic material is subjected to, when polarized.

Due to the complexity of this phenomena, an analytical model is not capable of accurately predict transformers noise level. Therefore empirical models [7] or numerical methods, such as the finite element method (FEM) or the boundary element method (BEM), are used to calculate the noise radiation of a power transformer. The development of such FEM/BEM models requires the characterization of the magnetomechanical behavior of electrical steel sheets used in the core, through representative experimental set-ups.

This paper presents an experimental setup in which magnetostriction measurements were carried out, based on an Epstein frame concept.

## 2    Background and Related Work

When magnetized, a ferromagnetic material is subjected to a mechanical deformation which varies with the magnetic polarization. This magnetomechanical effect, named magnetostriction, is one of the causes of transformers core vibration, along with the Maxwell forces (which occur when the magnetic field faces a material of different magnetic permeability). Magnetostriction is an anisotropic material property with non-linear behavior, which is specific of each type of electrical steel, and thus it may only be determined experimentally.

The measurement of these properties can be performed with different setups, one of them is the Epstein frame. An Epstein frame comprises a primary and a secondary winding, disposed in four coils, and the testing specimens, forming an unloaded transformer, whose specifications are defined according to IEC 60404-2 [8]. This device may also be used to characterise the magnetomechanical behavior of the tested specimen, besides Technical Report IEC TR 62581 [9] describes the general principles and technical details regarding magnetostriction measurements by means of an Epstein frame or a Single Sheet Tester (SST).

The major part of the work developed on magnetostriction measurements was carried by means of a SST, mainly because of its simplicity. Anderson [1] developed a SST which was capable to measure magnetostriction, under applied mechanical stress, using a piezoelectric accelerometer. Javorski studied the frequency characteristics of magnetostriction using a modified SST [11] and formulated a numerical magnetostriction model based on those measurements [10].

Klimczyk [14] improved the experimental setup idealized by Anderson to study the influence of the specimen thickness, coating and residual stresses on the magnetostrictive behavior of electrical steel. Ghalamestani [6] also used a SST to carry out magnetostriction measurements, but instead of using accelerometers to measure the deformation, the author used an heterodyne laser interferometer.

However, an Epstein frame resembles better a power transformer operation, since the effects of the lamination stacking, and clamping might not be neglected. Behlacen [2] studied magnetostriction by means of an Epstein frame, using a force transducer to compute the magnetostrictive forces and then converted them to deformation and strain values.

This work aims to acquire and to evaluate the anisotropic magnetostriction of an electrical steel sheet, where its frequency characteristics were addressed, as well as the influence of magnetic polarization and clamping loads applied on the joints in the magnetostriction curves. These measurements are the first step to compute the sound power level of a power transformer, providing inputs required by a commercial FEM software to predict magnetostriction along the transformer core, based on the magnetic field it is subjected to. The workflow of this numerical study is presented on Fig. 1. Future works also include experimental validation of numerical simulations under different conditions, which are representative of a full-size power transformer.

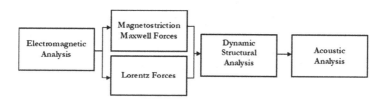

**Fig. 1.** Numerical simulations workflow.

## 3   Experimental Measurements

### 3.1   Experimental Set-Up

The magnetostriction measurements were carried out on an Epstein frame, by means of strain gauges. The strain data was acquired and then processed by a data acquisition system, which synchronized the strain signal with the current and voltage signals. The Epstein frame used in this work, Fig. 2, matches the characteristics listed on the IEC standard previously referred [8].

Tested specimens were assembled according to standards, in double lapped joints [8] and with their rolling direction parallel to the magnetizing direction [11].

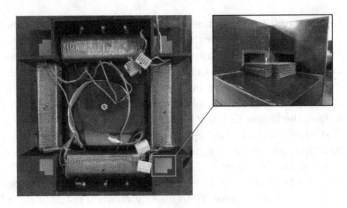

**Fig. 2.** Epstein frame.

**Electrical Steel Specimens.** In order to test electrical steel that is used in power transformers, several strips of grain oriented electrical steel *Power-Core*® H105-30 from ThyssenKrupp were collected. The characteristics of the tested electrical steel are shown in Table 1. Electrical strips dimensions were determined based on IEC/TR-62581, to ensure a magnetic path of 0.94 m [8].

**Table 1.** *PowerCore*® H105-30 properties.

| Parameter | Value | Units |
|---|---|---|
| Saturation polarization | 2.03 | T |
| Coercive field strength | 5 | A/m |
| Density | 7650 | $kg/m^3$ |
| Resistivity | 0.48 | $\mu\Omega m$ |
| Length | 300 | mm |
| Width | 30 | mm |
| Thickness | 0.3 | mm |

**Strain Gauge.** For a discrete and local measurement of magnetostriction, strain gauges were used and placed in one strip of the tested specimen. The strain rosette has a temperature response matched to steel (HBM K-XY31-3/350) and two measuring grids (0°/90° T rosette).

The coating of the electrical strip was removed allowing a direct contact with the steel. The strain gauge was attached to the strip using an HBM Z70 adhesive, and connected to the data acquisition system with AWM 2651 cables. These cables were twisted, like shown on Fig. 3, in an attempt to compensate any electromagnetic interferences. In addition, to avoid the effects of the double-lap joints (test specimen edges) the gauge was positioned in the middle of the strip, as shown on Fig. 3.

**Fig. 3.** HBM K-XY31-3/350 on the specimen.

**Autotransformer.** In order to better control the voltage and current fed into the circuit, a Zenith V8HM autotransformer was connected to the Epstein frame for power supply.

**Data Acquisition System.** For data acquisition, a National Instruments data acquisition system composed by a CompactDAQ-9188 Chassis was used. Data regarding current, voltage and strain were acquired using NI-9227, NI-9244 and NI- 9236 input modules, respectively, with a sampling time of 2 ms. Apart from data acquisition, the system allows the constant monitoring of magnetizing current and voltage supply in primary winding, with a PC and a dedicated software system developed in Labview. Through the data logging software, an interface algorithm was created to calculate magnetic field – $H(t)$ – and magnetic polarization – $B(t)$ – using Eqs. (1) and (2), where $N_1$ and $N_2$ are the number of turns of the primary and secondary windings, respectively, $l$ the magnetic path length, $I(t)$ is the current, $A$ the magnetic active area and $U_2(t)$ the voltage on the secondary winding [13,15]. As a result, magnetostriction could be plotted as a function of $B(t)$ or $H(t)$.

$$H(t) = \frac{N_1 \cdot I(t)}{l} \tag{1}$$

$$B(t) = -\frac{1}{N_2 \cdot A} \int U_2(t)dt \tag{2}$$

Figure 4 shows the experimental set-up scheme employed in this study.

## 3.2   Measurement Procedure

The excitation was made using the power grid ($f \approx 50$ Hz and $U_{rms} = 230$ V), by means of the autotransformer, which allows the step-down and control of the voltage applied to the primary winding.

Before measurements initialization, preliminary calculations were performed for variables definition. Peak magnetic polarization ($B_{peak}$) is predicted based on the effective secondary winding voltage ($U_{2rms}$). Finally, the power supply

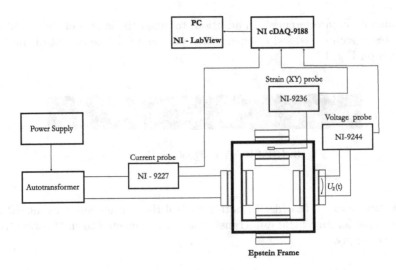

**Fig. 4.** Experimental set-up.

output should be slowly increased until the secondary voltage has reached the desired value [8]. When the desired peak magnetic induction is achieved, the data is collected.

Eighteen experimental measurements were conducted. On these tests, three parameters were evaluated: magnetic polarization, $B$; number of laminations, $n_l$; clamping load on the core joints, $F$. Three levels of magnetic polarization were considered: 1.5, 1.7, 1.9 T; as for the laminations three arrangement were tested: one, four and thirteen strips per limb.

## 4    Results and Discussion

Initially, magnetostriction frequency characteristics were studied. According with literature review [11], for an excitation frequency of 50 Hz, magnetostriction presents a fundamental component of 100 Hz (double the excitation frequency), and respective harmonics. However, the acquired signal exhibited a distorted behavior, possibly due to electromagnetic interference, especially when compared to those of IEC TR-62581 [9].

Therefore, to ensure a representative magnetostriction loop, a FFT (Fast Fourier Transform) analysis was conducted. Through this analysis, it was concluded that, in addition to the fundamental component, other harmonics were present, some of which were related with magnetostriction multiple harmonics, the others were related with the power grid (50 Hz and odd harmonics) and other parasite signals. To work around the problem, magnetostriction fundamental frequency and respective harmonics were identified and isolated. Moreover, rigid body motion (0 Hz) was also taken into account. Figure 5 shows the filtered magnetostriction spectrum for an iron core composed by thirteen steel sheets per

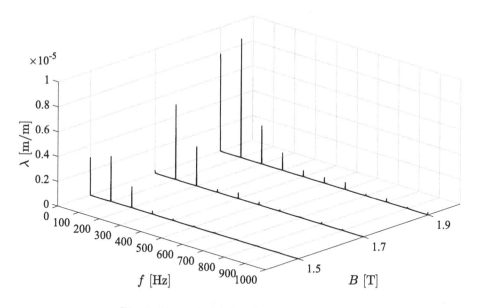

**Fig. 5.** Magnetostriction frequency spectrum.

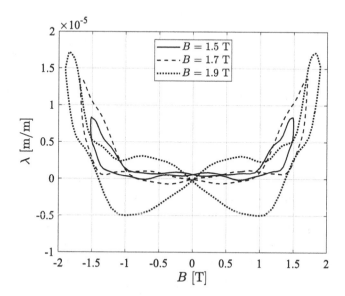

**Fig. 6.** Magnetostriction as a function of the magnetic polarization (13 strips per limb).

limb, under three induction levels. As it can be verified, the first two harmonics (100 and 200 Hz) show a greater contribution; however, for higher polarization values, the influence of higher harmonics rises.

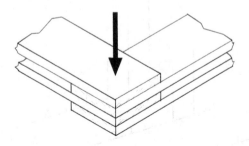

**Fig. 7.** Load applied on the lap joints

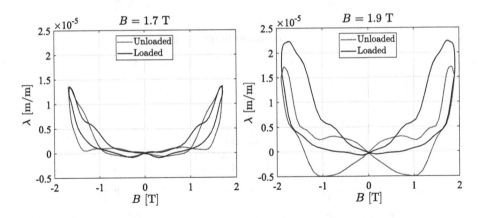

**Fig. 8.** Influence of a clamping load applied on the core joints.

The influence of the magnetic polarization on the magnetostriction of the test specimen was also addressed. According to previous studies [1,6], peak-to-peak magnetostriction rises when the magnetic polarization increases. This trend was verified in the tested specimen, as shown in Fig. 6. Moreover, the magnetostriction loop is distorted when polarization rises, especially when the polarization is beyond the knee point of the hysteresis loop (B-H). This fact may be explained by a greater influence of higher harmonics (300 Hz and higher) on the magnetostrictive behavior of the specimen, as can be seen in Fig. 5. The impact of a clamping load on the lap joints of the Epstein frame, like displayed on Fig. 7, was also investigated. In order to load the joints, four 1.6 N weights were used. Figure 8 shows the obtained results. It was verified that the magnetostriction loops were distorted, yet the peak-to-peak and zero-to-peak magnetostriction values remained the same. The curve of higher polarization was the most mis-shaped, to the extent that the compressive strain could no longer be observed.

Besides magnetic hysteresis, magnetic materials are characterized based on the mechanical hysteresis [12]. In Fig. 9, magnetostriction is represented as a function of the magnetic field, for an excitation of 1.5 T. The mechanical hysteresis due to the magnetic excitation can be observed on Fig. 9.

In fact, the characterisation of the mechanical hysteresis of electrical steel was one of the main concerns of this investigation. For numerical computation of magnetostriction along the laminated iron core, FEM software require the mechanical hysteresis loop, in order to correlate the magnetic field with magnetostriction.

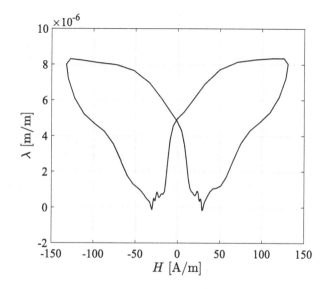

**Fig. 9.** Magnetostriction as a function of the magnetic field.

## 5   Conclusions and Future Work

Magnetostrictive behavior of grain oriented electrical steel was studied by means of an experimental set-up based on an Epstein frame. For the magnetostriction measurements, the generated signal of a strain rosette was acquired and processed via a dedicated software system. Current and voltage data was also acquired and synchronized with the strain data. Through the data software system, these two signals were processed in order to obtain the magnetic field and polarization, so that the magnetostriction curves could be extracted.

The frequency characteristics of magnetostriction were also addressed. The measured results allowed to conclude that the first two harmonics are the most significative, yet when the magnetic flux density gets closer to saturation, higher harmonics gain more influence.

In addition, this study revealed that the applied load on the core joints has influence on the hysteretic behavior of magnetostriction, since significant differences could be observed throughout the acquired data. With a view to further comprehend the influence of this load, additional measurements will be conducted with different weights.

Future research activities include additional magnetostriction measurements using Fiber Bragg Grating (FBG) sensors and a Laser Interferometer for comparison with previous results. Additionally, different types of grain oriented electrical steels will be tested, as to discern which are the optimal solutions to decrease power transformers noise radiation.

From this study and in order to simulate the real operation of a power transformer, a modified Epstein frame with a clamping system on two limbs will be created. The new system will allow the characterization of magnetostriction, tanking into account the clamping pressure and the stress state of the other limbs.

Regarding the obtained results, the magnetostriction loop as a function of the magnetic field can be applied to numerical simulations, allowing the evaluation of power transformer noise radiation.

**Acknowledgements.** This work is supported by the project POCI-01-0247-FEDER-024035, with the acronym *Quiet Transformer 2*, co-funded by the European Regional Development Fund (ERDF) through COMPETE2020 - Programa Operacional de Competitividade e Internacionalização (POCI) under the "Portugal 2020" Programme.

# References

1. Anderson, P., Moses, A., Stanbury, H.: An automated system for the measurement of magnetostriction in electrical steel sheet under applied stress. J. Magn. Magn. Mater. **215**, 714–716 (2000)
2. Belahcen, A.: Magnetoelasticity, Magnetic Forces and Magnetostriction in Electrical Machines. Ph.D. thesis, Helsinki University of Technology (2004)
3. Braña, L.F., Campelo, H.M., López-Fernández, X.M.: Quiet transformers: design issues. In: Advanced Research Workshop on Transformers (ARWtr) (2013)
4. European Comission: Special Eurobarometer 468: Attitudes of European citizens towards the environment, November 2017
5. Foster, S.L., Reiplinger, E.: Charcteristics and control of transformer sound. IEEE Trans. Power Appar. Syst. **PAS–100**(3), 1072–1077 (1981)
6. Ghalamestani, S.G.: Magnetostriction in electrical steel: numerical modelling and development of an optical measurement method. Ph.D. thesis, Ghent University (2013)
7. Girgis, R.S., Bernesjo, M., Anger, J.: Comprehensive analysis of load noise of power transformers. In: Power & Energy Society General Meeting, PES 2009, pp. 1–7. IEEE (2009)
8. IEC/60404-2: Methods of measurement of the magnetic properties of electrical steel strip and sheet by means of an epstein frame, June 2008

9. IEC/TR-62581: Electrical steel-methods of measurements of the magnetostriction characteristics by means of single sheet and epstein test specimens. Technical report, International Electrotechnical Commission (2010)
10. Javorski, M., Čepon, G., Slavič, J., Boltežar, M.: A generalized magnetostrictive-forces approach to the computation of the magnetostriction-induced vibration of laminated steel structures. IEEE Trans. Magn. **49**, 5446–5453 (2013)
11. Javorski, M., Slavič, J., Boltežar, M.: Frequency characteristics of magnetostriction in electrical steel related to the structural vibrations. IEEE Trans. Magn. **48**, 4727–4734 (2012)
12. Kaltenbacher, M., Volk, A., Ertl, M.: Anisotropic model for the numerical computation of magnetostriction in grain-oriented electrical steel sheets. COMPEL - Int. J. Comput. Math. Electr. Electron. Eng. **32**(5), 1620–1630 (2013)
13. Kis, P., Kuczmann, M., Füzi, J., Iványi, A.: Hysteresis measurement in labview. Physica B: Condens. Matter **343**, 357–363 (2004)
14. Klimczyk, P.: Novel techniques for characterisation and control of magnetostriction in GOSS. Ph.D. thesis, Cardiff University (2012)
15. Kulkarni, S.V., Khaparde, S.: Transformer Engineering: Design, Technology, and Diagnostics. CRC Press, Boca Raton (2013)

# Design of Compact LoRa Devices for Smart Building Applications

Sérgio I. Lopes[1,2]([✉]), Felisberto Pereira[3], José M. N. Vieira[3,4],
Nuno B. Carvalho[3,4], and António Curado[1,5]

[1] Instituto Politécnico de Viana do Castelo, Viana do Castelo, Portugal
sil@estg.ipvc.pt
[2] Instituto de Telecomunicações, Aveiro, Portugal
[3] Instituto de Telecomunicações, Campus Universitário de Santiago, Aveiro, Portugal
[4] DETI, University of Aveiro, Campus Universitário de Santiago, Aveiro, Portugal
[5] CONSTRUCT LFC, Faculty of Engineering (FEUP),
University of Porto, Porto, Portugal

**Abstract.** The use of smart devices in buildings is many times compromised by its form and size. Smart devices are composed of several components including sensors, boards, batteries, processing units, and antennas. However, the form and size of the smart devices are usually limited due to antenna restrictions. In this paper, we propose the architecture of a compact low-cost LoRa smart device designed for easy deployment in smart building applications. The proposed device architecture features a reduced size embedded antenna and an ultra-low-power microcontroller to interface several sensors and actuators. The results obtained have shown that the proposed design can be used for communication, between two compact LoRa devices, in line-of-sight for up to 4.2 km, in urban environments for up to 1.2 km and also for in-building communications for up to 152 m, without compromising the low-power features that LoRa supports.

**Keywords:** Green communications · LoRa · Smart buildings

## 1 Introduction

Green wireless communications are nowadays a hot topic in research that has been pushed by new ubiquitous applications in several application domains [1]. As a result, these communication systems have been designed for optimal spectrum efficiency and high transmission reliability [2]. Moreover, the need for energy efficiency with reduced environmental impact in radio communications increases the effort of reducing the communication cost and therefore, the power used for communications.

In [3], Buckman et. al. define a Smart Building as the harmonious integration of intelligent systems, control mechanisms, architecture and construction materials to operate as an entire building system, with adaptability at its core to enable

© ICST Institute for Computer Sciences, Social Informatics and Telecommunications Engineering 2019
Published by Springer Nature Switzerland AG 2019. All Rights Reserved
J. L. Afonso et al. (Eds.): GreeNets 2018, LNICST 269, pp. 142–153, 2019.
https://doi.org/10.1007/978-3-030-12950-7_12

continuous building improvement in terms of energy efficiency, longevity, comfort, and satisfaction. A central topic in the previous definition that is implicit and vital in the design of this type of systems is the selection of the communication technology, in order to enable a simple, non-invasive and transparent integration between the main elements of such systems.

In a smart building context, several sensors and actuators are deployed for data collection, reasoning, and building control. The lack of a widely accepted standard for low-power in-building communications opens a window of opportunity to use and adapt other standards with higher maturity levels that are already adopted by industry for long-range communications, e.g. SigFox or LoRa. Another common standard that has been very popular in this type of applications is Wi-Fi. Wi-Fi is a mature technology with a large ecosystem that is being integrated in several smart devices due to its easy deployment and simple integration with existing IP networks at an affordable price. However, the use of Wi-Fi faces two main drawbacks: (i) high power consumption that results in a reduced device autonomy and (ii) coverage bellow 40 m, making it difficult to perform effective in-building and inter-building communications.

Moreover, the use of smart devices in buildings is many times compromised by its form and size. Smart devices are composed of several components including sensors, boards, batteries, processing units, and antennas. However, the form and size of the smart devices are usually limited due to antenna restrictions.

Given this, in this work, we will evaluate the viability of using LoRa technology in the design of compact and ultra-low-power devices for smart building applications that demand reduced maintenance, i.e. battery operation over long periods of time (in the order of magnitude of the years) for in-building and inter-building connectivity. For this, we will focus on the design of a compact LoRa antenna with optimal performance without compromising the form and size of the smart sensor.

This paper is organized as follows. Firstly a discussion about the state-of-the-art in low-power wireless communication systems commonly used in smart building applications is undertaken. Secondly, the architecture of the proposed Smart device is introduced and its specification is presented. Thirdly the design and simulation of the LoRa embedded antenna are presented using a simplified model of the Printed Circuit Board (PCB) that includes its main components. Fourthly, real experiments are performed and the results are discussed. Lastly, final conclusions are undertaken and future work is pointed out.

## 2 Wireless Communication Technologies for Smart Buildings

When selecting a wireless communication technology for a smart building, four main criteria are commonly used: (i) cost; (ii) data rate; (iii) autonomy and (iv) communication range. Note that, when using these criteria, there is a strict and proportionally inverse relationship between data rate and autonomy and between communication range and autonomy, due to the increase in power consumption to communicate at higher bit rates or greater distances.

Given the scope of this paper, we will focus on low-power communication technologies. Table 1 compiles the five more promising standards that are being used in smart building applications, notably LoRa, Sigfox, NB-IoT, and Z-Wave. Note that, although the Wi-Fi technology was not designed for low-power applications, it has been included in this study, mainly due to its high maturity level and large ecosystem. The table includes the four main criteria introduced at the beginning of this section. The cost criterion has been estimated based on the average price of commercial off-the-shelf modules. Additionally, six technical criteria (modulation, bandwidth, frequency, etc.), have been added for a more effective comparison.

**Table 1.** Wireless technologies commonly used in smart buildings.

|               | LoRa[5]       | SigFox[6]               | NB-IoT [7]  | Z-Wave[8]  | Wi-Fi[9]    |
|---------------|---------------|-------------------------|-------------|------------|-------------|
| **Cost**          | 3–5€          | 2–5€                    | 10–20€      | 8–12€      | < 2€        |
| **Data Rate**     | <50 kbps      | <100 bps                | <200 kbps   | <40 kbps   | <300 Mbps   |
| **Autonomy**      | <10 years     | <10 years               | <10 years   | <2 years   | <10 days    |
| **Range (urban)** | <5 km         | <10 km                  | <1 km       | <100 m     | <40 m       |
| Modulation    | CSS           | BPSK                    | QPSK        | FSK        | BPSK/QAM    |
| Bandwidth     | 125/250 kHz   | 100 Hz                  | 200 kHz     | 300 kHz    | 20/40 MHz   |
| Frequency (EU) | 868 MHz      | 868 MHz                 | LTE bands   | 868 MHz    | 2.4/5.0 GHz |
| Spectrum Cost | Free          | Free                    | Very High   | Free       | Free        |
| Max. msg/day  | Unlimited     | $140(\uparrow), 4(\downarrow)$ | Unlimited | Unlimited | Unlimited |
| Max. payload  | 243 bytes     | $12(\uparrow), 8(\downarrow)$ bytes | 1600 bytes | 64 bytes | 64 KB |

LoRa technology combines long-range connectivity with a considerable increase of the battery lifetime at a low-cost using sub-GHz unlicensed spectrum. LoRa uses a Chirp Spread-Spectrum (CSS) modulation schema which results in a considerably higher resistance to noise, interference or jamming signals, and also presents known advantages in terms of multi-path fading and the Doppler effect [5]. Although it needs a specific infrastructure based on LoRa Gateways to connect the smart devices to the Internet, it is a good alternative to Wi-Fi when low-power devices need to be deployed inside a building.

Sigfox is a company with its own proprietary technology that was designed specifically for the IoT-era. It is a sub-GHz technology that takes advantage of ultra-low channel bandwidth in the communication process, offering a simple and very light protocol stack that imposes hard restrictions in the number and size of the messages exchanged [6], in a daily basis, cf. Table 1. The company has its own communication infrastructure, being its access offered as a paid service.

NB-IoT (Narrowband IoT) is an LTE-based synchronous protocol developed under the 3GPP (Third Generation Partnership Project), that has been designed to address the needs of very low data rate and low-power devices that need to connect to the Internet using standard mobile networks [7]. As major disadvantages, one can identify its high cost, not only the smart device cost but also the operational cost due to the use of licensed spectrum, which also compromises its ecosystem development.

Z-Wave is a wireless technology specifically designed for remote control and home automation applications. It is a low-power communication technology that works in the sub-GHz frequency range and was designed to operate in a source-routed mesh network topology, where each device is able to send and receive control messages through walls or floors taking advantage of intermediate devices to route around household obstacles or radio dead spots that might occur [8]. As major disadvantages, one can identify its intermediate cost, low range capabilities, and autonomy, when battery operation is considered, cf. Table 1.

Wi-Fi is a mature technology with a large ecosystem widely used in smart building applications. There are several suppliers of Wi-Fi modules, cf. Table 1, ready for smart device integration at an affordable price. Moreover, it is a technology easy to deploy and integrate with existing IP networks. However, it presents two major drawbacks, the first is related to its reduced autonomy an the second is related to a small in-building communication coverage.

Finally, and regarding QoS (Quality of Service), protocols that rely on ISM frequency bands, i.e. unlicensed spectra, are more susceptible to interference, multipath, and fading phenomena, which delivers lower QoS, when compared with protocols that use licensed spectrum, such as NB-IoT. Given this, NB-IoT is, therefore, more appropriate for applications that demand guaranteed QoS. In smart building applications, the devices used for sensing and actuation are mainly designed to achieve low cost and long battery lifetime, and not requiring high QoS demand or frequent communication, which places the LoRa technology in advantage when this type of application is considered [4].

## 3   Smart Device Architecture

Figure 1 illustrates a simplified block diagram of the proposed Smart Device architecture. It was specified to operate in two distinct modes: (i) Data Collection Unit (DCU) or (ii) Physical Actuation Unit (PAU). When configured as a DCU, it will be equipped with a set of sensors for data acquisition (e.g. $CO_2$, Relative Humidity, Temperature, Air Pressure, and Radon). These sensors will be connected to a low-power microcontroller using distinct interfacing methods (analog or digital). All the attached sensors will be digitally controlled using analog power switches that will enable a proper power management of the overall device. On the other hand, when configured to operate as a PAU, it will take advantage of two actuation possibilities: one for remote ON/OFF control and the second for remote PWM (Pulse Width Modulation) control, thus enabling the possibility to remotely control an electric motor for fine ventilation. The user interface will be based on a single push-button and an RGB led.

Several sensors have been interfaced to the microcontroller. To obtain a raw estimate of the $CO_2$ level, we opted for the low-cost SNS-MQ135 from Olimex. This is a resistive gas sensor that does not directly provide the $CO_2$ level, but it can be computed indirectly by software after a calibration process, being its

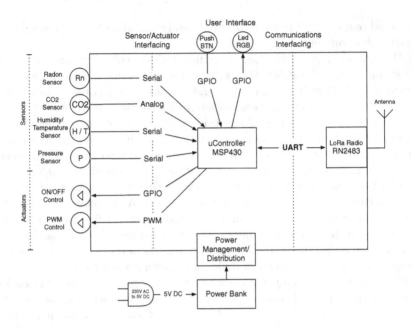

**Fig. 1.** Block diagram of the Compact LoRa Device.

precision highly dependent of this calibration process. The humidity and temperature are acquired using the HTS221 from STMicroelectronics, the maximum error for humidity is $\pm\,3.5\%$rH and for temperature is $\pm\,1°$C. The MPL3115A2 from NXP Semiconductors is used for air pressure measurements with a maximum error of $\pm\,0.4$ kPa. Lastly, the PCB provides a serial connection to an external Radon gas sensor through a specific connector. The Radon sensor considered was the RD200M that measures the radon level after stabilized for 1 hour with a precision of $\pm\,0.5$ pCi/l. The RD200M needs to operate in a continuous mode consuming approximately 60 mA and it will be only attached for specific application cases.

Regarding the power requirements and sensors specifications, we opted for an ultra-low-power microcontroller, i.e. the MSP430F247 from Texas Instruments. From the energetic point of view, the microcontroller consumes 270 $\mu$A in Active Mode at 1 MHz and just 0.3 $\mu$A in Standby Mode. In terms of digital and analog interfacing, it supports several serial communications protocols (UART, SPI, $I^2$C) and has multiple analog inputs that can be multiplexed to the input of an A/D module.

The Smart Device connectivity uses LoRa technology based on the RN2483 LoRa SoC (System-on-Chip), radio module manufactured by Microchip and designed to operate in Sub-GHz bands and therefore enabling long range, low power, and high network capacity [10]. The RN2483 LoRa SoC is equipped with a UART host interface for simple integration with a microcontroller via AT commands [10]. Its radio frontend can deliver to the antenna up to 14.0 dBm and presents a receiving input sensitivity of −148 dB.

The RN2483 LoRa SoC has no built-in antenna. The choice of an antenna involves the analyses of several aspects. For example, the direction of communication, the power gain required and the surrounding materials are some aspects that need to be considered in the antenna selection or design process. A list of requirements and a correct perception of the final application limitations is essential, especially in cases that include non-line-of-sight, such as in-building and inter-building communications.

## 3.1   Compact LoRa Antenna Design

The first aspect to be considered is the operating frequency. In Europe, LoRa operates in the 868 MHz ISM band. When using this ISM band the module operates with frequencies from 863 MHz to 870 MHz. The antenna should than be projected to operate in that frequency interval.

Furthermore, the smart device is supposed to operate inside buildings and, given the difficulty to predict the kind of environment that will be surrounding it, an omnidirectional radiation pattern should be considered. Nevertheless, it is also important to design the antenna having into account the metallic elements that are nearby, particularly in the PCB.

Given the necessity to design a small and compact device, all the metallic elements near the antenna, e.g. electronic components, microcontroller, and battery, must be carefully positioned. This proximity between parts may result in a great influence on the antenna performance and compromise the communication process. One possible solution is to use a commercial antenna. This approach has the advantage of achieving higher performance at a higher size and cost. Furthermore, a commercial antenna is not designed to be closer to metallic components and needs to be attached to the main board by means of a connector, which results in a lack of sturdiness and increased size. Another solution is to use a common monopole antenna. This type of antenna can be printed on the same board than the circuit and has an omnidirectional radiation pattern. However, this design is highly influenced by the surrounding environment and therefore not recommended for this application case.

In this work, we opted to use a Planar Inverted-F Antenna (PIFA), which is an alternative to the classic monopole antenna design. This design ensures more robustness regarding the surrounding environment without compromising the implementation and the omnidirectionality pattern. Besides the branch connected to the radiofrequency signal (RF), the PIFA also has a branch connected to the ground.

## 3.2   Simulation

The first step in the antenna design is to simulate the antenna based on its theoretical model. From this point, multiple adjustments in its dimensions are then made until the best results are achieved. This process is even more crucial when the antenna is close to a circuit or a ground plane, these elements have electrical characteristics that influence the antenna performance. More detailed information about the implications can be found in [11].

As we are focused on the design of a compact device, the PIFA antenna needs to be placed near the circuit, which can negatively impact the antenna performance. To mitigate this, the antenna was designed using the circuit presented in Figure 2 as the initial simulation model. The antenna was designed using the Computer Simulation Technology Studio Suite (CST Studio Suite).

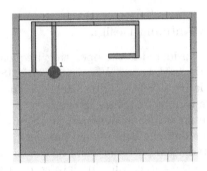

**Fig. 2.** Simulation model with groundplane and the PIFA antenna included.

In order to simplify the simulation process, the circuit has been imported to the simulator with a degree of abstraction, instead of representing all the circuit lines and components, the circuit was imported and converted to a ground plane. This abstraction does not compromise the results, since the metallic plane has the same influence represented by ground or lines, allowing a huge time-saving in the simulation.

Figure 3 illustrates the simulation results based on the $S_{11}$ parameter. In green is represented the theoretical model and in red the optimized model after multiple adjustments. Note that, the $S_{11}$ parameter represents the return loss, i.e. the reflected signal, and is directly related with the impedance mismatch from 50 ohms throughout the interconnection to the PIFA. In the frequency bands of interest, it is possible to observe an increase of performance of approximately 7.5 dB, between the theoretical and the optimized models.

The changes between the initial antenna and the optimized antenna are in terms of dimensions, the optimized antenna is more distant from the ground plane and the distance between branches are also different. Another important characteristic of the antenna is its omnidirectionality, cf. Fig. 4.

### 3.3   Field Experiments

The final circuit design and the assembled version can be seen in Fig. 5, where all relevant components can be observed, i.e. the PIFA antenna, the LoRa radio module, the microcontroller, sensors, and other passive components. The field

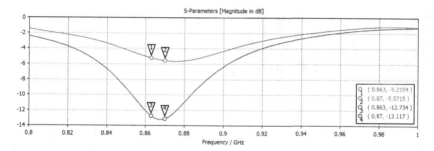

**Fig. 3.** $S_{11}$-parameter obtained after simulation. Green line represents the theoretical model and Red line represents the optimized model after multiple adjustments. (Color figure online)

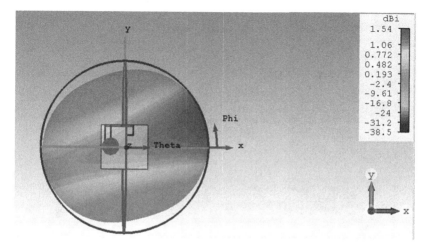

**Fig. 4.** Radiation diagram of the PIFA antenna using the PCB simplified model.

experiments were performed using two of these devices, one was configured as a transmitter and the other was configured as a receiver. The radio module used (RN2483) does not allow the measurement of any power indicator, such as the well-known RSSI, so the experiments were carried out to evaluate connectivity. The Printed Circuit Board dimensions are $91 \times 69$ mm.

Line-of-sight and urban environment connectivity were evaluated based on two field experiments, cf. Fig. 6. In both cases, one device was configured as a transmitter with an output power of 14 dBm and the second device was configured to operate as a receiver (sensitivity of $-143$ dBm). In both experiments, the receiver was placed in the roof of a building (blue marker). In the first experiment the transmitter was placed in line-of-sight situations (red markers), and in the second experiment, the transmitter was placed inside a car that was moving in an urban environment (green markers). The two devices presented successful

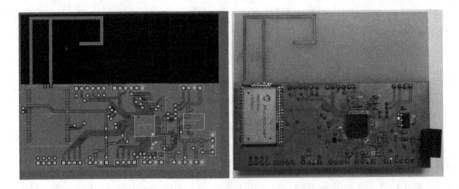

**Fig. 5.** PCB design with antenna and assembled version.

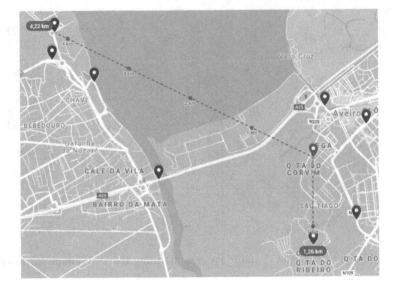

**Fig. 6.** Successful connectivity obtained for Line-of-sight (experiment 1) and urban environment (experiment 2) communications. (Color figure online)

communications up to distances of 4.2 km and 1.2 km, for the first and second experiment, respectively.

Indoor connectivity was evaluated based on two additional experiments, one to evaluate the in-building connectivity and other to evaluate the inter-building connectivity with neighbor buildings, cf. Fig. 7. In both experiments, the receiver was placed inside a building (blue marker) at the underground level. In the third experiment the transmitter was placed in distinct positions inside the same building at the same level in non-line-of-sight situations (green markers), and in the fourth experiment, the transmitter was placed in two distinct neighbor buildings (red markers) at upper levels. The longest distance that the devices were able to communicate in this environment was 152 m.

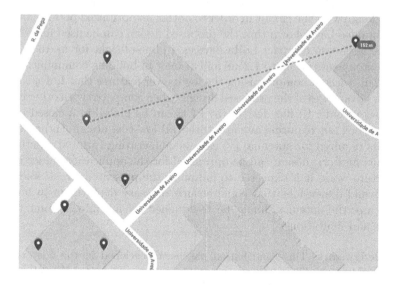

**Fig. 7.** Successful connectivity obtained for in-building (experiment 3) and inter-building (experiment 4) communications. (Color figure online)

Regarding the power consumption the device can be separated into three distinct modes: (1) Transmission mode - happens when a communication is performed and consumes approximately 39.2 mA; (2) Sensing mode - occurs when the sensors are acquiring data, the consumption depends on the sensor, being 40.2 mA for measuring $CO_2$, 280.6 $\mu$A for Temperature/Humidity and 542.1 uA for air pressure; (3) Sleep mode - when the device is not performing any task, consuming 9.4 $\mu$A.

Considering that the device performs one set of measurements per hour, i.e. sensing mode, and it takes around one second to do the job, the consumption in this mode is around 11.1 $\mu$A. Furthermore, and considering that the device transmits hourly with a transmission period of approximately one second, the consumption in the transmission mode is approximately 10.9 $\mu$A. In the remaining time, i.e. 3596 seconds per hour, the device is in Sleep mode consuming 9.4 $\mu$A. Adding these values we can estimate the overall average consumption of the device, i.e. 31.4 $\mu$A. Taking into account that the device can be powered by a CR2477 coin cell (that has a power capacity of 1000 mAh), and if we consider the profile of operation previously introduced, the device can operate for a period of approximately 3 years and 7 months. This power budget does not include the RD200M Radon sensor due to its power needs. In applications that demand Radon monitoring, the smart device must be continuously connected to the public power grid or powered by an alternative energy source, e.g. photovoltaic panel.

## 4  Conclusions and Future Work

Regarding the antenna design, it was proved that it is crucial to integrate the antenna design with the circuit in order to obtain an optimized performance. The results obtained have shown that the proposed design can be used for communication, between two compact LoRa devices, in line-of-sight for up to 4.2 km, in urban environments for up to 1.2 km and also for in-building communications for up to 152 m, without compromising the low-power features that LoRa supports.

Major advantages of the proposed design, when compared with other common approaches include: (i) flat design; (ii) PCB can be placed in a closed box, e.g. waterproof box not requiring any aperture; (iii) low-cost design; (iv) no external connectors required for antenna; (v) easy manufacturing (printed together with the circuit) and (vi) design can be optimized for the application under interest.

As future work, it is expected to minimize the presented circuit and to create forms and dimensions that could ensure and easy deployment in buildings. In that case, the antenna should be re-designed having into account the new materials and limitations.

**Acknowledgments.** This contribution has been developed in the context of the Project "RnMonitor - Online Monitoring Infrastructure and Active Mitigation Strategies for Indoor Radon Gas in Public Buildings on the Northern Region of Portugal (Ref: POCI-01-0145-FEDER-023997)" funded by FEDER (Fundo Europeu de Desenvolvimento Regional) through Operational Programme for Competitiveness and Internationalization (POCI).

## References

1. Kumar, A., Singh, K., Bhattacharya, D.: Green communication and wireless networking. In: 2013 International Conference on Green Computing, Communication and Conservation of Energy (ICGCE), Chennai, pp. 49–52 (2013). https://doi.org/10.1109/ICGCE.2013.6823398
2. Ramírez, I.U., Tello, N.A.B.: A survey of challenges in green wireless communications research. In: 2014 International Conference on Mechatronics, Electronics and Automotive Engineering, Cuernavaca, pp. 197–200 (2014). https://doi.org/10.1109/ICMEAE.2014.29
3. Buckman, A.H., Mayfield, M., Beck, S.B.M.: What is a smart building? Smart Sustain. Built Environ. **3**(2), 92–109 (2014). https://doi.org/10.1108/SASBE-01-2014-0003
4. Mekki, K., Bajic, E., Chaxel, F., Meyer, F.: A comparative study of LPWAN technologies for large-scale IoT deployment. ICT Express (2018). ISSN 2405–9595. https://doi.org/10.1016/j.icte.2017.12.005
5. Sornin, N., Luis, M., Eirich, T., Kramp, T., Hersent, O.: LoRaWAN Specification, v1.0, January 2015
6. Sigfox: Sigfox technical overview, May 2017

7. Zayas, A.D., Merino, P.: The 3GPP NB-IoT system architecture for the Internet of Things. In: 2017 IEEE International Conference on Communications Workshops (ICC Workshops), Paris, pp. 277–282 (2017). https://doi.org/10.1109/ICCW.2017. 7962670

8. Honeywell: Introduction to Z-Wave: An Introductory Guide to Z-Wave Technology, February 2013

9. Air802: IEEE 802.11 a/b/g/n Wi-Fi Standards and Facts. https://www.air802. com/ieee-802.11-standards-facts-amp-channels.html. Accessed 2 Aug 2018

10. Microchip: Low-Power Long Range LoRa Technology Transceiver Module, RN2483 Datasheet, March 2015. Accessed April 2017

11. Pereira, F., Pinho, P., Gonçalves, R., Carvalho, N.B., Lobato, J., Lopes, S.I.: Antenna design for ultra-compact Bluetooth devices. In: IEEE International Symposium on Antennas and Propagation & USNC/URSI National Radio Science Meeting, San Diego, CA, pp. 2619–2620 (2017). https://doi.org/10.1109/ APUSNCURSINRSM.2017.8073352

# Electro-Optical System for Evaluation of Dynamic Inductive Wireless Power Transfer to Electric Vehicles

Luiz A. Lisboa Cardoso[1,2(✉)], Dehann Fourie[2], John J. Leonard[2],
Andrés A. Nogueiras Meléndez[3], and João L. Afonso[1]

[1] Centro Algoritmi, University of Minho, Guimarães, Portugal
lisboa.cardoso@ieee.org, jla@dei.uminho.pt
[2] Marine Robotics Group, Massachusetts Institute of Technology,
Cambridge, MA, USA
[3] Department of Electronics Technology, University of Vigo, Vigo, Spain

**Abstract.** Inductive lanes that can wirelessly transfer power to moving electric vehicles is a research theme of worldwide interest. The goal is to provide on-the-road recharging, thus extending vehicle's autonomy and reducing battery capacity requirements. These lanes share, however, a common limitation: the power transfer is affected by the lateral displacement of the vehicle, with respect to the center of the lane. In the case of two-wheeled vehicles, such as electric scooters and bicycles, lateral inclination can also be pronounced enough as to interfere with power coupling. In order to experimentally evaluate the characteristics of such vehicular dynamic power transfer schemes, it is then necessary to synchronously log the vehicle's electric data, lateral displacement and attitude. In this paper, the design and implementation of an electro-optical measuring system with these capabilities, based on Light Detection and Ranging (LIDAR) technology and inertial sensors, is reported. A testing range with specific reference geometry, consisting of a corridor of parallel walls, is used to simplify the continuous and accurate estimation of lateral displacement. The design was validated by statistical characterization of the measurement errors, using simulated trajectories. A prototype was built and mounted on a non-electric bicycle, with the first tests confirming its positioning measurement qualities.

**Keywords:** Dynamic wireless power transfer · Inductive lanes ·
Vehicular power harvesting · LIDAR-based positioning

## 1 Introduction

Successful prototypes of dynamic inductive wireless power transfer (DIWPT) systems have been implemented [1, 2], but no dominant technical solution has been yet established. The prospective benefits of DIWPT, however, largely justify further research efforts to improve this technology. Firstly, the battery capacity requirements of electric vehicles (EV) will be reduced, thus reducing vehicle's initial and life-cycle costs. At the same time, their autonomy will be augmented, depending solely on the

© ICST Institute for Computer Sciences, Social Informatics and Telecommunications Engineering 2019
Published by Springer Nature Switzerland AG 2019. All Rights Reserved
J. L. Afonso et al. (Eds.): GreeNets 2018, LNICST 269, pp. 154–174, 2019.
https://doi.org/10.1007/978-3-030-12950-7_13

widespread use of inductive lanes (i-lanes) in the urban design. The use of multiple EV and i-lanes will, on the other hand, allow more flexible spatiotemporal options for the equilibrium of demand from the power grid, especially if smart vehicle-to-grid (V2G) technology is also considered [3]. All these factors combined shall favor the large-scale adoption of EV, in substitution of thermal-engine powered vehicles.

The great expectation around the future proliferation of dynamic inductive wireless power transfer as a standard technic for providing on-the-road charging [4–6] constitutes the motivation for developing a robust, accurate and inexpensive method for characterizing and evaluating the performance of such systems.

## 1.1  Dynamic Inductive Wireless Power Transfer Systems

In a DIWPT system, when the vehicle moves forward along its path, its pick-up (secondary) coil will cross the magnetic field generated by stationary primary coils placed underneath the floor, along the vehicle's path. The system effectiveness will depend on the appropriated time-spatial coil activation pattern, which is ensured by the power electronic design, but also and fundamentally by good magnetic coupling between the lane and the vehicle, which is ultimately influenced by distance and misalignment between primary and secondary coils.

Even with the use of precise autonomous navigation, some tolerance in the vehicle-to-lane lateral misalignment must be handled by the system [7], this parameter being perhaps the most critical one for human-driven EVs. The measurement of power availability on board of vehicle as a function of lateral displacement over the i-lane is then crucial for the evaluation of a DIWPT system.

## 1.2  Positioning Measurement Techniques

The evaluation of DIWPT requires tracking the position and attitude of an EV relative to the lane, while power is also being monitored. Desirable dynamic accuracies are in the order of one to two centimeters for positioning, and of a few degrees of arc for the estimation of attitude, this latter being achieved by inexpensive inertial measurement units (IMU). All position variables are expected to be sampled tens of times per second, to adequately represent EV trajectories.

In the FABRIC project [8], a recent representative effort in the quest for practical DIWPT, a 100 m long i-lane was tested for vehicle lateral misalignment using RTK Real-Time Kinematic (RTK) Global Positioning System (GPS). In this phase-sensing based variant of Differential GPS (DGPS), positioning accuracies in the order of one centimeter can be achieved [9]. However, current best commercial RTK-GPS receivers have a maximum positioning update rate in the order of 20 Hz [10, 11], which is just marginally acceptable for DIWPT analysis. These systems are also costly and relatively complex, requiring the transmission of a correction signal from a base station to the mobile station whose positioning is being measured.

Optical positioning measurements, using calibrated cameras and visual fiducial markers [12] and, often, infrared dot-markers, can deliver better accuracies at the required speed rates, in indoors tracking applications [13]. However, their simplicity is diminished when positioning of objects over longer paths, due to the need of increasing the number of coordinated cameras to cover extended areas.

In this work, a special reference geometry was imposed to the test site, allowing the use of LIDARs fixed on an instrument, which is attached to the EV, to directly measure its position. The calculus of the vehicle-to-lane lateral misalignment was significantly simplified by a robust computation neither involving computer vision processing techniques nor requiring inertial data, which are still required for determining vehicle's attitude and forward progress on lane.

## 2    System Design

### 2.1    Requirements

The current system implementation is to be used in the evaluation of DIWPT to lightweight electric vehicles, such as electrically assisted bicycles [14]. For this application, the nominal kinematic parameter limits are given in Table 1.

**Table 1.** Limit parameters assumed for the EV (electrically-assisted bike).

| Parameter | Maximum absolute value |
|---|---|
| Speed | 36 km/h (10 m/s) |
| Lateral acceleration | 3g (3 × 9.81 m/s$^2$) |
| Relative (to lane) yaw angle | 30° |
| Roll angle | 15° |

The range of measurements and the respective desirable order of error magnitude will vary with application and the objectives of the analysis, as well as the specific characteristics of the power train of the vehicle in test. For instance, typical nominal powertrain voltages for electrically assisted bikes are multiple of 12 V, often 24 V or 36 V. Without much information found on general DIWPT evaluation tools currently available, as well as on DIWPT systems specifically implemented for e-bikes [15], values from own experience guided the adoption of the representative values shown in Table 2:

**Table 2.** Target range and precision for vehicle onboard measurements.

| Parameter | Range | Std dev of error |
|---|---|---|
| Lateral displacement | −0.5 to 0.5°m | <2.5 cm |
| DC harvested voltage | 0 to 100 V | 2% of full scale |
| Power train voltage | 0–40 V | 2% of full scale |
| Powertrain demand | 0 to 500 W | 3% of full scale |
| Relative yaw | −30° to 30° | 5° |
| Pitch | −10° to 10° | 2° |
| Roll | −15° to 15° | 2° |

## 2.2   System Overview

The system is implemented as a remote sensing unit to be mounted onto an electric vehicle. Figure 1 shows its high-level block diagram representation: Positional and electric data from the vehicle's WPT receiver (WPT RX) and power-train are collected and wirelessly transmitted via a UHF channel, in real time, to a receiver unit that is connected to a computer (running the Analysis System) through a USB communication port. Electric data coming from the i-lane WPT transmitters (WPT TX) can optionally be monitored and synchronized to the vehicular data.

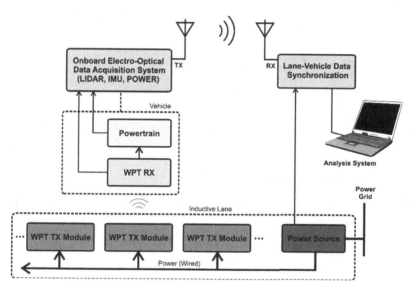

**Fig. 1.**   System global architecture, showing vehicle and lane subsystems. All data collected are synchronized and logged for off-line analysis.

## 2.3   Reference Geometry

The system works on the principle that the vehicle's position can be established by knowing the position of a fixed reference geometry. Three individual LIDAR sensors are simultaneously used to measure the lateral distance to the walls of a reference corridor, where the primary inductive modules of the i-lane to be tested lie underneath the floor. Figure 2 illustrates the top view of such configuration, where a single inductive module is under test. Inductive lane modules are aligned and centralized in between the parallel to the walls (A) of a reference corridor. The measurement unit is installed on the electric vehicle running over the inductive lane, indicated in Fig. 2 by a blue dashed curve (C). For lanes of short length, a rear flat surface (B) can be optionally used for referencing the rear LIDAR, if measurements of vehicle speed and longitudinal progress on lane are also required in the analysis.

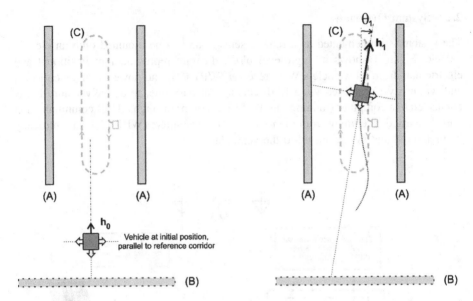

**Fig. 2.** Top view of test range: vehicle at initial position (left) and running in corridor (right). (Color figure online)

### 2.4 LIDAR-IMU Head Design

The heart of the measuring system is the LIDAR-IMU mounting head, drawn in Fig. 3, is a precision machined prismatic rectangular aluminum block of squared base, fixed to the vehicle's structure, mechanically solidary to the pick-up coil used to receive power from the i-lane, where all LIDARs and the IMU are mounted to.

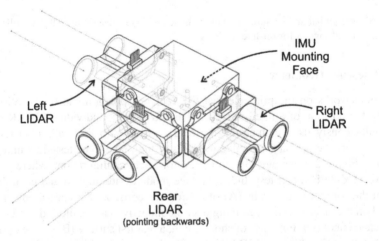

**Fig. 3.** Perspective view of the LIDAR head mounting. An inertial sensor, not shown in the figure, is fixed to the face of the block which is opposite to the face the rear LIDAR is mounted on, with its inertial refence axes orthogonal to the faces of the block.

The left and right LIDAR are align-mounted on opposite parallel faces of the block, with beams pointing opposite directions. A third rear LIDAR is mounted on a face of the block that is orthogonal to the faces of the left and right LIDAR, with its beam pointing backwards, in such a way that all the LIDAR beams are in the same plan, adjusted to be as horizontal as possible, when the assembly is fixed to the vehicle's frame, while the vehicle is resting in a neutral position.

## 2.5  Positional and Attitude Estimation

**Attitude.** The IMU embedded in the instrument continuously computes estimates for the spatial orientation of the vehicle, given by Euler angles, yaw, pitch and roll $(h_k, \rho_k, \gamma_k)$. By construction, yaw (horizontal orientation) and heading (direction of movement) will always coincide, unless the vehicle is skidding on the lane, so these terms are indistinctly used in this work. The last two of these angles, represent inclination with respect to the horizontal and vertical. The absolute yaw $h_k$ estimated by the IMU at any given measurement cycle $k$, however, has to be transformed in the relative orientation angle $\theta_k$, by subtracting the yaw reading obtained at the initially aligned start position ($h_0$, on the left side of Fig. 2) from the current yaw reading (for instance, $h_1$, as shown on the right side of Fig. 2):

$$\theta_k = h_k - h_0 \tag{1}$$

**Progress on Lane.** It is the distance $y$ from the vehicle (LIDAR-IMU head) to the back-wall, taken along the lane. It is measured by computing the projection of the back-LIDAR beam length $d_B(k)$ onto the lane longitudinal axis:

$$y = d_B(k) . \cos \theta_k . \cos \gamma_k \tag{2}$$

If the reference point on the vehicle is not the center of the LIDAR-IMU head, the corresponding coordinate transform should be additionally applied.

**Lateral Displacement.** Whereas the Euler angles are necessary to estimate the distance progressed on the lane, to correct the readings of back LIDAR beams to the back wall, (B) in Fig. 2, the lateral displacement can be directly computed as function of the lateral LIDAR measurements only: Due to deliberate construction of the LIDAR head (Sect. 2.4) and control circuit, beams of the left and right LIDAR at cycle $k$ are both simultaneous and colinear, so the lateral displacement $x_k$ of the EV with respect to center line of the lane can be determined by the proportion of the left and right LIDAR readings, according to (3):

$$x_k = \frac{w_c}{2} \frac{(d_L(k) - d_R(k))}{(d_L(k) + d_R(k) + w_L)} \tag{3}$$

where $d_L(k)$ and $d_R(k)$ are respectively the calibrated readings of the left and right LIDAR (as in Fig. 12), $w_c > 0$ is the width of the corridor and $w_L > 0$ is the distance between opposite external faces of the housing of the measurement unit, from where LIDAR distances are calibrated.

## 2.6 Modeling of Errors

Using (3) to compute the raw lateral displacement, $x_k$, which is a sample of the associated aleatory variable $X_k$, has one more benefit other than not depending on the inertial sensor data processed at the IMU: the standard deviation for $X_k$ can be smaller than those of individual measurements coming from any of the LIDARs, left or right.

Let's assume that both lateral LIDARs have the same behavior and are statistically independent. So, $d_L(k)$ and $d_R(k)$ are samples of aleatory variables $D_L(k)$ and $D_R(k)$, such that:

$$D_i(k) = T_i(k) + E_i, \qquad E_i \sim N(0, \sigma_L^2), \ i \in \{L, R\} \tag{4}$$

where $T_L(k)$ and $T_R(k)$ are the true, but unknown, beam lengths from each LIDAR to its respective target wall, and $E_L$ and $E_R$ are aleatory errors that can be modeled by independent identical normal distributions with zero mean and standard deviation $\sigma_L$. Under these simplifying assumptions, a vehicle running parallel to the corridor will have a normalized standard deviation $\sigma/\sigma_L$ varying according to its relative lateral displacement, as shown in the plot of Fig. 4 (obtained by numerical simulation).

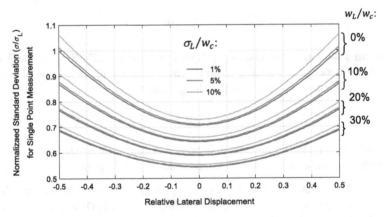

**Fig. 4.** Normalized standard deviation of lateral displacement estimation, given by (2), as a function of the true relative lateral displacement in the corridor (−0.5 means vehicle at left wall and +0.5, at right wall). The curves are shown for different constructive $w_L/w_c$ ratios and relative standard deviations $\sigma_L/w_c$ of the LIDAR measuring errors.

At the limit condition $w_L/w_c = 0$, for small $\sigma_L/w_c$ ratios (5% or less), the standard deviation of $X_k$ can still be up to approximately 30% smaller than $\sigma_L$, when the vehicle is close to the center of the lane, thus improving the quality of the lateral displacement measurement with respect to a single LIDAR measurement, as expected under the assumption of statistical independence of the errors on the two measurements $d_L(k)$ and $d_R(k)$. For the LIDAR components used in the design, the standard deviation errors $E_i$ of are proportional to the distances to be read, $T_i(k)$, ranging around 1% for distances 1 m and above. So, by using calibrated LIDARs, the standard deviation of a single measurement of the lateral displacement can be reduced up to approximately 0.7%, when the vehicle lies in the central region of the corridor. That corresponds to a ±7 mm error for 2 m wide corridor, when travelling parallel to the reference walls. By filtering or smoothing a series of consecutive measurements along a trajectory, the random error can be further minimized, depending on vehicle kinematics.

In the analysis of DIWPT applications, rather than logging the position of the mounting head itself, often the center of the pick-up coil installed on the EV will be the point of reference for measuring misalignment. Since the pick-up coil is also mechanically solidary to the frame of the vehicle, a simple transform can compute the movement of the coil center (or any other point fixed on the vehicle), based on the estimated position of the center of the LIDAR-IMU block.

## 2.7   Reduction of Error Variance

Assuming a smooth and flat lane with no obstacles, and no intrinsic vehicle vibration due to the power train or other factors, the perturbation on the vehicle movement can be entirely attributed to the human control when riding (or steering), which is ultimately related with human skeletal muscles movements. Since the fastest human hand or finger movements that can be produced lie in the range between 6 to 12 Hz [16], $f_{pos}$, the sampling rate for measuring the vehicle position, can be conservatively set at 60 Hz. A low-pass filter matching this expected bandwidth, with cutting frequency of 12 Hz, is used to condition the sequence of calibrated readings of each LIDAR, reducing the standard deviation of distance estimations.

A Finite Impulse Response (FIR) smoothing window, associated with a low-pass filter with a cutting frequency of 12 Hz and maximally flat response over the pass band, was designed and integrated in the analysis software. Filter coefficients and frequency magnitude response characteristics are shown in Fig. 5.

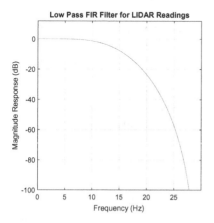
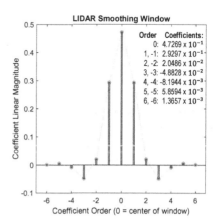

**Fig. 5.** Characteristics of the smoothing window for the LIDAR readings, implemented as a low-pass FIR filter of order 12, for the design LIDAR sampling frequency of 60 Hz.

Assuming an error modeling as in Sect. 2.6, for all LIDARs in the system, the statistical behavior of the error in lateral displacement (3) estimation for any known vehicle trajectory can then be computed by Monte Carlo simulations. Results in Fig. 6 were obtained for the case of a vehicle at the limit design maximum speed of 10 m/s (36 km/h), maneuvering in a sinusoidal pattern along the lane with maximum lateral acceleration of 29.4 m/s$^2$ (3g, three times the acceleration of the gravity on Earth's surface), within the walls of corridor with width $w_c = 178$ cm.

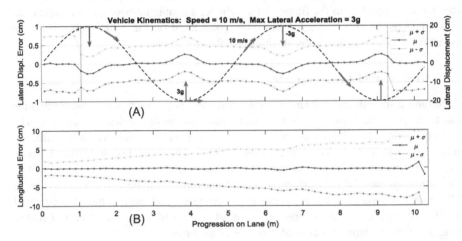

**Fig. 6.** Simulated statistics of positioning error, showing expected mean and standard deviation error for a vehicle on sinusoidal trajectory at limit design kinematics. (A) Upper graph shows error behavior in vehicle's lateral displacement measurement, as the vehicle progresses forward on the lane; (B) lower graph shows tendency for errors in longitudinal position.

The error pattern in lateral displacement is regular along the vehicle's trajectory, with mean $\mu$ zero most of the time, except at maximum excursions, when the measurement will lag the movement, resulting in a biased error up to approximately 3 mm. The standard deviation of the error remains practically constant, about 5 mm along all the lane, except for the first and last $N/2$ measurements on the lane, due to the smoothing window filter order N, where it raises to values of the standard deviation of a single measurement. These values will vary proportionally to the intrinsic standard deviation characteristic of the LIDAR readings, which will depend on the actual LIDAR model and the geometry ($w_c$) of the reference corridor being used.

## 2.8   Longitudinal Error

In Fig. 6(B), the longitudinal error can be noted to be unbiased along all the vehicle's path. The standard deviation, however, starts with a minimum value $\sigma_L$ in the order of 2 cm, and increases approximately in proportion to the progression on the lane, due to the dependency of the forward displacement estimation on a single back LIDAR reading, which has a standard deviation that is also proportional to the distance to the back wall, set 2 m behind the corridor entrance, the point of zero progression.

This behavior limits the application of the proposed configuration to lane modules up to about 6 m long, in the case secondary measurements related to forward movement of a vehicle are to be performed. For lateral displacement measurements, there is no such limitation, if the reference corridor is long enough to enclose the lane module to be evaluated.

## 2.9   System Block Diagram

**Onboard Wireless Electro-Optical Monitor.** This unit, as detailed in the block diagram of Fig. 7, has three LIDARs, one pointing right, one pointing left and one pointing backwards. All these LIDAR (Garmin Lite v3) and the IMU (Bosch BNO-055) are connected by a 400 kbit/s I2C bus to a master 32-bit STM32F103 microcontroller, the "Position Processor", which runs a supervisor program that every 16.67 ms gets the distance measurements from the LIDAR sensors, the Euler angles from the IMU, and the vehicle electric data coming through a dedicated 230.4 kbaud/s asynchronous serial bus from another 32-bit microcontroller, named the "Electric Data Processor". To accommodate different timing requirements, data from different sensors are buffered in one cycle and transmitted in the next cycle.

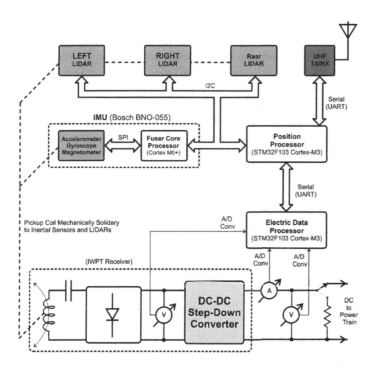

**Fig. 7.** Electro-optical data acquisition system architecture on board of the electric vehicle.

The adoption of a sampling period $T_{pos} = 16.67$ ms for the positional data, corresponds to a sampling frequency, $f_{pos}$, of 60 Hz, which implies (Nyquist Theorem) in a maximum tolerable bandwidth for the vehicle movement $B_{pos} = f_{pos}/2 = 30$ Hz.

Based on the predicted bandwidth limitation of 6 to 12 Hz, as seen in Sect. 2.7, all LIDAR calibrated measures can be further subjected to a low pass filter to reduce the variance of measurement errors.

The Electric Data Processor, on the other hand, performs analog-to-digital conversion on the signals coming from two voltmeter channels, which share a common ground reference, and a third channel sending data from a galvanically isolated Hall-effect amperemeter. When monitoring the electric vehicle, the amperemeter channel is intended to be associated with one of the voltage channels in a series-parallel connection. Power is computed by discrete integration of the product of these readings. The sample rate of the electric signals, $f_{power}$, was set to 6 kHz, a hundred times greater than $f_{pos}$. A new power estimate, integrated over the most recent 16.67 ms interval, is produced every $T_{power} = 166.7\,\mu s = 16.67\,ms/100$, and becomes available to be asynchronously read upon request of the Position Processor. The rms values for all other electric signals are similarly computed. In this manner, although the electric data is read just once every 16.67 ms, there will be no loss of information on the total power and average effective values of voltages and current, except where induced by noise or arithmetic rounding errors, if the maximum electric data bandwidth is limited to $B_{power} = f_{power}/2 = 3$ kHz.

The power transferred in a DIWPT configuration is expected to depend mostly on: (i) the relative position of the WPT receiver (in the vehicle) and the WPT transmitter (in the lane), which is also assumed to be bandwidth limited to $B_{pos}$; (ii) the fluctuations on the power demand of the powertrain; and (iii) the switching state (ON/OFF) and time response of the power electronics driving the WPT transmitter and receiver. To facilitate evaluating the profile of the maximum WPT as a function of lateral displacement, the WPT transmitter should be kept always activated, and the load coupled to the WPT receiver, on board of the vehicle, should be made constant. The system developed is then furnished with a dummy DC load to momentarily replace the power train during maximum transferred power profile tests.

Positional and electric data are packed together into 26-byte frames, including a time tag and a check-sum word, and periodically transmitted over UHF at 38400 baud/s. The UHF radio-modem used can be programmed to output power levels up to 20 dBm (100 mW), using any of 100 channels in the 433.4–473.0 MHz band. This is enough power to achieve virtually errorless transmission up to 30 m range in free space, a distance by design much larger than the length of the inductive modules and lane segments the equipment was built to monitor.

**Remote Vehicle Data Logger.** This unit receives and logs the vehicle data to a "Data Log Computer", as shown in the block diagram of Fig. 8. It can also optionally monitor and log electric data coming from the i-lane. A "Lane Activity Log Processor" acquires electrical data from the lane and merges it into data frames coming from the electro-optical measuring system installed on board of the vehicle. Because of the delays involved in measuring and transmitting over the UHF link the positional and electrical data coming from the EV, the "Lane Activity Log Processor" has to introduce compensatory delays in the lane data stream, to time-align both data sources.

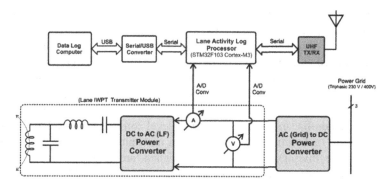

**Fig. 8.** System architecture on the lane side: real time data coming from vehicle is received and associated with simultaneous electric data sampled from the lane WPT transmitter module.

## 2.10   Supplementary System Sensors

Beyond the LIDAR-IMU based power and positioning monitoring system, other two independent subsystems were integrated into the developed equipment as general tools for future use, in support of the evaluation of DIWPT of EVs:

**Scanning LIDAR.** A short range (8 m) scanning LIDAR that rotates continuously at 5 to 15 Hz (300 to 900 rpm), providing 360° horizontal scan, with up to 4000 distance readings per second (model A2M8, manufactured by Shanghai Slamtec Co., Ltd.) It will allow future investigation of simultaneous localization and mapping (SLAM) techniques [17] as an alternative for positioning determination. Its current function is solely to provide panoramic LIDAR scene visualization, for checking consistence of the positioning data logged in the test runs.

**Voltage Data Logger.** A four-channel, differential analog-to-digital converter, of up to 40 kSamples/s per channel, data-logging system, for monitoring other electrical signal on board of the vehicle was also installed in the rack. The gain of each channel can be independently programmed to allow measuring signals up to ±100 V in amplitude. Data can be logged locally on disk, for posterior analysis, or relayed over a Wi-Fi link, for remote real-time system monitoring. It can, for instance, be used as a redundant power logging system, if additional current sensors are installed on the EV.

## 3   Implementation

### 3.1   Power Measurement Module

The implementation of power measurement subsystem was conceived and cost-optimized to evaluate electrically assisted DIWPT bicycles [14, 15]. It has two independent voltmeters and one amperemeter. One of the two voltmeter channels is associated with the amperemeter channel to provide power readings of the input to the power train or the substitute dummy load. The other voltmeter channel can be used, for instance, to measure the voltage at the DC output of the WPT receiver and pattern the voltage and power availability at any given position. All channels and the power product are sampled at 6 kHz and integrated over the most recent period of 16.67 ms, to provide readings of rms values over the positioning measurement cycles. The Hall sensor used in the design (ACS-712-30A, from Allegro MicroSystems, LLC) converts current to voltage with a factor of 66 mV/A, and a worst-case output accuracy of 1.5% at 25 °C, due to non-linearity. The zero current level corresponds to a 2.5 V output of the Hall sensor. The voltmeter channels have a maximum 0.5% error due to restive networks (voltage divisor). All conditioned signals are presented before the A/D (analog to digital) converter inputs of the microcontroller (STM32F103, from ST Microelectronics), with a reading range from 0 to 3.3 V at 12-bit, with a maximum total conversion error of $\pm$ 7.5 LSB (least significant bit) and a typical maximum error of $\pm4.3$ LSB at 25 °C, as shown in Table 3.

**Table 3.** Electric data typical maximum errors at 25 °C for uncalibrated single measurements.

| Channel | Reading | Range | Multiplier | Uncalibrated error |
|---------|---------|-------|------------|--------------------|
| $V_H$ | High side voltage | 0 to 134.2 V | 1/41.6667 | 0.5% + 4.3/4096 = 1.6% |
| $V_L$ | Low side voltage | 0 to 45.1 V | 1/13.6667 | 0.5% + 4.3/4096 = 1.6% |
| $I$ | Current | −12.1 to 30 A | 66 mV/A | 1.5% + 4.3/2703 = 3.1% |
| $P_H$ | High side power | −1.6 to 4 kW | (indirect) | 1.6% + 3.1% = 4.7% |
| $P_L$ | Low side power | −545 to 1353 W | (indirect) | 1.6% + 3.1% = 4.7% |

The instantaneous maximum power error (of a single measurement), given by the product of $I \times V_k$, can be computed by adding the relative errors of $I$ and $V_k$, that is, 1.6% + 3.1% = 4.7%. System calibration, however, can greatly compensate errors due to non-linearity, leaving practically only the typical random A/D conversion errors of respectively 1.1% and 1.6% for voltages and current. This gives a precision of 2.7% for instantaneous power readings, a figure that, for slow varying signals, can be further reduced when integrating the $N = 6\,\text{kHz}/60\,\text{Hz} = 100$ power samples in the average power calculation performed on the Electric Data Processor.

## 3.2  Attitude, Positioning and Electric Data Synchronization

Each single LIDAR measurement computed and logged at $f_s = 60$ samples per second, is obtained from the integration of individual pulse readings at a faster rate (>10 kHz), until a good correlation peak is detected in the return signal, backscattered by the reference walls. The maximum number of scan pulses used in this scan process can be programmed, and was experimentally optimized at 16, for a good balance between fast, stable and accurate readings. The correlation analysis of each of these pulse trains is accomplished in the mean time $t_{corr} = 2$ ms.

Euler angles are also logged at 60 samples per second, but their readings come from an inner data fusion estimation process running on the IMU, at a rate $f_{IMU} = 100\,\text{Hz}$. Since $f_s$ and $f_{IMU}$ are asynchronous, the IMU data can be up to $1/f_{IMU} = 10\,\text{ms}$ "old" with respect to the reading time. Similarly, the supervisor program running on the Position Processor executes several tasks along each 16.67 ms cycle, in such a manner that different sensors are not read at the same time. UHF transmission is not an instantaneous process as well: beyond the almost negligible propagation delay, the data is cached into a dedicated modulation processor and transmitted at 38.4 kbaud/s. Careful analysis and experimental timing evaluation of all processes involved in the computation of measurements resulted in the simplified timing diagram in Fig. 9, which shows the main events of the system, from LIDAR reading start until all data from vehicle is available at the stationary receiver on the lane side. A new data set of measurements is available every 16.67 ms.

Precise analysis of the logged data should take these delays into consideration, to time-align the lagging lateral displacement measurement (based only on LIDAR readings), the attitude measurements, the EV electrical measurements and the electric measurements coming from the i-lane.

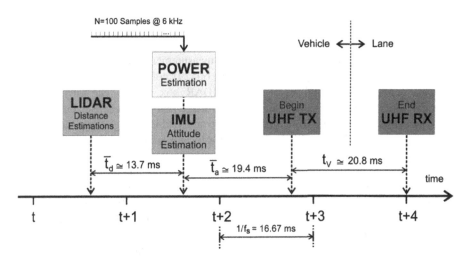

**Fig. 9.** Time line of main events in the system, from measurements on board of EV to UHF transmission and synchronization with lane data.

### 3.3   Prototype Integration

The electronics of the system were organized into two printed circuit board units, one for the LIDAR-IMU control and the other for power measurement, both using STM32F103 32-bit microcontrollers (Cortex-M3 core architecture), with a clock speed of 72 MHz (Fig. 10).

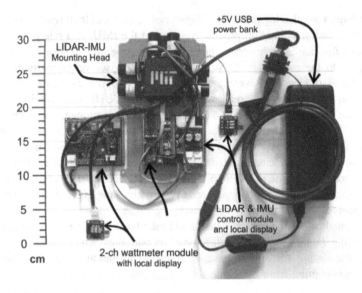

**Fig. 10.** Modules of the electro-optical measurement unit electrically connected during functional tests, before being mechanically integrated (except the power bank) into an IP68 housing.

The LIDAR-IMU control and the power measurement units were stacked and housed in an IP68 (according to IEC standard 60529) polycarbonate enclosure with clear lid, resulting in a total $w_L = 14$ cm (LIDAR box width). The only external electrical wired connections, those for power, voltage and current sensor inputs, uses IP68 compatible connectors. Inside the enclosure and visible through the clear lid were installed two organic LED (OLED) displays, for local reading of measurements made by each of the two modules. The watertightness of the assembly was, however, severely impaired by the holes drilled to let the LIDAR beams and their respective back scattering rays pass through the laterals of the box. For dust protection, 2 mm cast transparent acrylic windows were introduced to cover the LIDAR beam holes. These acrylic windows are also transparent (>85% transmission) at the 905 nm wavelength (infrared) emission of the LIDAR type used. Their effect in attenuating and delaying the LIDAR signals can be compensated by calibration procedures, with the maximum detection range being degraded, but experimentally verified to be still over 10 m, enough for the application. For testing vehicles outdoors in arbitrary weather, it would be necessary to redesign the LIDAR protection windows, so that the adequate water-tightness grade is met.

The power demand of the electric powertrain will depend on the acceleration and mechanical drag forces imposed to the vehicle, greatly varying along the vehicle progression on its path. A useful test condition is then to force the power consumption to the nominal maximum power demand of the powertrain. This can be achieved by momentarily replacing the powertrain circuit by a resistive dummy load of appropriated value. Such resistive load was also integrated in the prototype, as seen in Fig. 11(C), to facilitate the evaluation tests.

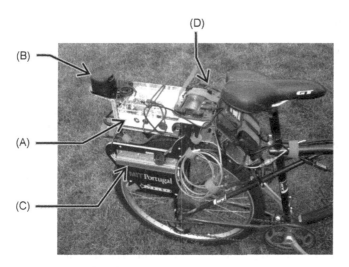

**Fig. 11.** UHF wireless electro-optical measurement unit (A) installed on a non-electric bicycle, for the initial positioning tests. Other system elements on the same assembly: (B) rotating LIDAR; (C) resistive loads and heatsink, mounted on both sides of vehicle; and (D) redundant voltage data logger model DI-1120, from DATAQ Instruments Inc., and management system, running on a Microsoft Windows 10 Pro PC Stick, manufactured by Azulle Tech.

## 4   Experiments and Results

### 4.1   LIDAR Calibration

The lateral LIDARs were calibrated using 9 reference distances from approximately 25 cm to 145 cm, and the back LIDAR using 5 reference distances from 112 cm to 766 cm. According to fabricant (GARMIN) of the LIDARs model Lite v3 used, the non-linearity in the LIDAR readings, as seen in Fig. 12, is expected, when measuring distances of 1 m and shorter (yellow shaded area). An observed increase in the standard deviation of readings at distances less than 0.45 m, however, strongly restricts practical operation of these LIDARs at too short range (gray shaded area).

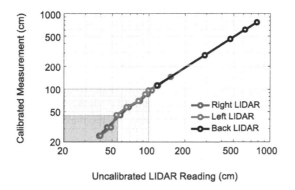

**Fig. 12.** LIDAR calibration curves experimentally obtained. (Color figure online)

## 4.2   Test Site Configuration

The ideal dimensions of the reference corridor depend on: (i) the range of magnitude of the lateral displacements to be measured; (ii) the maximum expected tilt angles of the vehicle, with respect to the corridor longitudinal axis; and (iii) the characteristics of the LIDAR used in the design.

According to the manufacturer (GARMIN) of the LIDARs used (model LIDARLite v3), the maximum range of detection, $d_{max}$, is 40 m, with an error of $\pm1\%$ in the mean value read, and another $\pm1\%$ error due to dispersion, for distances above 1 m, with non-linear behavior when reading distances less than 1 m. From experimentation, it was verified that the standard deviation of the distance measurements is reduced (down in the 7 mm to 9 mm range) at the distances of approximately 0.6 m to 1.2 m, increasing rapidly as the distance falls below 0.5 m, and proportionally to distance itself, at distances above 1.2 m.

Non-linearity in the readings can be compensated by calibration procedures, if operation distances are kept above $d_{min} = 0.5\,\mathrm{m}$. The reference corridor width $w_c$ should be such that the minimum distance from the LIDAR head to the wall, at the condition of maximum displacement from the center of lane, should be not less than the above marked minimum recommended operation distance $d_{min}$ for the LIDAR. Thus, a good choice $w_{min}$ for the minimum value of the corridor width, without experimenting LIDAR increased dispersion errors, would be expressed by:

$$w_{min} = d_{min} + d_L + w_L + d_{min} = 2d_{min} + d_L + w_L, \qquad (5)$$

where $d_L$ is the maximum anticipated lateral displacement width for the vehicle and $w_L$ is an equipment parameter, as defined in (3).

The maximum detection range $d_{max}$ also restricts the maximum corridor width, $w_{max}$. Considering the vehicle can assume relative heading ($\alpha$) and pitch ($\beta$) angles limited in absolute values respectively to $\alpha_{max}$ and $\beta_{max}$, then:

$$w_{max} \le d_{max} \cdot \cos(\alpha_{max}) \cdot \cos(\beta_{max}), \qquad (6)$$

There is, however, one more condition on the maximum value of $w_c$, that can be derived by requiring the LIDAR beam not to touch the floor, what would invalidate the simple expression in (3) for calculating the lateral displacement. The limit condition is when the vehicle is maximally tilt (roll angle) inside the corridor:

$$\frac{w_{max}}{\cos(\alpha_{max})} \le \frac{h_{LIDAR}}{\sin(\beta_{max})}, \qquad (7)$$

where $h_{LIDAR}$ is the height of the center of the LIDAR mounting head above the floor plane. So, reuniting conditions given in (6) and (7), the maximum corridor width, $w_{max}$, can be expressed by:

$$w_{max} = cos(\alpha_{max}).\min \left\{ d_{max}.\cos(\beta_{max}), \frac{h_{LIDAR}}{\sin(\beta_{max})} \right\}, \tag{8}$$

For a bicycle, a typical $d_L$ of interest will be around 1 m, so the desirable minimum corridor width to be used with measurement unit, as given by (5), should be 2.15 m. During the experiments with the bicycle, it was verified that heading (relative to lane longitudinal axis) and roll angles, under normal ridging conditions, were respectively limited to 30° and 15°. Using (8) and considering a mounting height of 1 m and the characteristic $d_{max}$ of the LIDAR used in the design, results that the maximum corridor width should be approximately 3.35 m.

In the first test runs herein reported, a corridor 1.778 m wide (Fig. 13) was used, due to its prompt availability (near our lab). This value lies outside the calculated ideal corridor width range. The consequence is that, for this width, lateral displacements estimations $d_L > 1.778 - 2 \times 0.5 - 0.15 = 0.628$ m are expected to have increased

**Fig. 13.** Left: experimental setup temporarily established during night time, in one of the corridors of MIT Computer Science and Artificial Intelligence Laboratory. Right: tracking the bicycle on the video, as a reference for data consistency check.

dispersion errors. In practice, however, there was no problem with that, because, for such a narrow corridor, its is difficult to ride with lateral misalignments much greater than 0.63 m, due to the increased risk of collision with the walls.

### 4.3   Trajectory Reconstitution

As a simplification, without any loss of generalization, we assume that the pick-up coil is parallel to the LIDAR (beam) plan, and its center is located at a fixed distance $H_C$ below the center of the LIDAR-IMU mounting head. The chart on Fig. 14(C), shows a trajectory reconstruction generated by the interactive analysis program written in MATLAB, from MathWorks, using $H_C = 62$ cm. The green dots are computed applying (2) and (3) to the IMU (B) and raw LIDAR data. The black curve on (C) is the estimated trajectory using filtered LIDAR data (A) instead. Since the bicycle in which the measurement unit was installed for the initial tests had neither electric power train nor energy harvesting devices, no electric data is associated to the trajectory.

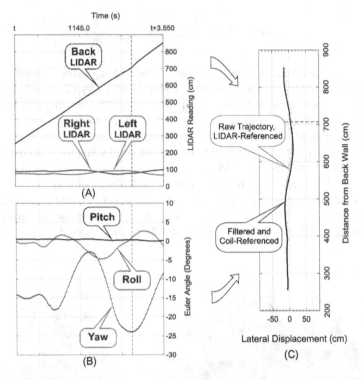

**Fig. 14.** Reconstitution of the trajectory of the center of a pick-up coil fixed on vehicle frame (C), based on LIDAR readings (A) and Euler angles (B). (Color figure online)

The unavailability of an accurate reference instrument also capable of dynamically measuring the trajectories, in the same way the presently developed instrument does, made it difficult to verify experimentally the measurement errors, currently only estimated by simulation. The computed trajectories were still compared to those obtained by video tracking Open Source Physics software [18], as shown in Fig. 13 (right), with consistent qualitative results. In this fist experiments, the low resolution of the camera used, however, limited the accuracy of trajectory estimation by the video tracking software, so far not permitting a useful numeric comparison with trajectories measured by the developed electro-optical equipment.

## 5    Conclusion

An electro-optical measurement instrument for analyzing dynamic wireless power transfer configurations was designed, implemented and tested for positioning. The combined use of LIDARs, IMU and a testing range with controlled geometry resulted in a simple, robust and potentially accurate technique to log the power transfer profile as function of lateral misalignment, critical for assessment of DIWPT schemes.

Statistical simulations indicate the capability of lateral displacement measurements with errors smaller than the base precision of the LIDAR components used, when testing vehicles with speeds up to 36 km/h and lateral accelerations up to three times the acceleration of gravity. Initial experiments with a prototype, specifically built for evaluating electrically assisted bicycles running on short inductive lanes (<10 m), confirm its adequacy of use, and indicate potential to achieve dynamic accuracies better than 1 cm, provided a calibration procedure is previously executed. Testing of the prototype will continue to fully explore its qualities as a DIWPT evaluation tool.

The measurement technique developed can be extended to larger and faster electric vehicles, and longer lane segments. For that, it is required that an appropriated reference corridor is set around the inductive lane under evaluation.

**Acknowledgments.** This research was partially supported by grant SFRH/BD/52349/2013 and project ESGRIDS – Enhancing Smart GRIDs for Sustainability, POCI-01-0145-FEDER-016434, both from FCT, the Portuguese funding agency supporting science, technology and innovation, and the MIT-Portugal Program. The authors are also thankful to R. Wiken, for his support with the mechanical implementation of the prototype at the MIT-CSAIL Machine Shop, to M. Brennan, for her generous donation of the bike used in the tests, and to L. Zvereva, who volunteered as a pilot in the first runs.

# References

1. Mi, C.C., Buja, G., Choi, S.Y., Rim, C.T.: Modern advances in wireless power transfer systems for roadway powered electric vehicles. IEEE Trans. Ind. Electron. **63**, 6533–6545 (2016)
2. Song, K., Koh, K.E., Zhu, C., et al.: A review of dynamic wireless power transfer for in-motion electric vehicles. In: Coca, E. (ed.) Wireless Power Transfer. IntechOpen, Rijeka (2016)
3. Yu, R., Zhong, W., Xie, S., et al.: Balancing power demand through EV mobility in vehicle-to-grid mobile energy networks. IEEE Trans. Ind. Inform. **12**, 79–90 (2016)
4. Covic, G.A., Boys, J.T., Budhia, M., Huang, C.: Electric vehicles – personal transportation for the future. World Electr. Veh. J. **4**, 693–704 (2010)
5. Ahn, S., Cho, D.-H.: Future wireless power transportation system. In: 2013 Asia-Pacific Microwave Conference Proceedings (APMC), pp. 468–469 (2013)
6. Bosshard, R., Kolar, J.W.: Inductive power transfer for electric vehicle charging. IEEE Power Electron. Mag. 22–30 (2016). https://doi.org/10.1109/mpel.2016.2583839
7. Mazharov, N.D., Hristov, S.M., Dichev, D.A., Zhelezarov, I.S.: Some problems of dynamic contactless charging of electric vehicles. Acta Polytech. Hungarica **14**, 7–26 (2017)
8. Laporte, S., Coquery, G., Revilloud, M., Deniau, V.: Experimental performance assessment of a dynamic WPT system for future EV in real driving conditions. In: 3rd Workshop on EV Systems, Data, and Applications (EV-Sys 2018), Proceedings of the 9th ACM International Conference on Future Energy Systems, Karlsruhe, Germany, pp. 570–578 (2018)
9. Feng, Y., Wang, J.: GPS RTK performance characteristics and analysis. J. Glob. Position Syst. **7**, 1–8 (2008)
10. Supej, M., Čuk, I.: Comparison of global navigation satellite system devices on speed tracking in road (Tran)SPORT applications. Sensors **14**, 23490–23508 (2014)
11. Leica Geosystems AG: Leica GS18 T Data sheet, pp. 1–2 (2017)

12. Lightbody, P., Krajník, T., Hanheide, M.: A versatile high-performance visual fiducial marker detection system with scalable identity encoding. In: Proceedings of the Symposium on Applied Computing, pp. 276–282. ACM, Marrakech (2017)
13. Mossel, A.: Robust 3D position estimation in wide and unconstrained indoor environments. Sensors **15**, 31482–31524 (2015). https://doi.org/10.3390/s151229862
14. Association française de normalisation (AFNOR): European Standard NF EN 15194(2009)
15. Cardoso, L.A.L., Martinez, M.C., Melendez, A.A.N., Afonso, J.L.: Dynamic inductive power transfer lane design for e-bikes. In: 2016 IEEE 19th International Conference on Intelligent Transportation Systems (ITSC), pp. 2307–2312 (2016)
16. Freund, H.-J.: Time control of hand movements. Prog. Brain Res. **64**, 287–294 (1986)
17. Thrun, S., Leonard, J., Siciliano, B., Khatib, O.: Simultaneous localization and mapping. In: Siciliano, B., Khatib, O. (eds.) Springer Handbook of Robotics, pp. 871–889. Springer, Heidelberg (2008). https://doi.org/10.1007/978-3-540-30301-5_38
18. Brown, D.: Tracker - Video Analysis and Modeling Tool, version 5.0.6 (2018)

# On the Effects of Parameter Adjustment on the Performance of PSO-Based MPPT of a PV-Energy Generation System

André Luiz Marques Leopoldino[(✉)] [ID], Cleiton Magalhães Freitas [ID], and Luís Fernando Corrêa Monteiro [ID]

Rio de Janeiro State University, Rio de Janeiro, Brazil
andre.leopoldino@gmail.com, {cleiton.freitas,lmonteiro}@uerj.br

**Abstract.** The growing concern on environmental issues caused by fossil fuels and, indeed, on the availability of such energy resources in a long-run basis have settled the ground for the spreading of the so called green energy sources. Among them, photovoltaic energy stands out due to the possibility of turning practically any household into a micro power plant. One important aspect about this source of energy is that practical photovoltaic generators are equipped with maximum power point tracking (MPPT) systems. Currently, researchers are focused on developing MPPT algorithms for partial shaded panels, among which, particle swarm optimization (PSO) MPPT stands out. PSO is an artificial intelligence method based on the behavior of flock of birds and it works arranging a group of mathematical entities named particles to deal with an optimization problem. Thus, this work focus on analyzing the performance of this algorithm under different design conditions, which means different amount of particles and different set points for the constants. Besides that, the article presents a brief guideline on how to implement PSO-MPPT. Simulations of an array with three photovoltaic panels, boost-converter driven, were carried out in order to back the analyzes.

**Keywords:** Photovoltaic energy generation ·
Maximum power point tracking · Particle swarm optimization

## 1 Introduction

The growing concern on environmental issues caused by fossil fuels and, indeed, on the availability of such energy resources in a long-run basis have settled the ground for the spreading of the so called green energy sources. Among them, photovoltaic (PV) energy stands out due to the possibility of turning practically any household into a micro power plant [11]. In views of that, countries such as Germany, China and Japan have taken the lead, powered either from environmental or commercial aims, of the movement of solar photovoltaic energy spreading [1, 20].

© ICST Institute for Computer Sciences, Social Informatics and Telecommunications Engineering 2019
Published by Springer Nature Switzerland AG 2019. All Rights Reserved
J. L. Afonso et al. (Eds.): GreeNets 2018, LNICST 269, pp. 175–192, 2019.
https://doi.org/10.1007/978-3-030-12950-7_14

From the technical point of view, it is important to highlight that, in addition to PV panels, electronic converters, and others hardware components, PV-based power generation systems should be equipped with Maximum Power Point Tracking (MPPT) controllers, otherwise they may not extract the maximum amount of energy from the panel. In fact, the lack of such controllers can even turn the effective power generation impracticable. In short, the amount of power harvested from a panel depends on the voltage in the terminal of the panel itself and this relationship varies with environmental variables such as solar radiance and temperature. Thus, MPPT controllers act searching in real time for the voltage which may lead to the Maximum Power Point (MPP) of the panel. It is worthwhile noticing that methods such as Perturb and Observe (P&O), Hill Climbing, Incremental Conductance, and plenty of others based in artificial intelligence have already been extensively tested, and are considered to be reliable for this purpose [2,9,15]. Nonetheless, these methods are prone to fail in face of partial shading of the panel, situation in which the panel might present multiple maximum power points.

Regarding the operation under partial shading, a couple of other methods have already been proposed for MPPT [10], among which Particle Swarm Optimization (PSO) [7]. This method belongs to the Artificial Intelligence (AI) branch and is based on the behavior of flock of animals. Its characteristic make it possible to search for the global MPP (GMPP) without being trapped into local maxima, which would possible reduce the amount of energy harvested. A brief review of the literature shows that researchers have widely used different forms of PSO algorithms in different configurations of PV generation systems. Some authors have used PSO-MPPT for reducing steady-state oscillations [5] in a single-converter system, while other have developed algorithms for multi-converter distributed systems [14]. Besides that, it is also found in the literature PSO-MPPT applied to grid-tied systems [13]. Furthermore, some researchers have combined PSO with other techniques [8] or modified the basic concept of PSO with intention to cut off the random characteristic of the algorithm [16]. Although some authors have analyzed the influence of some parameters, such as number of particles used in the MPPT, it lacks a full analyze of the influence of the algorithm settings into the performance of the PSO-MPPT. In views of that, this work aims at analyzing how the number of particles and the tuning of constants used in a PSO algorithm affect the performance of MPPT of an array of partially shaded PV panels. In short, the performance of the PSO-MPPT was analyzed through simulation for different number of particles and settings for the constants. For this matter, it was considered a system comprised of an array of three series-connected panels, a boost converter and a 96 V battery. Apart from these analyses, it is also in the scope of this article to present a detailed description of the PSO-MPPT used in the simulations.

This work is organized in seven sections as follows: The Sect. 2 presents a review on how PV panel is modeled and the effects of the partial shading on the power × voltage (P-V) relationship. Section 3 aims at presenting the scenario proposed for analysis. After that, an introductory discussion on PSO algorithm is carried out in Sect. 4 and, in the sequence, the PSO-MPPT algorithm analyzed in this work is detailed in Sect. 5. Section 6 presents the methodology used for analysis along with the simulation results. Finally, conclusions are drawn in Sect. 7.

## 2  Photovoltaic Panels

This section aims at depicting the mathematical model used for representing the PV panels, along with describing its behavior under different radiance and temperature levels. Besides that, it is also explained the effects of partial shading on the P-V curve.

### 2.1  PV Panel Modeling

The single diode model approach [19] was used to represent the PV panel in the simulation environment. With this model, the PV panel is represented by current source, $I_{ph}$, paralleled with direct biased diode and a shunt resistor, $R_{sh}$, as it is presented in Fig. 1. Besides that, a series resistor, $R_s$, is inserted in the circuital model so as to modeling the conduction losses of the panel. As the shunt resistance tends to assume high values [3], the current flowing out of the PV panel may be expressed by:

$$I_{pv} = I_{ph} - I_d \tag{1}$$

where $I_d$ is the current flowing through the diode.

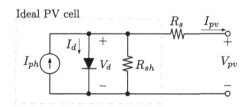

**Fig. 1.** Single-diode equivalent circuit of a photovoltaic cell

Basically, the current source $I_{ph}$ model the panel response to solar irradiation and, of course, the effect of temperature on the power generation. Thus, this current can be represented as:

$$I_{ph} = \frac{G}{G_{ref}} I_{sc,ref} + C_T (T - T_{ref}) \tag{2}$$

where $G$ and $T$ are, respectively, the radiance in $W/m^2$ and temperature in $K$ which the panel is submitted, whereas $G_{ref}$ and $T_{ref}$ are the reference values of these variables for which the short-circuit current $I_{sc,ref}$ was measured. Regarding these last parameters, that is, $G_{ref}$, $T_{ref}$ and $I_{sc,ref}$, they generally are empirical values provided by the manufacturer of the panel. As for the constant $C_T$, it is simply a temperature coefficient that accounts the effect of this variable into the short circuit current.

The diode current, on the other hand, can be expressed by:

$$I_d = I_o \left( e^{\frac{V_d}{aV_t}} - 1 \right) \tag{3}$$

where $I_o$ is the saturation current of the cell, $V_t$ is the thermal voltage of the PV and $a$ is a factor which depends on the doping of the silicon used in the panel [4]. Different from $I_o$ and $a$, which are constants provided by the manufacturer in the data-sheet, $V_t$ is computed by means of the following formula:

$$V_t = \frac{kT}{q} \tag{4}$$

where $k$ is the Boltzmann constant, $1.38 \times 10^{-23}$ J/K and $q$ is the electron charge, $1.6 \times 10^{-19}$ C. The main data of the panel considered throughout this work is summarized in Table 1.

**Table 1.** Parameters of the used panel

| Parameter | Symbol | Value |
|---|---|---|
| Referential radiance | $G_{ref}$ | $1000\,\mathrm{W/m^2}$ |
| Referential temperature | $T_{ref}$ | 298.15 K (25 °C) |
| Short-circuit current | $I_{sh,ref}$ | 3.8 A |
| Saturation current | $I_o$ | $2.16 \times 10^{-8}$ A |
| Diode coefficient | $a$ | 1.12 |
| Thermal constant | $C_T$ | 0.0024 A/K |
| Rated power | – | 60.53 W |
| Rated voltage | – | 17.04 V |
| Number of cells | – | 36 |

Considering the PV panel, for which the technical parameters are presented in Table 1, one may find out the I-V and P-V characteristic curves displayed in Fig. 2. The dots highlighted on the curves indicates either maximum power or current in which the maximum power is achieved. It is possible to notice from Figs. 2(b) and (d) that changes in the radiance and, more significantly, in the temperature which the panel is submitted shifts the voltage in which the maximum power point is achieved.

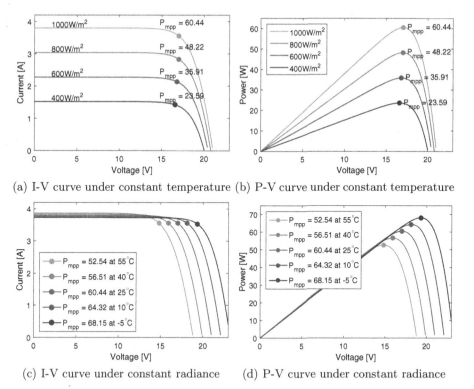

(a) I-V curve under constant temperature (b) P-V curve under constant temperature

(c) I-V curve under constant radiance     (d) P-V curve under constant radiance

**Fig. 2.** I-V and P-V curves of a PV panel. (a) and (b) presents the I-V and P-V curves for different values of radiance keeping temperature constant at $25\,°C$. (c) and (d) presents the I-V and P-V curves for different values of temperature keeping radiance level at $1000\,W/m^2$.

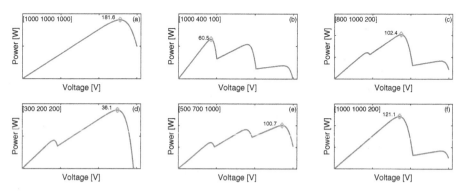

**Fig. 3.** P-V curve shapes for an array of three series-connected panels under partial shading. The vector $[G_1\ G_2\ G_3]$, placed on each upper left corner, represents the radiance distribution in the panels for that case and the diamond-shaped mark spot the GMPP.

## 2.2 Characteristics of the PV Panel Under Partial Shading Condition - PSC

The partial shading occurs when an PV panel or an array of panels is submitted to non-homogeneous distribution of radiance. It means that, due to some external factors such as clouds, leaves or even birds and others animals covering part of the panels, the radiance received by part of the cells of a panel is different from the others. In this situation, either cells or even full panels turn into loads for those associated to them, which requires the use of bypass diodes for enhancing power generation [17]. Nonetheless, the result of having panels bypassed when under PSC is that of changing the characteristic of the P-V curve of the group, making room for multiple maximum points as illustrated in Fig. 3. It must be pointed out that the position of the maximum points and quantity of them depends on factors such as number of cells/panels shaded and unshaded, radiance and temperature. It is also important to realize that the peak value of each maximum not necessarily matches the others and that there is no straightforward rule to determine which maximum point is the greatest. Hence, MPPT algorithms can be trapped into local maxima rather than the global.

# 3    Proposed Scenario and Methodology

Figure 4 presents the scenario considered for evaluation of the PSO-based MPPT. Basically, an array of three series-connected PV panels is feeding a battery through a boost converter. It is important to notice that an input capacitor, $C_{in}$, is paralleled with the PV array just on the input of the converter. This capacitor plays an important role in the circuit because it is the storage element responsible to sustain the voltage across the PV array, $v_{pv}$. It is also important to notice that it is possible to change $v_{pv}$ by means adjusting the duty cycle, $d$, of the converter. Still on the Fig. 4, the block named *Control Algorithms* contains

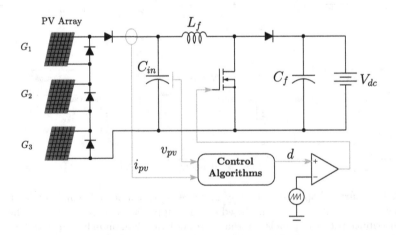

**Fig. 4.** Reference circuit used throughout the simulations.

the PSO-MPPT algorithm. As it can be seen, both voltage $v_{pv}$ and current $i_{pv}$ of the panels are measured and used to compute the power generated. The output of this block is the duty cycle $d$ which is used to drive the converter. Table 2 presents the parameters used during this paper.

**Table 2.** Reference for parameters used throughout simulations

| Parameter | Symbol | Value |
|---|---|---|
| Input capacitance | $C_{in}$ | $30\,nF$ |
| Filter inductance | $L_f$ | $0.5\,mH$ |
| Filter capacitance | $C_f$ | $50\,\mu F$ |
| Battery voltage | $V_{dc}$ | $96\,V$ |

# 4   Particle Swarm Optimization

Basically, the PSO is an AI-based method, similar to genetic algorithms, based on the behavior of flock of birds and others animals [6]. It was observed that the individuals of such groups take advantage of the so call group intelligence to achieve their collective goal, something like finding shelter or food. To cut the long story short, if the objective is to find food, rather than concentrating all the individuals together, the flock is spread over a large area and, as the members communicate with each other, all of them converge to the place which is supposed to have more food available. In the same way, a group of individuals, in this case called particles, is part and parcel of the PSO method. These particles are spread all over the domain of the problem, and they are programmed to gather information and to interact with each other in order to find the solution, which, in general, is the point in the domain which minimizes a previously-established cost function. As the cost function may present local minimum, finding the global inflection point requires well setting of the PSO algorithm, besides the widespread placement of particles.

The PSO algorithm runs on an iterative-approach basis, which means that each particle is initially placed at different spots and, turn after turn, they move around, with changing velocity, towards the solution of the problem [18]. It is important to notice that all spots are mapped on the domain of the problem and, as it has already been stated, the problem itself is to find the minimum point of a user-defined cost function. The velocity $u_i$ with which a certain particle moves is given by:

$$u_i[k] = w\ u_i[k-1] + \underbrace{C_1 r_1(pbest_i - x[k-1])}_{\text{cognitive component}} + \underbrace{C_2 r_2(gbest - x[k-1])}_{\text{social component}} \quad (5)$$

where $i$ is the number of the particle, $k$ is the number of the iteration, $w$ is the inertia weight, $C_1$ and $C_2$ are positive constants, $r_1$ and $r_2$ are random numbers ranging from 0 to 1, and $x$ is the position of the particle. Besides that, the variables *pbest* and *gbest* correspond to the best positions (positions which returned the best results) achieved, respectively, by this particle and by the whole group, accounting all the previous iterations.

As it can be seen in (5), the velocity of a particle changes with two main parts named cognitive and social. The former is intended to draw upon the particle's own experience, whereas the later focus on the group acquired knowledge. It is worth noticing that the chosen values of the constants $C_1$ and $C_2$ are straight-forwardly linked with the dynamic of the algorithm and, because of that, these values must be adequately tuned according to the objective. As for the random variables $r_1$ and $r_2$, they play an important role in the searching process, avoiding the particles to rapidly settle on an unchanging direction of movement [6]. Other point noteworthy is the role of inertia weight $w$. The greater this coefficient is, the wider the domain is explored. In other words, bigger values of $w$ promotes better the searching for global minimum of the cost function [18]. Finally, the position of the particle $i$ in the $k^{th}$ iteration is given by:

$$x_i[k] = x_i[k-1] + u_i[k] \tag{6}$$

## 5  PSO-MPPT

As the voltage across the panels can be controlled by means of changing the duty cycle, $d$ was chosen to be the variable representing the domain of the problem. Thus, the position of each particle, this last being referred as $q_i$ in some graphs, represents a duty cycle and was chosen to be updated as follows:

$$d_i[k] = d_i[k-1] + u_i[k-1] \tag{7}$$

It should be borne in mind that $d_i[k]$ must be bounded within the interval $[0, 1]$, otherwise the PSO algorithm may command a searching outside the domain of the problem. The same way, (5) can be rewritten as:

$$u_i[k] = u_i[k-1] + \underbrace{C_1 r_1(d_{best,i} - d[k-1])}_{\text{cognitive component}} + \underbrace{C_2 r_2(d_{best,g} - d[k-1])}_{\text{social component}} \tag{8}$$

where $u$, in this case, is the rate of change of the duty cycle, which means the velocity of the particle, $d_{best,i}$ and $d_{best,g}$ take the role of *pbest* and *gbest* in (5). Although they are not used in (8) it is important to point that the values of power associated to $d_{best,i}$ and $d_{best,g}$ shall be stored, respectively, in $P_{max,i}$ and $P_{max,g}$. Unfortunately (8) has no bounds and must not be used in this form, otherwise it could threaten the performance of the algorithm. Among different methods for limiting the rate of changing of the duty cycle, it was chosen the trigonometric approach used in [12]. Thus, (8) must be rewritten as:

$$u_i[k] = \frac{2}{\pi} tg^{-1}\Big(w u_i[k-1] + C_1 r_1(d_{best,i} - d_i[k-1]) + C_2 r_2(d_{best,g} - d_i[k-1])\Big) \tag{9}$$

since the image of the inverse tangent is $[-\pi/2, \pi/2]$ and it only returns $\pm\pi/2$ in case the argument reaches $\pm\infty$, this formula bounds the velocity within the interval $(-1, 1)$.

When it comes to the cost function, the approach presented in (Sect. 4) was changed according to the current objective—find the MPP. Hence, the algorithm was arranged to search for a maximum instead of a minimum of a function, and this function was considered to be the power produced by the converter.

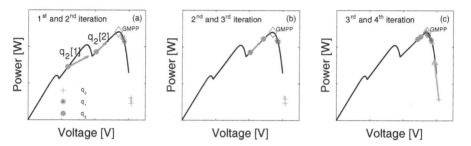

**Fig. 5.** Particle swarm convergence for three particles, $q_0, q_1$ and $q_2$. The size of the arrows are proportional to the velocities and the graphs show the paths from (a) 1st to $2^{nd}$, (b) $2^{nd}$ to $3^{rd}$, and (c) $3^{rd}$ to $4^{th}$ iterations.

Once explained how the position and velocity of each particle is computed, it is time to present the PSO-MPPT algorithm. Firstly, all particles have to be initialized and this takes an important role in the process. For proper convergence it is necessary not only a certain minimum number of particles, but also that these are properly spread throughout the domain of the problem. To better understand this process, Fig. 5 exemplifies the desired behavior for a case with three particles. In the leftmost square is presented the particles in their initial position, notice that rather than displaying actually the position (duty cycle) it was chosen to spot the point into the P-V curve associated to it. After a couple of turns, the particles move to the positions shown on the central graph and latter on they converge to the global maximum point, as shown in the graph on the right. In order to have a faster and more accurate convergence process it was assigned different ranges for the initialization of each particle. It means that in case we have $n$ particles, their initial position might be a random number within specific intervals, as follows:

$$d_1[0] = rand\left(\left(0, \tfrac{1}{n}\right]\right)$$

$$d_2[0] = rand\left(\left(\tfrac{1}{n}, \tfrac{2}{n}\right]\right)$$

$$\vdots$$

$$d_n[0] = rand\left(\left(\tfrac{n-1}{n}, 1\right]\right)$$

(10)

where $rand()$ is a function which returns a random number within the interval given. This approach guarantee the widespread placement of the particles in the first turn. It was also chosen $u_i[0] = 0$ as initial velocity for each particle.

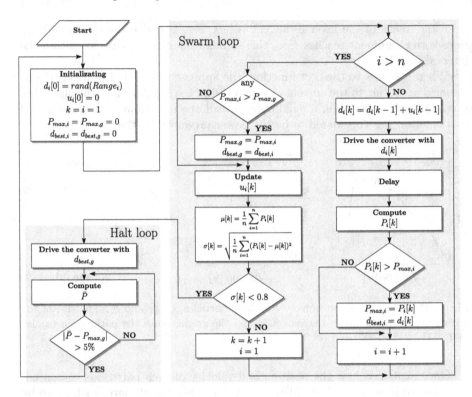

**Fig. 6.** Particle swarm algorithm flowchart for $n$ particles. The *swarm loop* represents the process of going from particle to particle testing the power response. The *halt loop* goes off whenever the particles converge to GMPP.

After setting the initial states of the particles, the iterative process goes off. In every cycle $k$, the positions $d_i[k]$ of all $n$ particles are updated according to Eq. (7) and, then, the converter is driven with each value in sequence to compute the generated power $P_i[k]$, from $v_{pv}$ and $i_{pv}$, associated to each particle. Notice that whenever the duty cycle is changed the circuit undergoes transient state. That is why the measurement of the power is delayed in 4.5 ms. In addition to that, instead of using the instantaneous power, it was chosen to be used the average power computed over 50 samples (covering a period of 0.5 ms) to guarantee that any oscillation or noise in the signals do not compromise the proper work of the algorithm. In case the $P_i[k]$ surpass the maximum power, $P_{max,i}$, achieved by the particle so far, $d_i[k]$ is assigned to $d_{best,i}$, and $P_i[k]$ to $P_{max,i}$. Before finishing the iteration, after all particles have been tested, $P_{max,g}$ and $d_{best,g}$ are updated, case any $P_{max,i}$ surpass its previous value, and the velocities $u_i[k]$ are computed. Attention have to be raised to the fact that even after converging to the MPP, the particles still continue changing position due to the random characteristic of the process and it can cause oscillations on the power generated. Thus, it was chosen to halt the algorithm, and drive the converter with $d_{best,g}$, whenever the particles crowd each other in a small neighborhood. To infer if the particles are next to each other is used the standard deviation of the average point of $P_i[k]$, given by:

$$\sigma[k] = \sqrt{\frac{1}{n} \sum_{i=1}^{n} (P_i[k] - \mu[k])^2} \qquad (11)$$

where

$$\mu[k] = \frac{1}{n} \sum_{i=1}^{n} P_i[k] \qquad (12)$$

is the average power of all particles after the $k^{th}$ iteration. The halt loop is commanded to arise whenever $\sigma[k] < 0.8$ is satisfied. The flowchart in Fig. 6 summarizes the algorithm. Notice that once halt, the searching process only restarts if occurs a fluctuation in the generated power $\overline{P}$ bigger than 5%.

# 6    Methodology and Analysis of Results

This section aims at analyzing the performance of the PSO-MPPT under different setting conditions, it means, different number of particles, values of the constants $w$, $C_1$ and $C_2$. Firstly, it was defined a set of values of the parameters for which the PSO algorithm was to be analyzed. The number of particles, for instance, was set for 3, 5, 7 and 9, on a row, the constants $C_1$ and $C_2$, on the other hand, were varied from 1 to 2 with steps of 0.2 and the inertia constant $w$ from 0.2 to 1.0 with the same step size, totaling 720 different combinations of setting points. Considering this space, a set of eight simulations were carried out for each combination to access the performance of the algorithm under different environment conditions. Half of these considered partial shading condition, each one with a different pattern, and the other half full coverage of the sun, with different levels of radiance. The temperature, on the other hand, was held constant at 25 °C for all the aforementioned cases. In summary, it was carried out 5760 simulations, 2880 of which considering partial shading condition. Table 3 summarizes the ranges in which each variable of the simulations were varied.

**Table 3.** PSO search range parameters

| Parameter | Range | Step | Unit |
|---|---|---|---|
| $w$ | $(0.2, 1)$ | 0.2 | – |
| $C_1$ | $(1, 2)$ | 0.2 | – |
| $C_2$ | $(1, 2)$ | 0.2 | – |
| $n$ | $(3, 9)$ | 2 | – |
| $G_1, G_2, G_3$ | $(400, 1000)$ | 200 | $Wm^{-2}$ |
| $T_{env}$ | 25 | 0 | °C |

For the sake of classifying the results, were binarily classified into group A, for those which reached accuracy higher than 99% (virtually 100% accuracy), and group B, for all the other results. In this context, accuracy represents the per unit value of the power produced by the converter taking as reference the theoretical MPP for each case. The global results of simulations and classification are shown in histogram in Fig. 7. As expected, the experiments in scenarios without shading produced virtually 100% accuracy for all the cases. Meanwhile, under partial shading the tests unveiled that only 87.67% (2525) were classified into the group A. Here it is important do state that among those nearly 12% which were classified into the group B, some ended up in a local maxima and others did not converge.

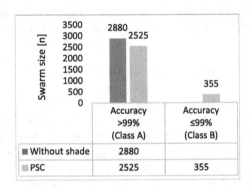

**Fig. 7.** Accuracy and classification of simulation results independently of the settings

Thenceforth, to compare performance of parameters it was defined the success rate, $SR$, of the MPPT as follows:

$$SR(i,j,m,l) = \left.\frac{|A|}{|A| + |B|}\right|_{C_1(i),C_2(j),w(m),n(l)} \quad \begin{cases} i, j \in \mathbb{N}^* \mid i, j < 7 \\ m \in \mathbb{N}^* \mid m < 6 \\ l \in \mathbb{N}^* \mid l < 5 \end{cases} \quad (13)$$

Where $|A|$ and $|B|$ represents the number of cases classified in groups A and B for a specific combination or parameters $n$, $C_1$, $C_2$ and $w$. In short, $SR(i,j,m,l)$ informs the percentage of cases which were classified in the group A for each combination of parameters.

Since the swarm size $n$ is the principal hyper-parameter in the algorithm, we partitioned the $SR$ using this metric. For each number of particles we tested 720 scenarios and the success rate $SR$ for them is shown in Fig. 8. In these graphs, the colors blue and yellow represent the extremities of the results: the lowest and the highest levels of $SR$. Thus, it was possible to find from Fig. 8(b) that there are 13 combinations of $C_1$ and $C_2$ regarding the case with $n = 5$ which the success rate achieved 100%, indicating that all these tests (260) converged to the GMPP. Notice that the inertia constant varies among all these tests and it is going to be analyzed in the sequence. Due to the fact that the chart for five particles presented the greatest yellow area amongst all, it was decided that the best tracking performance is achieved with $n = 5$.

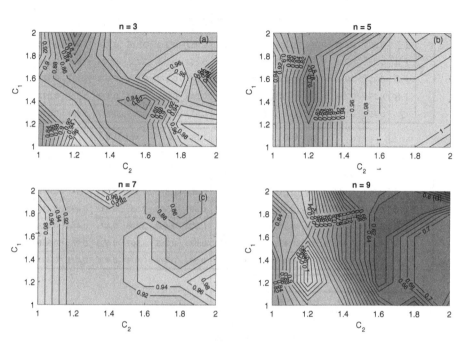

**Fig. 8.** Success rate mapping for different number of particles (a) $n = 3$: 5 pairs with $SR = 100\%$. (b) $n = 5$: 13 pairs with $SR = 100\%$. (c) $n = 7$: 7 pairs with $SR = 100\%$. (d) $n = 9$: 2 pairs with $SR = 100\%$. (Color figure online)

Considering the 260 successful cases, it means, those detailed in the previous paragraph ($n = 5$), it was analyzed the average convergence time and the results presented in the Table 4. It is observed that the average time grows with the value of the inertia constant $w$. This happens because, once $w$ goes bigger, the velocity of the particles tends to significantly increase and, thus, the particles jump around the GMPP, leading the PSO algorithm into a larger settling time. It is noticeable, as well, that there is an optimum region on the domain $C_1$–$C_2$, represented in Table 4(a) by dashed cells. In this region, the tracking process reaches its lowest value, 0.251 s. It is important to notice that the bounding technique used in (9) is responsible for making different values of $C_1$ and $C_2$ produce the same settling time.

In summary, the best results were achieved when swarm size was set for five particles, the constants for cognitive and social components $C_1$ and $C_2$ were both set for 1.6, and the inertia weight $w$ for 0.2.

**Table 4.** Average time in seconds to reach GMPP for class A with size $n = 5$, partitioned by $w$. The parameters $C_1$ and $C_2$ already identified are in boldface inside the dashed cells.

| | $C_1$ | w = 0.2 | | | | | (a) | w = 0.4 | | | | | (b) |
|---|---|---|---|---|---|---|---|---|---|---|---|---|---|
| | | 1 | 1.2 | 1.4 | 1.6 | 1.8 | 2 | 1 | 1.2 | 1.4 | 1.6 | 1.8 | 2 |
| $C_2$ | 1 | 0.345 | 0.471 | 0.439 | 0.408 | 0.439 | 0.377 | 0.283 | 0.314 | 0.314 | 0.314 | 0.283 | 0.283 |
| | 1.2 | 0.251 | 0.251 | 0.251 | 0.251 | 0.251 | **0.251** | 0.911 | 0.251 | 0.314 | 0.314 | 0.314 | **0.314** |
| | 1.4 | 0.251 | 0.251 | 0.251 | 0.251 | 0.251 | **0.251** | 0.251 | 0.251 | 0.251 | 0.314 | 0.314 | **0.345** |
| | 1.6 | **0.251** | **0.251** | **0.251** | **0.251** | 0.251 | **0.251** | **0.377** | **0.377** | **0.377** | **0.408** | 1.003 | **0.377** |
| | 1.8 | **0.251** | **0.251** | **0.251** | 0.283 | 0.283 | 0.314 | **0.345** | **0.314** | **0.314** | **0.377** | 0.377 | **0.377** |
| | 2 | 0.251 | 0.251 | 0.251 | 0.251 | **0.251** | 0.251 | 0.377 | 0.377 | 0.345 | 0.377 | **0.439** | 0.377 |

| | $C_1$ | w = 0.6 | | | | | (c) | w = 0.8 | | | | | (d) |
|---|---|---|---|---|---|---|---|---|---|---|---|---|---|
| | | 1 | 1.2 | 1.4 | 1.6 | 1.8 | 2 | 1 | 1.2 | 1.4 | 1.6 | 1.8 | 2 |
| $C_2$ | 1 | 0.314 | 0.283 | 0.345 | 0.377 | 0.377 | 0.377 | 0.418 | 0.377 | 0.418 | 0.418 | 0.377 | 0.439 |
| | 1.2 | 0.377 | 0.544 | 0.377 | 0.314 | 0.377 | **0.377** | 0.408 | 0.377 | 0.439 | 0.408 | 0.377 | **0.439** |
| | 1.4 | 0.418 | 0.418 | 0.418 | 0.418 | 0.418 | **0.377** | 0.533 | 0.533 | 0.565 | 0.533 | 0.460 | **0.439** |
| | 1.6 | **0.377** | **0.377** | **0.345** | **0.345** | 0.377 | **0.408** | **0.502** | **0.439** | **0.439** | **0.471** | 0.460 | **0.533** |
| | 1.8 | **0.439** | **0.377** | **0.408** | **0.439** | 0.439 | **0.408** | **0.533** | **0.565** | **0.502** | **0.659** | 0.953 | **0.596** |
| | 2 | 0.439 | 0.439 | 0.439 | 0.408 | **0.408** | 0.533 | 0.502 | 0.471 | 0.471 | 0.471 | **0.471** | 0.471 |

| | $C_1$ | w = 1 | | | | | (e) |
|---|---|---|---|---|---|---|---|
| | | 1 | 1.2 | 1.4 | 1.6 | 1.8 | 2 |
| $C_2$ | 1 | 0.502 | 0.502 | 0.471 | 0.471 | 0.502 | 0.533 |
| | 1.2 | 0.502 | 0.502 | 0.544 | 0.585 | 0.565 | **0.565** |
| | 1.4 | 0.502 | 0.471 | 0.502 | 0.533 | 0.565 | **0.502** |
| | 1.6 | **0.502** | **0.471** | **0.471** | **0.502** | 0.502 | **0.533** |
| | 1.8 | **0.502** | **0.502** | **0.471** | 0.439 | 0.533 | **0.565** |
| | 2 | 0.533 | 0.471 | 0.502 | 0.558 | **0.502** | 0.621 |

Figure 9 shows the convergence process observed in the best scenario addressed in the simulation and Fig. 10 shows the search domain. It is highlighted in Fig. 9(c) the final value of $d_{best,g}$ and in (a), the system reached the GMPP at 120 W, for this case. It is possible to notice that it took about 0.25 s, which correspond to 10 swarm cycles, for the system reach to the GMPP. Thus, the hatched areas on the graphs corresponds to the period in which the PSO algorithm was halted for there was not changes into the position of the MPP. These chart also allow us to visualize the heart of the PSO algorithm: the changing values observed in the power and duty cycle shows the algorithm testing the position of each particle on a row, cycle after cycle. Notice that both variables are related to the converter, which means they comprise the results for all the particles of the swarm. As the time moves on, the particles start searching in a

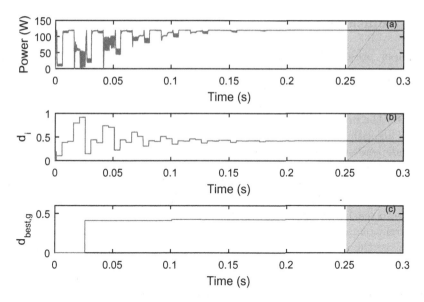

**Fig. 9.** Convergence process. (a) Output power of PV. (b) Duty cycle. (c) Best duty cycle during search process. After time 0.25 s the search algorithm halts and $d_{best,g}$ is steadily delivered to the power converter.

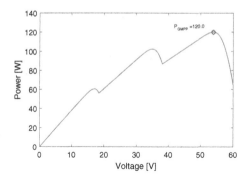

**Fig. 10.** $P$-$V$ curve showing the tracked global power point with success rate of 99.9% (best set of parameters found).

narrower neighborhood, which means the difference of duty cycle from particle to particle and from cycle to cycle gradually fade, and eventually they converged to the MPP. It is also worthwhile noticing that $d_{best,g}$ is only changed twice and this results comes from the widespread placement of the particles during the initialization process.

# 7  Conclusions

This paper presented a general review of the use of PSO in MPPT and the influence of the adjustment of parameters into the performance of the MPP tracking. In a nutshell, it has been presented a grid search over a space of 5760 scenarios for the best combination of parameters, number of particles, $C_1$, $C_2$ and $w$, for the proposed algorithm. From the results, it was possible to conclude that the algorithm is effective and reached the GMPP in almost 88% of proposed cases independently of the settings (number of particles and chosen values for $C_1$, $C_2$ and $w$). It was also noticed that the rate of non-convergence, which in fact, for this analysis, means not reaching the GMPP before $t = 3$ s, was low with only 39 out of 5760 cases reporting this behavior. Of course, the algorithm was able to reach the GMPP nearly 100% of the cases for $n = 5$, $C_1 = C_2 = 1.6$ (best setting arrangement). It was also spotted that the best performances, when it comes to the convergence time, led the algorithm to reach GMPP in about 0.25 s.

Besides that, it is also possible to draw some conclusions about the relationship between parameter adjustment and tracking performance:

– Swarm size ($n$): large number of particles leads to a slower convergence time.
– Inertia coefficient ($w$): larger value can slow the convergence time since it might require more cycles for all particles get closer to the GMPP.
– Cognitive and social components: inside the algorithm $C_1$ and $C_2$ contributes either for local and global maximum searching.

One last point to be made concerns the effect of the general configuration on the results achieved. Since in the present analysis was considered only cases with one, two or three local maxima, it is not possible to guarantee that the performance will be the same for the cases where more than three maxima occurs.

# References

1. Arantegui, R.L., Jäger-Waldau, A.: Photovoltaics and wind status in the European Union after the Paris agreement. Renew. Sustain. Energy Rev. **81**, 2460–2471 (2018). https://doi.org/10.1016/j.rser.2017.06.052
2. Bendib, B., Belmili, H., Krim, F.: A survey of the most used MPPT methods: conventional and advanced algorithms applied for photovoltaic systems. Renew. Sustain. Energy Rev. **45**, 637–648 (2015). https://doi.org/10.1016/j.rser.2015.02.009
3. Dolara, A., Leva, S., Manzolini, G.: Comparison of different physical models for PV power output prediction. Sol. Energy **119**, 83–99 (2015). https://doi.org/10.1016/j.solener.2015.06.017
4. Hasan, M., Parida, S.: An overview of solar photovoltaic panel modeling based on analytical and experimental viewpoint. Renew. Sustain. Energy Rev. **60**, 75–83 (2016). https://doi.org/10.1016/j.rser.2016.01.087

5. Ishaque, K., Salam, Z., Amjad, M., Mekhilef, S.: An improved particle swarm optimization (PSO)-based MPPT for PV with reduced steady-state oscillation. IEEE Trans. Power Electron. **27**(8), 3627–3638 (2012). https://doi.org/10.1109/TPEL.2012.2185713
6. Kennedy, J., Eberhart, R.: Particle swarm optimization. In: Proceedings of ICNN 1995 - International Conference on Neural Networks, vol. 4, pp. 1942–1948, November 1995. https://doi.org/10.1109/ICNN.1995.488968
7. Khare, A., Rangnekar, S.: A review of particle swarm optimization and its applications in solar photovoltaic system. Appl. Soft Comput. **13**(5), 2997–3006 (2013). https://doi.org/10.1016/j.asoc.2012.11.033
8. Koad, R.B., Zobaa, A.F., El-Shahat, A.: A novel MPPT algorithm based on particle swarm optimization for photovoltaic systems. IEEE Trans. Sustain. Energy **8**(2), 468–476 (2017). https://doi.org/10.1109/TSTE.2016.2606421
9. Liu, F., Kang, Y., Zhang, Y., Duan, S.: Comparison of P&O and hill climbing MPPT methods for grid-connected PV converter. In: 2008 3rd IEEE Conference on Industrial Electronics and Applications, pp. 804–807, June 2008. https://doi.org/10.1109/ICIEA.2008.4582626
10. Liu, L., Meng, X., Liu, C.: A review of maximum power point tracking methods of PV power system at uniform and partial shading. Renew. Sustain. Energy Rev. **53**, 1500–1507 (2016). https://doi.org/10.1016/j.rser.2015.09.065
11. Malinowski, M., Leon, J.I., Abu-Rub, H.: Solar photovoltaic and thermal energy systems: current technology and future trends. Proc. IEEE **105**(11), 2132–2146 (2017). https://doi.org/10.1109/JPROC.2017.2690343
12. Mirhassani, S.M., Golroodbari, S.Z.M., Golroodbari, S.M.M., Mekhilef, S.: An improved particle swarm optimization based maximum power point tracking strategy with variable sampling time. Int. J. Electr. Power Energy Syst. **64**, 761–770 (2015). https://doi.org/10.1016/j.ijepes.2014.07.074
13. de Oliveira, F.M., da Silva, S.A.O., Durand, F.R., Sampaio, L.P., Bacon, V.D., Campanhol, L.B.: Grid-tied photovoltaic system based on PSO MPPT technique with active power line conditioning. IET Power Electron. **9**(6), 1180–1191 (2016). https://doi.org/10.1049/iet-pel.2015.0655
14. Renaudineau, H., et al.: A PSO-based global MPPT technique for distributed PV power generation. IEEE Trans. Ind. Electron. **62**(2), 1047–1058 (2015). https://doi.org/10.1109/TIE.2014.2336600
15. Rodriguez, E.A., Freitas, C.M., Bellar, M.D., Monteiro, L.F.C.: MPPT algorithm for PV array connected to a hybrid generation system. In: 2015 IEEE 24th International Symposium on Industrial Electronics (ISIE), pp. 1115–1120, June 2015. https://doi.org/10.1109/ISIE.2015.7281628
16. Sen, T., Pragallapati, N., Agarwal, V., Kumar, R.: Global maximum power point tracking of PV arrays under partial shading conditions using a modified particle velocity-based PSO technique. IET Renew. Power Gener. **12**, 555–564 (2018). https://doi.org/10.1049/iet-rpg.2016.0838
17. Shepard, N.: Diodes in photovoltaic modules and arrays. Final report, prepared for JPL by General Electric Company Advanced Energy Systems and Technology Division, King of Prussia, Pennsylvania, 15 March 1984
18. Song, M.P., Gu, G.C.: Research on particle swarm optimization: a review. In: Proceedings of 2004 International Conference on Machine Learning and Cybernetics (IEEE Cat. No.04EX826), vol. 4, pp. 2236–2241, August 2004. https://doi.org/10.1109/ICMLC.2004.1382171

19. Villalva, M.G., Gazoli, J.R., Filho, E.R.: Comprehensive approach to modeling and simulation of photovoltaic arrays. IEEE Trans. Power Electron. **24**(5), 1198–1208 (2009). https://doi.org/10.1109/TPEL.2009.2013862
20. Yu, H.J.J., Popiolek, N., Geoffron, P.: Solar photovoltaic energy policy and globalization: a multiperspective approach with case studies of Germany, Japan and China. Prog. Photovolt. Res. Appl. **24**(4), 458–476 (2014). https://doi.org/10.1002/pip.2560. https://onlinelibrary.wiley.com/doi/abs/10.1002/pip.2560

# Multi-temporal Active Power Scheduling and Voltage/var Control in Autonomous Microgrids

Manuel V. Castro[1]([✉]) [ID] and Carlos L. Moreira[1,2] [ID]

[1] INESC TEC (Institute for Systems and Computer Engineering,
Technology and Science), Porto, Portugal
{manuel.v.castro, carlos.moreira}@inesctec.pt
[2] Faculty of Engineering, University of Porto, Porto, Portugal

**Abstract.** This paper presents a multi-temporal approach for the energy scheduling and voltage/var control problem in a microgrid (MG) system with photovoltaic (PV) generation and energy storage devices (PV-battery MG) during islanded operation conditions. A MG is often defined as a low voltage (LV) distribution grid that encompasses distributed energy resources and loads that operate in a coordinated way, either connected to the upstream distribution grid or autonomously (islanded from the main grid). Considering the islanded operation of the MG during a given period, it is necessary to develop proper tools that allow the effective coordination of the existing resources. Such tools should be incorporated in the MG control system hierarchy in order to assure proper conditions for the operation of the autonomous MG in terms of active power, voltage and reactive power management. Energy storage devices are essential components for the successful operation of islanded MG. These devices have a very fast response and are able to absorb/inject the right amount of power. For the operation of the MG in islanding conditions during a longer period, it is necessary to integrate information related to the forecasting of loads and PV-based generation for the upcoming hours for which is intended to maintain MG in islanded operation. Therefore, this paper presents a tool to be integrated in the Microgrid Central Controller (MGCC) that is responsible to perform a multi-temporal optimal power flow (OPF) in order to schedule the active and reactive power within the MG for the next time intervals.

**Keywords:** Microgrid · Voltage/var control · Storage dispatch ·
Renewable energy integration · Autonomous operation

## 1 Introduction

Environmental concerns, political instability in fossil fuels exporting countries and a rapid technological development on energy conversion systems are the main factors for a rapidly integration of small-scale Renewable Energy Sources (RES) in the structure of power distribution systems [1, 2]. This lead to a paradigm shift of power systems in which generation became distributed throughout the various voltage levels and grew closer to the consumption points with the increasing connections of technologies such

J. L. Afonso et al. (Eds.): GreeNets 2018, LNICST 269, pp. 193–207, 2019.
https://doi.org/10.1007/978-3-030-12950-7_15

as PV panels, wind turbines, fuel cells, microturbines and combined heat and power (CHP) applications [3–5]. The smaller modular generation units that have lower power outputs than 100 kW can be denominated as Microsources (MS). They exploit RES or fossil fuels in high efficiency local CHP applications and are usually connected to the LV level. Because of the nature of their electric energy output, they are often coupled to the grid via power electronic interfaces and as consequence have very low inertia [4].

The large-scale integration of Distributed Generation (DG) based on RES in the distribution network increases the uncertainty of the power flows because of the high variability and intermittency of sources like wind and solar [3]. As consequence of the unpredictability nature of DG, there could be, in the system, sudden dips and peaks in the steady state voltage profile and branches overload. These challenges drove an implementation of multiples changes in the electrical system, especially at the LV level, to increase controllability and improve the management of several resources in order to incorporate DG without the need for massive grid reinforcements.

It is in this context that emerges the concept MG. A MG is regarded as distribution network that integrates a communication infrastructure with the aim of promoting the active management and control between MS, storage devices and loads [3]. The MG can operate in an autonomous mode for a significant period of time. This requires several features of controllability and management of storage devices and DG units in order to guarantee an adequate steady state voltage profile and no violation of technical limitations. The deployment of MG could be the key to increase the network security and resilience when extreme natural disasters or extreme weather conditions occur and prevent major blackouts because of their ability to work islanded from other grids providing a self-healing functionality [3]. The concept of the MG was studied and explored, evolving into a more general concept, which is the SmartGrid (SG) and nowadays is seen as the basic component of a SG.

Storage devices are a key component for the successful operation of autonomous power systems that do not have synchronous generators to regulate frequency. These devices are able to absorb/inject the right amount of power, if necessary in very short time [3, 6]. The operation of a PV-battery MG relies on the power-frequency and voltage-reactive power droop control concepts that can be programmed in power converters associated to energy storage devices, such that these devices can operate as a grid-forming unit, or, in other words, as a Voltage Source Inverter (VSI). During islanded operation, the primary control layer (based on the droop control) is responsible for frequency and voltage regulation strategies that will assure the continuous power balancing with minimum dependence of communication system. Then, the secondary control layer will be responsible to dispatch the available resources according to a given objective in order to restore frequency and node voltages to reference set-points [3]. Therefore, in the proposed approach, it is assumed the steady state operating conditions of the system, such that the grid frequency is at the nominal value.

The main contribution of this paper is related to the development of a multi-temporal approach for the energy scheduling and voltage/var control problem of a PV-battery MG system during islanding operating conditions. The proposed approach takes into consideration forecasts of PV production and load for the next time steps and performs an energy scheduling and voltage/var control problem for an islanding MG operating with several VSI coupled to energy storage devices.

# 2 Microgrid Concept and Control Architecture

The MG concept was first introduced in the United States of America by the Department of Energy, more specifically, the Consortium for Electric Reliability Technology Solutions (CERTS) while studying the implications of DG penetration in power systems. CERTS defines the MG as being a single and self-controlled entity that supply energy to its consumers and also manages, controls and maintains the local necessities [3]. This concept was fully developed and expanded by the European Union (EU), Canada and Japan [5]. In the EU, the MG concept was designed to safely integrate the MS based RES in high levels of penetration because of environmentally concerns and economic benefits. A clear definition of a MG system, was developed by the CIGRE working group WG C6.22 following concept: "MicroGrids are electricity distribution systems containing loads and distributed energy resources, (such as distributed generators, storage devices, or controllable loads) that can be operated in a controlled, coordinated way either while connected to the main power network or while islanded" [7].

The operation of a MG requires high levels of flexibility and control. For this purpose, it was essential to establish a hierarchical management and control scheme supported by a communication infrastructure. In the higher level of MG management and control is the Microgrid Central Controller (MGCC) located in LV side of the MV/LV transformer. The MGCC communicates with the lower level controllers and is responsible for a proper technical and economic management of the MG. The secondary hierarchy control is located near each of controllable MS, storage devices and controllable loads (Fig. 1). The controllers of MS and storage are called Microsource controllers (MC) and usually are housed in within power electronic interface of the MS. The controllable loads or groups are regulated and adjusted by load controllers (LC). The MGCC provides power set-points to the secondary controllers (LC and MC) according to a pre-defined strategy. The MC responds in milliseconds to the demands from MGCC and from local information and have autonomy to optimize local generation, during interconnected mode, and fast load following, during islanding of the MG. The LC responds to demands of the MGCC like implement load-shedding features during emergency circumstances. It is also the information available in the MC and LC terminals that indirectly determined a set of operation and control actions that guarantee the stability of the system during transitional periods [4].

## 2.1 Microgrid Operation Modes

Through the exploitation of its control and management system, the MG can operate in two distinct modes: normal interconnected mode and autonomous/islanded operation mode. These modes of operation are briefly addressed hereafter.

**Normal Interconnected Mode.** In interconnected mode, the MG is connected to the medium voltage network (MV) and can partially or totally be supplied by the MV and inject the exceeding power in the MV [6]. This mode of operation can have different objectives: minimize the costs of operation or maximize revenue (economical), maintain voltage levels and/or minimize branch losses (technical) and reduce $CO_2$ emissions (environmental) [3]. In this mode, the MG is operated and controlled by the MGCC that

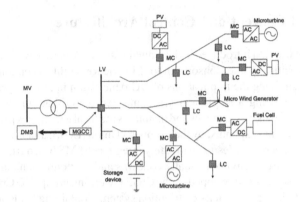

Fig. 1. MG architecture [4].

communicates with Distribution Management System (DMS). The DMS is located upstream, in the distribution network, and the MGCC is installed in the LV side of the MV/LV transformer (see Fig. 1) [5]. The DMS enables the possibility of information exchange and establishment of contractual agreements between the MG and the Distribution System Operator (DSO). The MG can be seen as an aggregation of loads and MS operating as a single entity in order to simplify their interaction with the DSO.

**Islanded or Emergency Operation Mode.** The islanded or emergency mode (also known as autonomous) can be triggered by a disturbance in the upstream network or by a planned action. The disturbance in the network can be as simple as a line fault to an event like a tornado or an earthquake that severely damages electrical equipments of the power system and can cause a general blackout. A planned action of disconnection can be executed in order to perform maintenance or reparations on the system. When a MG is disconnected from the MV network, operates autonomously in a similar way to the electric power systems of the physical islands [6]. In this mode, the stability of the MG is assured by the coordination between the MGCC and the MC and LC [3]. The disconnection from the MV network requires an instant change in the output power control of MC, switching from power dispatch mode to a frequency and voltage control mode (primary control). Afterwards, the MGCC needs to implement a secondary control loop that performs an optimized dispatch of the MS and storage units [4]. This optimization can have as an objective to reduce system losses and maintenance of the profile of steady state bus voltage [5]. Furthermore, in case of a blackout due to an extreme event the MG can perform the local power restoration. By operating autonomously, the MG allows a reduction on interrupting times on LV levels. In addition, the MG can perform a black start, which is a service restoration that restarts the system after a blackout. This process relies on the availability of self-starting units like a battery [5].

The autonomous operation of a MG is successfully guaranteed by the implementation of adequate frequency and voltage control functionalities and after that a competent dispatch of the power reserve in the grid. These features are generally established in two levels of control: the primary and secondary control.

## 2.2    Microgrid Autonomous Operation

Since most of the MS connected in the MG have power electronics interfaces and there is usually not a synchronous generator installed, the primary control level of the MG (acting locally at the power electronic interface connected to the grid) depends on two fundamental types of control strategies that are available for those interfaces: PQ inverter control and VSI inverter control.

The PQ inverter control is a control mechanism that enables the power converters to be synchronized with an energized grid and it is intended to feed a given active and reactive power set point. Through this type of control, the converter operates as a current-controlled voltage source that is kept in synchronism with the grid (grid-tied inverter). Given this operational characteristic, this type of converters is usually installed in RES of energy conversion systems that has a relatively slow response to power control signals (such as microturbines) [4, 6].

The other type of control (Voltage Source Inverter (VSI), also known as a grid-forming inverter) is the one implemented for the inverters used in energy storage devices, because of their ability of acting as an independent voltage source with very fast response capabilities to load changes [6]. In principle, this control mechanism is designed by controlling voltage and frequency through the following droop functions:

$$\omega = \omega_0 - k_P \times P \tag{1}$$

$$V = V_0 - k_Q \times Q \tag{2}$$

where,

$\omega$ – Reference angular frequency value (rad/s).
$\omega_0$ – Idle value of angular frequency (rad/s) at no load conditions.
$k_P, k_Q$ – Droop slopes (rad/s.W and V/var).
$P$ – Inverter active power output (W).
$V$ – Reference voltage value (V).
$V_0$ – Idle value of voltage (V) at no load conditions.
$Q$ – Inverter reactive power output (var).

With this P-f droop function when there is a decrease/increase of load the frequency increases/decreases according to (1) and Fig. 2(a). The Q-V droop function (2) and Fig. 2(b) allows a reactive power sharing between VSI [4]. This control principle lets the VSI to react with only the information at its terminals [3].

In a long-term operation as an autonomous system, a MG must have a secondary control to ensure the dispatch of resources with a certain objective after the transient period from connected operation to islanded operation. The secondary control dispatches DG sending set points to the MC to compensate the frequency deviation due to the power injected by the storage devices and possibly leading to restoration of nominal frequency (or at least close enough). There were identified two secondary load-frequency strategies: one strategy implemented locally at each MC and another more centralized managed by the MGCC [3].

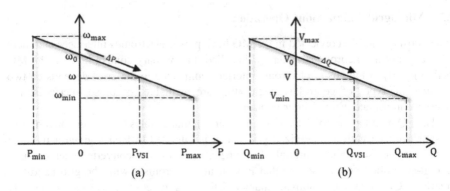

**Fig. 2.** VSI droop characteristics: P-f droop (a) and Q-V droop (b) [1].

# 3  Microgrids Active and Reactive Power Scheduling and Voltage/var Control During Autonomous Operation

MG are typically established in LV distribution systems and the associated feeders have a predominant resistive component. As a consequence there is an important influence of the active power in the voltage profiles (while traditionally, the reactive power controls the voltage if reactance is higher than the resistance). Consequently, it is not possible to decouple the active and reactive power in the MG operation in practical terms. To overcome this issue, there are many studies and researches, such as [8], that propose the implementation of virtual impedance in the power electronic interfaces operated as VSI (grid-forming type-unit with droop control functions as previously discussed) and using the droop control concepts. The introduction of virtual impedance for droop-based controls of MG can provide mechanisms for P-Q decoupling by artificially changing the X/R ratio through the emulation of a virtual inductor in the output impedance of VSI-type droop controlled power converters.

## 3.1  Power Flow in Islanded Microgrid

The active and reactive power scheduling and voltage/var control study assumes that the frequency is controlled and maintained using the frequency control strategies mentioned previously. Therefore, the frequency is considered to remain at the nominal value (50 Hz). Consequently, the key concern prior to the development of any strategy is solving the power flow problem in autonomous droop-controlled MG comprise both grid-tied and grid-forming inverters (with virtual inductances).

**VSI Power Flow Model.** As shown in Fig. 3, a VSI can be regarded as an AC voltage source connected to the grid through a coupling inductance. In this figure, the VSI is assumed to be connected to a LV cable (negligible inductance) being represented only the cable resistance ($R_C$). The VSI coupling inductance corresponds to the physical one plus the virtual inductance value added to the VSI control system.

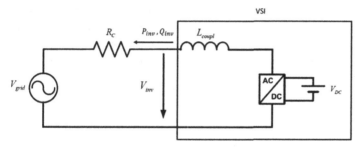

**Fig. 3.** VSI connected to the grid through a LV feeder [4].

The active and reactive power inverter in a LV grid can be calculated by (3) and (4).

$$P_{inv} = \frac{V_{inv}}{R_C^2 + X_C^2} \left[ R_C \left( V_{inv} - V_{grid} \cos \delta \right) + X_C V_{grid} \sin \delta \right] \quad (3)$$

$$Q_{inv} = \frac{V_{inv}}{R_C^2 + X_C^2} \left[ R_C \left( V_{inv} \sin \delta \right) + X_C \left( V_{inv} - V_{grid} \cos \delta \right) \right] \quad (4)$$

Where,

$P_{inv}$ – Inverter active power output (W).
$Q_{inv}$ – Inverter reactive power output (var).
$V_{inv}$ – Inverter terminal voltage (V).
$R_C$ – Cable resistance (Ω).
$X_C$ – Coupling reactance ($\omega \cdot L_{coupl}$) (Ω).
$V_{grid}$ – Grid voltage (V).
$\delta$ – Phase difference between inverter output voltage and grid voltage (rad).

Regarding steady state conditions, the operation of these type of inverters in LV MG includes also the "virtual inductance" concept [8] that is responsible for increasing the output inductance of the power converter and its proper operation in grids with high R/X factor. Therefore, the VSI is regarded as a voltage source linked to a reactance, being represented in power flow studies using two buses (Fig. 4): an internal VSI bus and VSI output bus that acts as an interface with the grid. This model also allows a certain decoupling of active and reactive power.

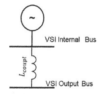

**Fig. 4.** VSI power flow studies model.

According to the droop Eq. (1), voltage control at each VSI terminal depends on the reactive power loading. Being $k_Q$ a fixed characteristic of each VSI, voltage and reactive power control requires the proper adjustment of the idle voltage $V_0$ in each unit. From the two-bus model, the idle voltage $V_0$ can be determined as in (5):

$$V_0 = V_{int} + k_Q \cdot Q_{out} \tag{5}$$

where,

$V_{int}$ – Internal VSI bus voltage.

$Q_{out}$ – VSI reactive power output.

### 3.2    A Multi-temporal Based Approach for Active and Reactive Power Scheduling and Voltage/var Control

Taking into consideration the VSI power flow model previously discussed and taking into account as well the energy capacity of the batteries, it is possible to formulate a multi-temporal based approach for active and reactive power scheduling and the voltage/var control problem to be integrated into the MGCC. This problem can be seen as an OPF based on [9] that has an objective function (OF) (6) and is subjected to the constraints (7) to (17). Equations (7) to (9) are referring to the power and energy balance for the $N$ nodes of the network. The constraints (10) to (17) refer to the technical limits of the devices or technical operation limits of the MG.

The OF considered in this formulation is the minimization of the quadratic bus voltage deviations from the nominal voltage value (1 p.u.):

$$\min \sum_{h=1}^{H} \sum_{i=1}^{N} \left(V_i^h - 1\right)^2 \tag{6}$$

subject to:

$$P_{DG_i}^h + P_{D_i}^h - P_{C_i}^h - P_{L_i}^h = V_i^h \sum_{h=1}^{H} \sum_{k=1}^{N} V_k^h \cdot \left( \begin{array}{c} G_{ik} \cdot \cos\left(\theta_i^h - \theta_k^h\right) \\ + B_{ik} \cdot \sin\left(\theta_i^h - \theta_k^h\right) \end{array} \right) \tag{7}$$

$$Q_{DG_i}^h + Q_{D_i}^h - Q_{C_i}^h - Q_{L_i}^h = V_i^h \sum_{h=1}^{H} \sum_{k=1}^{N} V_k^h \cdot \left( \begin{array}{c} G_{ik} \cdot \sin\left(\theta_i^h - \theta_k^h\right) \\ - B_{ik} \cdot \cos\left(\theta_i^h - \theta_k^h\right) \end{array} \right) \tag{8}$$

$$SoC_i^h = SoC_i^{h-1} + \left( \eta_{C_i} \cdot P_{C_i}^h - \frac{P_{D_i}^h}{\eta_{D_i}} \right) \tag{9}$$

$$V_i^{min} \leq V_i^h \leq V_i^{max} \tag{10}$$

$$P_{DG_i}^{min} \leq P_{DG_i}^h \leq P_{DG_i}^{max} \tag{11}$$

$$P_{D_i}^{min} \leq P_{D_i}^{h} \leq P_{D_i}^{max} \tag{12}$$

$$P_{C_i}^{min} \leq P_{C_i}^{h} \leq P_{C_i}^{max} \tag{13}$$

$$Q_{DG_i}^{min} \leq Q_{DG_i}^{h} \leq Q_{DG_i}^{max} \tag{14}$$

$$Q_{D_i}^{min} \leq Q_{D_i}^{h} \leq Q_{D_i}^{max} \tag{15}$$

$$Q_{C_i}^{min} \leq Q_{C_i}^{h} \leq Q_{C_i}^{max} \tag{16}$$

$$SoC_i^{min} \leq SoC_i^{h} \leq SoC_i^{max} \tag{17}$$

where,

$V_i^h$ – Voltage magnitude at bus $i$ at hour $h$
$V_k^h$ – Voltage magnitude at bus $k$ at hour $h$
$B_{ik}$ – Susceptance from bus $i$ to bus $k$
$G_{ik}$ – Conductance from bus $i$ to bus $k$
$\theta_i^h$ – Voltage angle at bus $i$ at hour $h$
$\theta_k^h$ – Voltage angle at bus $k$ at hour $h$
$P_{DG_i}^h$ – Active power output of DG $i$ at hour $h$
$P_{D_i}^h$ – Active power provided from discharging the storage unit (VSI) $i$ at hour $h$
$P_{C_i}^h$ – Active power provided from charging the storage unit (VSI) $i$ at hour $h$
$P_{L_i}^h$ – Active load at the bus $i$ at hour $h$
$Q_{DG_i}^h$ – Reactive power output of DG $i$ at hour $h$
$Q_{D_i}^h$ – Reactive power provided while discharging the storage unit (VSI) $i$ at hour $h$
$Q_{C_i}^h$ – Reactive power provided while charging the storage unit (VSI) $i$ at hour $h$
$Q_{L_i}^h$ – Reactive load at bus $i$ at hour $h$
$SoC_i^h$ – State of charge of VSI $i$ at hour $h$
$N$ – Total number of buses in the MG
$H$ – Total number of hours expected for MG autonomous operation.

In this formulation, the control variables are the active and reactive from the storage units ($P_C, P_D, Q_C, Q_D$), active power form PV systems ($P_{DG_i}^h$), that will be lower than the maximum available power in case of grid technical constrains violation or violation of state of charge (SoC) conditions in energy storage devices, and the injected/absorbed reactive power in the PV panels ($Q_{DG}$). The state variables are the voltage magnitude and angle at each bus ($V, \theta$).

# 4 Case Study

## 4.1 Test System Description

In order to illustrate de exploitation of the tool that can be used for active and reactive power scheduling and voltage/var control in autonomous MG, the test system from [3] was adopted. This MG test system – LV grid (400 V nominal voltage) – includes 3 VSI, 17 buses, 13 loads and 8 PV generators (Fig. 5). The lines of the MG test system are predominantly resistive (R/X ratio in the range of 3 to 5), as it is a typical characteristic of LV distribution grids. In the overall procedure that is proposed, a three-phase balanced operation of the system is assumed.

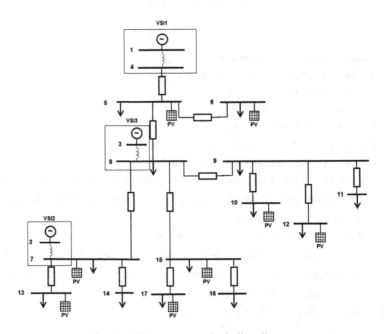

**Fig. 5.** MG test system single-line diagram.

The admissible range for the buses voltage magnitude is presented in Table 1.

**Table 1.** Admissible bus voltage range

| Bus | Vmin (p.u.) | Vmax (p.u.) |
|-----|-------------|-------------|
| 1–3 | 0.90 | 1.10 |
| 4–17 | 0.95 | 1.10 |

The active and reactive power range for all the power converters (VSI) is presented in Table 2. The charging and discharging efficiency considered for the energy storage devices is 80% (a typical value), which takes into account not only the efficiency of the battery in itself but also the efficiency of the inverters and the energy wasted in the auxiliary services [10]. The maximum storage capacity of each VSI is exhibited in Table 3, as well as the initial value assumed for the SoC of each unit. In addition, the SoC's lower limit is assumed to be 20% of the unit nominal energy capacity.

**Table 2.** Active and reactive power range in VSI

| VSI | Pmax (kW) | Qmax (kvar) | Pmin (kW) | Qmin (kvar) |
|-----|-----------|-------------|-----------|-------------|
| 1 | 200.0 | 130.0 | −200.0 | −130.0 |
| 2 | 100.0 | 65.0 | −100.0 | −65.0 |
| 3 | 50.0 | 32.5 | −50.0 | −32.5 |

The envisioned MG integrates also solar PV generation systems. This type of source is assumed to have the capability of providing reactive power injection the grid (inductive or capacitive) within a given range (in this case, ±20% of the active power). Therefore, PV generators total installed power capacity is 138 kW (±28 kvar). The total peak load present in the system is 67 kW (active) and 15 kvar (reactive).

It is assumed that this MG becomes isolated at a given time and that will remain in those operating conditions for 24 h onwards. For this time interval, it is necessary to define the energy scheduling and voltage and reactive power control for the overall system. Therefore, it is assumed forecasted load and PV production profiles for the MG, which are represented in Fig. 6 (normalized values with respect to the maximum load and PV generation installed capacity previously defined).

**Table 3.** Storage capacity limits and initial values.

| VSI | Max (kWh) | Min (kWh) | Initial SoC (kWh) |
|-----|-----------|-----------|-------------------|
| 1 | 210 | 42 | 105 |
| 2 | 160 | 32 | 80 |
| 3 | 120 | 24 | 60 |

The proposed approach tool was developed using Matpower [11] and its solvers and the simulations were performed in a MATLAB® (R2016b) environment on a PC with an Intel Core i7-2600 CPU @ 3.4 GHz and 8.0 GB of RAM.

## 4.2  Obtained Results

**Active Power Scheduling.** The obtained results regarding the scheduled VSI active power output and the SoC of the associated energy storage devices (Fig. 7) demonstrate that the storage devices are predominantly injecting power to the grid when there

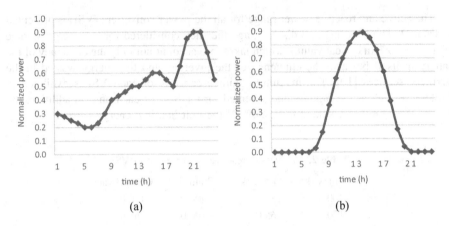

**Fig. 6.** Load profile forecast (a) and PV generation profile forecast (b).

is low PV generation (from hour 1 to 9 and from hour 19 to 24) and high power consumption (from hour 20 to 22). The batteries charge mostly during the time of high sunlight exposure, which is during hour 12 until hour 19.

**Reactive Power Scheduling.** The objective function of this problem forces the PV generators and VSI to adjust their reactive power output (Fig. 8) in order to minimize voltage deviations from the nominal value (1 p.u.).

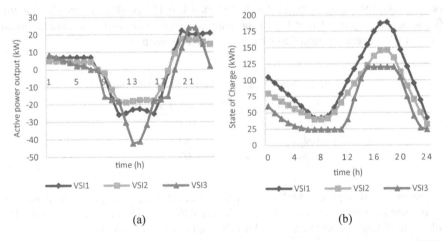

**Fig. 7.** VSI's active power output (kW) (a) and energy storage devices capacity (kWh) (b) evolution over time.

**Bus Voltages.** Regarding the bus voltages, it is possible to infer from Fig. 9 that there is little variation (in terms of magnitude) from the nominal value, especially from the VSI's internal bus. This is because of the OF used in this OPF. Some variability

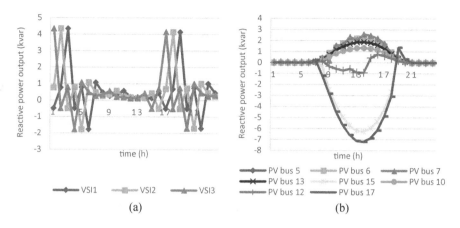

(a)                                                            (b)

**Fig. 8.** Reactive power output of VSI (a) and PV generators (b).

specially occurs in hours of high PV generation (maximum deviation of 5.5% from hour 11 to 15 at bus 15) and peak load values (maximum deviation of 2.5% from hour 20 to 22 at bus 4).

**Active Power Losses.** Regarding the active power losses over time there is the evident conclusion from Fig. 10: charging and discharging the storage devices wastes more energy than the power exchanges in the feeders (because of the charging and discharging efficiencies that were considered). Regarding the grid active power losses, the reduced values that can be observed are a consequence of the relatively small power transactions and the reduced length of the cables.

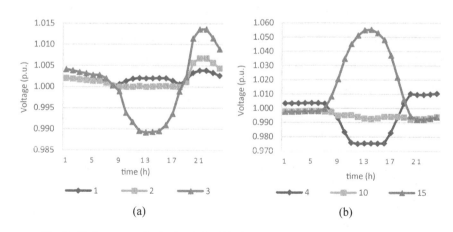

(a)                                                            (b)

**Fig. 9.** Voltage magnitude (p.u.) for VSI buses (a) and buses 4, 10 and 15 (b).

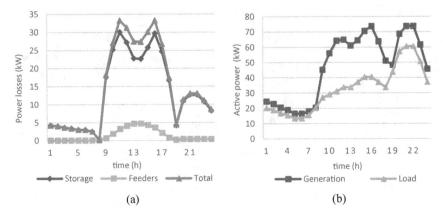

**Fig. 10.** Active power losses (a) vs total active power generation and load (b) (kW).

## 5   Conclusions and Future Works

To support the autonomous operation of a MG, this paper presents a multi-temporal approach that allows the scheduling of active and reactive power/voltage control for storage devices and DG units. This approach exploits a multi-temporal formulation since it is necessary to take into account the SoC of the storage devices. This SoC depends not only of the amount of power that is necessary to output in a specific moment but also is subjected to the energy left in store from the previous period. Additionally, the problem formulation took into consideration the specific characteristics of a droop-controlled MG operating in islanded mode, in particular regarding the voltage and reactive power droop implemented in VSI-type converters.

After the successful validation of the proposed approach, additional work is necessary in order to consider new issues such as the unbalanced operation of the LV MG due to the presence of a significant number of single phase devices (loads and small generation systems), as well as the need of exploiting possible flexibility ranges that can be provided by resources (responsive loads) and that can have a beneficial contribution to support islanding operation of the MG system. For example, the consideration of specific strategies for the consideration of flexible loads that can be adjusted over time is a valuable feature in order to provide additional support the overall energy management problem in the islanded MG.

**Acknowledgments.** This work was financed by the ERDF – European Regional Development Fund through the Operational Programme for Competitiveness and Internationalization - COMPETE 2020 Programme and by National Funds through the FCT – Fundação para a Ciência e a Tecnologia (Portuguese Foundation for Science and Technology) within project "ERANETLAC/0005/2014".

# References

1. Simpson-Porco, J., Shafiee, Q., Dörfler, F., Vasquez, J., Guerrero, J., Bullo, F.: Secondary frequency and voltage control of islanded microgrids via distributed averaging. IEEE Trans. Industr. Electron. **62**(11), 7025–7039 (2015)
2. Han, H., Hou, X., Yang, J., Wu, J., Su, M., Guerrero, J.: Review of power sharing control strategies for islanding operation of AC microgrids. IEEE Trans. Smart Grid **7**(1), 200–215 (2016)
3. Gouveia, C.S.T.: Experimental validation of microgrids: exploiting the role of plug-in electric vehicles, active load control and micro-generation units. Ph.D. Thesis, University of Porto, Faculty of Engineering, Porto (2014)
4. Moreira, C.C.L.: Identification and development of microgrids emergency control procedures. Ph.D. Thesis, University of Porto, Faculty of Engineering, Porto (2008)
5. Nascimento, I.L.A.: Voltage and reactive power control in autonomous microgrids. M.Sc. Dissertation. University of Porto, Faculty of Engineering, Porto (2017)
6. Lopes, J.A.P., Moreira, C., Madureira, A.G.: Defining control strategies for microgrids islanded operation. IEEE Trans. Power Syst. **21**(2), 916–924 (2006)
7. Marnay, C., et al.: Microgrid evolution roadmap. In: 2015 International Symposium on Smart Electric Distribution Systems and Technologies (EDST), Viena (2015)
8. Wu, X., Shen, C., Iravani, R.: Feasible range and optimal value of the virtual impedance for droop-based control of microgrids. IEEE Trans. Smart Grid **8**(3), 1242–1251 (2017)
9. Meirinhos, J.L., Rua, D.E., Carvalho, L.M., Madureira, A.G.: Multi-temporal optimal power flow for voltage control in MV networks using distributed energy resources. Electr. Power Syst. Res. **146**, 25–32 (2017)
10. McKay, C.: Energy storage networks, WTWH Media LLC and its licensors, 25 January 2018. https://www.energystoragenetworks.com/three-battery-types-work-grid-scale-energy-storage-systems/. Accessed 18 Oct 2018
11. Zimmerman, R., Murillo-Sánchez, C.: Matpower 6.0 User's Manual, PSerc (2016)

# Author Index

Printed in the United States
By Bookmasters